D0146446

EDUCATING FOR FREEDOM

THE ARNOLD AND CAROLINE ROSE BOOK SERIES
OF THE AMERICAN SOCIOLOGICAL ASSOCIATION

The Rose Book Series was established in 1968 in honor of the distinguished sociologists Arnold and Caroline Rose, whose bequest makes the Series possible. The sole criterion for publication in the Series is that a manuscript contribute to knowledge in the discipline of sociology in a systematic and substantial manner. All areas of the discipline and all established and promising modes of inquiry are equally eligible for consideration. The Rose Book Series is an official publication of the American Sociological Association.

The Editor and Editorial Board gratefully acknowledge the contributions of Jane Hood, University of New Mexico; Jeffrey L. Obler, University of North Carolina at Chapel Hill; and Jonathan Rieder, Barnard College, as expert reviewers of this manuscript.

EDUCATING FOR FREEDOM

The Paradox of Pedagogy

DONALD L. FINKEL
WILLIAM RAY ARNEY

RUTGERS UNIVERSITY PRESS
New Brunswick, New Jersey

Library of Congress Cataloging-in-Publication Data

Finkel, Donald L., 1943–
Educating for freedom : the paradox of pedagogy / Donald L. Finkel, William Ray Arney.
p. cm. — (The Arnold and Caroline Rose book series of the American Sociological Association)
Includes bibliographical references and index.
ISBN 0-8135-2201-3 (cloth : alk. paper)
1. Education—Philosophy. 2. Teacher–student relations. 3. College teaching. I. Arney, William Ray. II. Title. III. Series.
LB14.7.F56 1995
370'.1—dc20

94-25231
CIP

British Cataloging-in-Publication information available

Published by Rutgers University Press, New Brunswick, New Jersey
Manufactured in the United States of America

To Susan Finkel

The crux is freedom. Liberal education aims at the free mind. . . .
If we could force men to be free, we would. As it is. . . .

—Joseph Tussman, *Experiment at Berkeley*

CONTENTS

ACKNOWLEDGMENTS

OVER THE YEARS it took to complete this project we received many helpful comments and reactions from friends and colleagues. We especially want to thank Susan Finkel, Bernard Bergen, Jutta Mason, Judy Gardner, Charlie Teske, Rita Pougiales, Kirk Thompson, Nancy Koppelman, Patrick Hill, Mark Weisberg, Ron Manheimer, John Parker, and Peter Elbow. Colleagues who were on teaching teams with the two of us influenced this work. They include (in addition to Kirk Thompson) Nancy Taylor, Sandie Nisbet and Willie Parson.

Many members of the faculty of The Evergreen State College participated in a large seminar on a portion of the manuscript. We are grateful for the discussions that seminar provoked.

Our conversations on collegial teaching included many Evergreen students, especially those in an academic program called "The Paradox of Freedom." Talks with students provided an indispensible ingredient in this effort.

Tom Parker and the administration of Drury College provided one of us the opportunity to discuss these ideas in a two-week faculty seminar. The Sponsored Research Fund of The Evergreen State College supported some of the work that led to this book.

We extend special thanks and appreciation to all members of the faculty of The Evergreen State College—to the founding faculty and administrators who made the place possible and to everyone else whose work sustains it today.

INTRODUCTION

> All the instruments [of education] have been tried save one, the only one precisely that can succeed: well-regulated freedom.
>
> —Jean-Jacques Rousseau, *Emile*

"IF WE COULD FORCE men to be free, we would; as it is we can only try to help them."[1] So writes Joseph Tussman in his account of his experimental program at Berkeley during the late 1960s. But if we *could* force students to be free, would we do so? What kind of freedom arises from coercion? Teachers who seek to set their students free through education find themselves in a puzzling and problematic situation. *Teaching* freedom is a paradox, the paradox of pedagogy.

Of course, Tussman knew there was no way to make people free: "As it is," he writes, "we can only try to help them." This work is an exploration of Tussman's "as it is." What are the terms in which pedagogy has framed for itself the problematic project of teaching freedom? How has pedagogy confronted the paradox of teaching freedom? Is there a way to resolve the paradox of pedagogy? If not, are there interesting ways to respond to it and live with it?

More than two hundred years ago, Rousseau set for himself the task of designing an education for freedom, a liberating education. In his book *Emile, or On Education,* he struggled heroically with this project, brilliantly attempting to try "the one instrument" that had not been tried, "well-regulated freedom." The very phrase seems an oxymoron; the paradox of pedagogy is contained within it. The free individual must be so well instructed that he will be able to fully realize his individuality in society. His free mind must be so well disciplined that he will choose wisely and freely for himself, and for others, too. His teacher must regulate the student's freedom even as he gives it to him. As Tussman argues, "A healthy mind, a functioning mind, a free mind, is not a mind which believes as it pleases."[2] Teaching freedom is a paradox of the first rank.

The goal of individual education is good government. Individuals must develop the authority to govern themselves, and at the same time develop a responsiveness to the authority of other individuals sufficient to allow them to form together a well-governed, enriching collective. The paradox is that most teaching begins with a form of governing that undermines the achievement of this end: the governing of the thoughts and actions of dependent students by institutionally authorized (but not necessarily authoritative) teachers. The well-schooled individual is taught to be governed by institutional authority and forfeits the possibility of entering freely and authoritatively into a self-governing society.

Rousseau's response to the paradox of pedagogy was to write a treatise showing how a well-wrought relationship between one tutor and one pupil, a relationship crafted outside of institutions and, as far as possible, removed from society altogether, can produce that paradoxical being, the "social individual." Since Rousseau we have cast every pedagogical proposal and have discussed every pedagogical reform in terms that are variations and permutations on that one carefully cultivated relationship between student and teacher.

The discourse on education in this country has always been a discourse of emergency, but recently, the discussion of our problems of education has reached a fever pitch. We have had educational debates, exhortations, a barrage of recommendations on teaching, model schools, innovative curricula; we have had policy councils, educational research, national reports, and journalistic exposés. And we can expect a stream of more of the same. Most reports on education focus on one part of the student-teacher dyad or on that which seemingly connects the two, the curriculum. The Carnegie Commission, for example, finds that the American professoriate is dispirited. Most faculty members would leave the profession if they could, and many find the intellectual vitality of their campuses wanting, according to Ernest Boyer.[3] Popular books like *ProfScam: Professors and the Demise of Higher Education* claim faculty members are interested in using their time for anything but teaching.[4] On the other side, students are characterized (or caricatured) by people like Allan Bloom, E. D. Hirsch, and Diane Ravitch as illiterate, ignorant, and uninterested in learning.[5] And, of course, the curriculum is implicated in all of this as being unresponsive to national concerns, too trendy, anachronistic, disjointed, ungrounded, or otherwise in need of repair. Campus reform is big business. The National Institute for Education asserted several years ago that if institutions simply applied extant knowledge concerning the conduct of the classroom experiences involving teachers and students, "the quality of undergraduate education could be significantly improved."[6] College and university administrators are embracing novel teaching/learning configurations, including federated collections of courses, integrating academic curricula around skill building, forming small "freshman interest groups" within large courses, and even trying thematic, collaboratively taught coordinated studies programs of the sort Tussman developed at Berkeley.[7] At the root of all these criticisms and reforms is a kind of faith—now more than two centuries old—that if one can get the student-teacher relationship right, education will proceed smoothly from there. Even Tussman, for all his farsightedness, thought of his efforts as a restructuring of that relationship. His concern was that coordinated studies programs shift the focus from the question, What should I do with my students to What should we do with *ours?*[8] The student-teacher(s) relationship(s) still was central to his innovative pedagogical endeavor.

In the rush to "meet the educational emergency" no one has asked, "Into what kind of relationship are you inviting a student when you undertake to educate him through a student-teacher relationship?" Rousseau, for example, acknowledged that the student-teacher relationship is erotic. Instead of inquiring into the implications of such an assessment for the education of students, we usually recoil and try to solve, in advance, the problems that can arise in such a relationship. But it might be that in our rush to solve problems we run away from something essential to education.

We begin this book with a review of thinkers who have kept their eyes open to the nature of the relationship into which teachers invite students. All of them—Rousseau, Sigmund Freud, Paulo Freire, Ivan Illich, and Michel Foucault—remind us that modern pedagogy, based as it is on the personal relationship between student and teacher, is inherently paradoxical, and will always be, to some degree, self-defeating. You cannot teach a student to "be free." There will always be some more-or-less debilitating dependence remaining in an education that has proceeded from a close student-teacher relationship.

The second part of this book is about our reaction to this insight. After realizing that the promise of a liberating, personal pedagogy may be lost in paradox, we turn our attention to that first, most paradoxical pedagogue, Socrates. By considering our own separate, very different reactions to him, we are led to the view that the *best* response to the paradox of pedagogy is teaching that has at its heart not the relationship between teacher and student, but the relationship between two teachers. Teachers who differ in fundamental ways but yet remain equals can engage in *collegial teaching* with students they have in common. Collegial teaching entails turning away from the student-teacher relationship and turning toward one's colleagues in a way that enables the relationship between colleagues—not the relationship between a teacher and students—to become the driving educational force in the classroom.

We are not interested in driving eroticism out of education (but that is to say simply that we are not interested in attempting the impossible). In the end, we favor an approach that does not try to manage the eroticism of the classroom but gives eroticism a place where its "problems" have fewer effects on the people who are in institutionally dependent positions, the students. If pedagogy is to enable freedom, we think the mutuality of the relationship between colleagues—not the dependency of the relationship of student to teacher—is the place to begin.

Genesis of This Book

This is a report on a conversation between the two of us. We have worked together at an unusual college, The Evergreen State College in Olympia, Washington. Early in our conversation we found that we shared similar concerns about the aims of teaching and about what happens to students. But we also found that we had very different approaches to dealing with those concerns. We were so different in our approaches to teaching and learning that our conversation could have ended early. That it did not is largely attributable to the place where it occurred. To understand the conversation on which we report here the reader must from the outset know a little about the circumstances that gave rise to this work.

We have been Members of the Faculty of The Evergreen State College, one of us since 1976, and the other since 1981. We became genuine colleagues in 1983 when, quite by accident, we found ourselves on the same "teaching team" (consisting of three faculty members in all) in an "academic program" at Evergreen. A number of years after that experience we chose to teach together on another teaching team, this time in a program with five faculty members and one hundred students. Four years later, and after writing a draft of this book, the two of us taught a program called "The Paradox of Freedom." Our conversation about pedagogy flourished in those three years together.

As the quotation marks around "academic program" and "teaching team" suggest, Evergreen is not a typical institution of higher education. It is a descendant of the Tussman experiment at Berkeley and, before that, of Alexander Meiklejohn's college at the University of Wisconsin. The Evergreen State College was one of the experimental, alternative, innovative colleges that emerged from the debates on higher education in the 1960s. Evergreen was, and remains, a public institution, created and funded by the state of Washington, and partly for that reason it is one of the few alternative institutions to have survived the enrollment crises of the 1970s and early 1980s and the ensuing cascading conservatism in higher education. At this writing, Evergreen is thriving and growing. The school has achieved a national reputation as a liberal arts college with a different approach to undergraduate education.

In addition to its being a public institution, there are two other facts about the college that must be appreciated at the start. The first is that Evergreen was not to be a "school within a school." Many similar experiments in higher education foundered because programs or "colleges" were created within the institutional confines of larger, traditional institutions. Evergreen was a college unto itself from the beginning. Its first president and his trio of academic deans had no higher or surrounding set of administrators to contend with. Second, the founding administrators had the courage to cut the school free from traditional academic structures, which would have drastically curtailed the possibility of the college's doing anything very different or important. The constraining structures that were renounced from the founding of the college included, for the faculty, academic departments, tenure, academic ranks, merit pay increases, differential pay according to "market demands" for one's field, and the imperative to publish and gain a scholarly reputation in a discipline. For students, structures overthrown at the start included grades, majors, distributional requirements, and linked sequences of courses.

The effect of these circumstances was to have a college without a predetermined vision for itself—neither one coming "from above" nor one deriving from historically forceful structures. The founding vision of the college was entirely *negative.*[9] Charles McCann, the college's first president, made it very clear to the twenty-one men (three deans and eighteen faculty members) who had been hired to spend academic year 1970—71 "planning" the college before the first batch of students arrived in the fall of 1971 that there were to be "no grades, no majors, no departments, etc., etc." But he never commented on what there would or should be. That was up to the planning faculty and the three deans to decide. This "negative" approach with its lack of direction led one founding faculty member to write to a friend:

> My major reservation at the top is the probably unreasonable one that McCann is not a Meiklejohn. He has shaped a quite modest legislative mandate of purely local reference (to build a new State College which is not a carbon copy of others existing in the State of Washington) into a sweepingly innovative effort of national significance. But in this McCann is more negatively than positively inspired.[10]

Out of the rich, "negative" soil prepared by the college's chief administrator, the faculty and deans together cultivated something positive—not a curriculum, but a curricular vehicle. What they decided during the planning year was that the center and chief raison d'être of Evergreen would be a curriculum consisting not of individual courses or course sequences but of integrated academic programs called Coordinated Studies Programs.[11] These programs were to constitute full-time work for both the students and faculty. That is, a student was to take only one academic program at a time, and faculty were to teach but one at a time, usually for a full academic year.

In the beginning years of the college, programs were always yearlong and created from scratch at the start of each academic year. They were also interdisciplinary (or in some cases, a-disciplinary or antidisciplinary) and each was organized around a theme or problem. A program's teaching team consisted of three to seven faculty members who wished to investigate together some theme, problem, or question—like the connection of human development to history, or the meaning of political action in today's world, or whether there are new ways to think about health and health care. Each faculty member would inevitably bring to bear on the common inquiry the perspective of his academic discipline, but in most cases there would be no a priori prescribed subset of his discipline he would have to cover. The faculty team members had complete liberty to set up the schedule for the program and could design classes of whatever length and style they deemed fit. The two "requirements" in programs were (1) a "book seminar," regular meetings (usually twice a week) of twenty students and one teacher to discuss together a book read in common and (2) a faculty seminar, a weekly meeting where all faculty on a team would discuss a reading among themselves with no students present. Students received written narrative evaluations in the place of grades. All, some, or none of the academic credits signed up for by the student could be awarded by the faculty at the completion of the program, but there was to be no record on a student's transcript of any unearned credits (i.e., there were to be no formal signs of "failure").

The details may seem both trivial and overwhelming, but they are important. Taken together they created a new kind of teaching and learning environment, one which offered different opportunities for both students and teachers. An ideal Coordinated Studies Program is demanding for its students and faculty, but for both it can be intellectually vitalizing and rewarding.

It was in such a program that Arney and Finkel first met in 1983. The program was called "Human Health and Behavior," and the two of them, trained in sociology and psychology, were joined by a biologist to teach this two-quarter-long program. They were surprised to discover how much they enjoyed working together, how much they relished teaching together. The reason they were surprised is that they proceeded in such strikingly different ways as teachers. One of them loved to prepare and deliver formal lectures. The other avoided such lecturing as much as possible, believing as he did that lecturing was ineffective as a teaching device. One of them liked to engage personally with students; the other, though quite capable of making a lasting friendship with a particular student, generally kept students at a distance and refused to satisfy their demands for contact and support. One of them practiced a developmental pedagogy; the other eschewed any notions of natural development, and pursued instead, what he called a "pedagogy of refusal." From a student's point of view, the two of them could not appear more different. It might have been expected that they would have trouble teaching together.[12] It certainly might have been expected that they would have trouble in the weekly planning meetings agreeing on assignments, class activities, and all the countless details that together constitute an academic program.

But we had no difficulty at all. The fact is we thrived in each other's professional company and slowly began to realize that it was our difference as teachers (and, more fundamentally, as thinkers) that attracted us to each other. First of all, we respected and admired each other's work in the program. Second, each of us found that the other provided a kind of foil, so that we could be even more strongly what we were as teachers, knowing that the opposite base was covered, as it were, and covered with just as much force. Finally, both of us discovered in ourselves a kind of shadow teacher who was quite the opposite of our dominant teaching self. The developmentalist took a kind of secret vicarious joy in watching his colleague frustrate students with cryptic utterances they could not understand. The "refusalist" had to admit the force and appeal of the developmental perspective, and even took pleasure in watching someone shape his interactions with students in a way that was so artfully guided by this perspective. Thus, we discovered that because we were so different, and because we were teaching together, we were able at one and the same time to be more ourselves and something other than ourselves. This is a singular pleasure, and it is also a condition that leads somewhere.

Where it led was to a decision to teach together again. In 1988—89 we were two members of a five-person teaching team in a year-long "Core program" (i.e., designed for first-year students) called "Classical and Modern: An Integrated Approach to Education." It was during that program that our plans for this work crystallized.

The conversation reported on in this book was conducted partly in front of students and colleagues (in the two academic programs) and partly in private. It was also conducted partly in an extracurricular faculty seminar group of six colleagues who met monthly for several years to discuss readings in philosophy and social theory. And partly it was conducted internally in each of our own heads on and off over the years as we read books, taught with other colleagues, and worked with our students.

This book charts that conversation. Writing this book became a way both to reveal what we discovered through teaching together and to sustain it. The writing of the book is ultimately inseparable from the teaching of the programs; there is no clear demarcation between the two activities. Thus, this book is, in the final analysis, less a book *about* teaching than a *reflection of* teaching.[13] But it is a reflection of a different kind of teaching than most of us usually experience. This book is a reflection of—and a reflection on—collegial teaching, teaching where the personal relationship between colleagues replaces the personal relationship between student and teacher as the energizing and focusing center of the project we call pedagogy.

Our Argument

Before we can begin to make sense of the meaning or purpose of such a radical recentering of pedagogical space in higher education, we must examine what has long been accepted as the appropriate center of the college classroom: the student-teacher relationship. By calling this relationship the "center," we do not mean that it is an end of education, or even a conscious device used by teachers as a means.

We mean rather that it has come to be an unquestioned, often unspoken, structuring assumption of the human setting within which education is supposed to happen. There is near-universal agreement that the most desirable arrangement to promote learning would be the pairing of a single teacher with a single student. As Finkel and Monk put it:

> Most teachers and students conceive of the heart of education as a two-person relationship. The ideal relationship is that of tutor and tutee alone in a room. Classes are seen only as an economic or pragmatic necessity in which one person—the teacher—either simultaneously engages in ten or three hundred two-person relationships with separate individuals or addresses a single undifferentiated entity—the audience.[14]

Most discussions of pedagogy have an air about them that suggests that anything less than a one-on-one learning/teaching relationship is an unfortunate compromise.

This grounding assumption of contemporary educational discourse has it that the best kind of education is mediated by a personal relationship between the student and the teacher. Where does this assumption come from? What implications lie buried within it? These are the questions we pursue in part 1.

This foundational idea goes back at least to our "founding" texts on education: the Socratic dialogues of Plato. In these dialogues, Socrates' interlocutors learn something (if they learn anything) by being, for a time, in a face-to-face relationship with Socrates. In its weakest form, this assumption is not very interesting, for it asserts simply that the young of a species cannot provide education entirely for themselves without some assistance from the more mature. In its stronger versions, the assumption becomes more interesting and more familiar to the modern ear. The stronger versions assert not just that adults must be somehow involved in educating the young, but more pointedly that the teaching adult must cultivate a *personal* relationship of a specific content—a relationship aimed toward freedom and structured by care, concern, and above all, attention to and respect for the *individuality* of the pupil. This assumption would seem to be our modern bellwether for judging a pedagogy to be humane and liberal. It is this strong version that we examine here.

The idea that a humane and liberal pedagogy must be mediated by a close and caring personal relationship between student and teacher is actually a modern idea, one connected to the set of ideas that emerged in Europe in the seventeenth and eighteenth centuries and led to the Enlightenment. It is in some way tied to the very concern of intellectuals with education that manifested itself in the publication of John Locke's *Some Thoughts Concerning Education.*[15] Locke's book was widely read at the time and led to his being regarded as an authority on education.[16]

Since Locke argued that the education of "gentlemen" is best undertaken privately—preferably by the young man's father—the assumption of education's mediation by a one-to-one personal relationship was built into his discussion from the start. This relationship stressed the importance of shaping educational experiences to meet the *individual* needs of the child. But Locke's ultimate aim was to shape the individual to fit into society;[17] education was to tame impulsive human nature so that a child could eventually take his place as a responsible and respectable citizen of liberal, bourgeois society.

It is only with Rousseau that we find the full blossoming of the strong version of our founding educational assumption, for Rousseau was concerned with the individual first. Whereas Locke considered the educator to be society's agent, Rousseau's educator becomes the child's ally in the war society inevitably wages against developing children. Rousseau places his pedagogue on the side of the child from the outset. Although the child, through the tutor's guidance, will eventually find his way into society, he is not shaped solely for that purpose.

Locke's book, influential though it was, was not strikingly original. It was, rather, "a distillation of the best educational thinking of his time by a man of varied experience, keen intelligence and deep human sympathy."[18] Rousseau's text on education, *Emile,* though it was influenced in many ways by Locke, is a strikingly original text. It is the first education text to invert the long-accepted Christian view that human nature is defective (fallen) and in need of taming before it is fit to enter into society. Rousseau assumed that human nature was just fine and that it was society that was corrupt and corrupting. His insight was that fallen and defective human nature as we know it does not result from nature or God's imprint on children, but is the effect of the actions of society and social agents on them. Rousseau thus set out to develop a pedagogy that was liberating, not taming. He wanted the child to retain all the good that nature put into him, while still learning to manage himself in the social world where, for better or worse, he would have to live his life.

Although Locke's book is "modern" in the sense of being connected with the ideas that came with the rise of rationalism, science, and liberalism, Rousseau seems almost our contemporary in his aims and assumptions. Rousseau not only assumed the importance of the close personal relationship between pupil and teacher, but he developed this idea to its most extreme form. In so doing, he unpacked its many implications. His is the first pedagogy that aimed to be guided by the *natural* development of the student, the first that attempted to help the child develop his natural potentials in the face of a society that would limit and constrict him. Rousseau's was the first pedagogy that can be termed progressive, humane, and liberating, in the contemporary senses of those terms. It was the first that showed fully how such goals require the systematic and careful cultivation of a close personal relationship between the child and his teacher.

Since the promise of pedagogy (as we have it from Rousseau, at least) is a promise of freedom, a promise of liberation from society (or liberation for society[19]), the investigation we are undertaking must be seen as falling within the liberal wing of educational thought. One influential contemporary philosopher, Richard Rorty, captured the difference between a "liberal" and a "conservative" approach to education this way:

> When people on the political right talk about education, they immediately start talking about the truth. Typically, they enumerate what they take to be the familiar and self-evident truths and regret that these are no longer being inculcated in the young. When people on the political left talk about education, they talk first about freedom. The left typically views the old familiar truths cherished by the right as a crust of convention that needs to be broken through. . . . The right usually offers a theory according to which, if you have truth, freedom will follow automatically. . . . On the leftist's inverted version of Plato, if you take care of freedom—especially political and economic freedom—truth will take care of itself.[20]

The conversation we intend to construct is a conversation intended for people interested in the promise of freedom, not the promise of truth, offered to the individual through education. Since it was Rousseau, we believe, who started this conversation about education's liberatory potential in the modern era, we ground our conversation in his *Emile.*

We then move on to explore more carefully the paradox inherent in any liberatory pedagogy based on the student-teacher relationship explicated in its ideal form in *Emile.* We use Freud's central concept of "transference" as a means to this end. Freud's psychoanalytic view puts a sharp edge on the problematic dimension of Rousseau's educational project. Rousseau dimly anticipated these problems in the closing pages of *Emile;* Freud drives them home.

The third step in our four-part inquiry into the student-teacher relationship requires us to consider the educational writings of the Brazilian liberatory educator, Paulo Freire, for Freire appears to offer a way out of the impasse that Freud's analysis reveals so sharply. Freire attempts to shift liberatory pedagogy away from its focus on the individual onto, instead, the social and cultural group. This restructuring offers new hope for progressive pedagogy and appears to sidestep the problems of transference that mired the Rousseauian project.

Then the institutional analyses of Ivan Illich and Michel Foucault, examined next, do to Freire's hopeful project precisely what Freud's understanding did to Rousseau's. At the end of that section, we find ourselves in a bleak spot: no form of liberatory education seems to lead people to freedom. But in the process of getting to that point we will have shown how complicated and problematic is the student-teacher relationship, the personal relationship at the center of all education that calls itself progressive, humane, or liberating. We will have discovered, by means of this examination, that behind the promise of modern progressive pedagogy there lies a fundamental paradox.

A paradox, one scholar says, is "a dilemma inherent in the thing itself." It "enhances rather than degrades its matter."[21] Our arrival at a paradox in our consideration of pedagogy based on the student-teacher relationship permits us a new start. In part 2 we go back to the origin of the conversation about education in our tradition—back to

Socrates—in an attempt to explore how educators might respond to paradox once they have discovered it at the center of their project. We find in our own responses to Socrates not one, but two, approaches to paradox. Out of this difference, we formulate our orientation to pedagogy, one that turns away from the student-teacher relationship and turns toward the relationship between teacher-colleagues. We call our approach "collegial teaching."

PART 1

STUDENT AND TEACHER

One repays a teacher badly if one remains only a pupil.

—Friedrich Nietzsche, *Ecce Homo*

1

THE PROMISE OF A PERSONAL PEDAGOGY: ROUSSEAU'S *EMILE*

Emile is an orphan. It makes no difference whether he has his father and mother. Charged with their duties, I inherit all their rights. He ought to honor his parents, but he ought to obey only me. That is my first, or rather, my sole condition.

I ought to add the following one, which is only a consequence of the other, that we never be taken from one another without our consent. This clause is essential, and I would even want the pupil and the governor to regard themselves as so inseparable that the lot of each in life is always a common object for them. . . . But when they regard themselves as people who are going to spend their lives together, it is important for each to make himself loved by the other; and by that very fact they become dear to one another. The pupil does not blush at following in his childhood the friend he is going to have when he is grown. The governor takes an interest in concerns whose fruit he is going to harvest, and whatever merit he imparts to his pupil is an investment he makes for his old age.

—Jean-Jacques Rousseau, *Emile*

ROUSSEAU'S *Emile, or On Education*, published in the earliest days of the modern era, offers the promise of pedagogy that we moderns have been trying to cash for more than two hundred years.[1] Rousseau's pedagogy is built upon the foundation of a carefully cultivated personal relationship between one teacher and one student. From this foundation, Rousseau shows us how to conduct an education that will benefit both the child and society. This education will take its cues from Nature, structuring itself around the natural stages of development any child must traverse. At the same time, it will prepare a social being, a citizen fit for living with fellow citizens. In *Emile,* Rousseau gives us an extended thought experiment in how to educate the good person, one who will be free to live in society but who will not be of society.

Rousseau's masterwork on education frames all the debates it seems possible for us to have about pedagogy. We continue to struggle with the problem of how to implement an education that is individually developmental and socially responsible. Rousseau's answer to the problem is as clear as it can be. Education must be based in the one-to-one relationship of the master and the pupil. It must respect the developmental program Nature has written for all human beings, but it must acknowledge that what is natural to a person who would live in society is not what would be "natural" outside of or before the existence of society. It must recognize the crucial importance of the environment that impinges on the student and conditions his education. This ideal education must not be imperialistic; it must endow the pupil with a sense of limits, limits of self, knowledge, and action. And finally, education must be liberal and liberating. That is, a good education will make a person who is good, who will find friendship, who will not hurt others, and who will hold all social forms suspect because they are likely to be harmful to someone. There is hardly a contemporary dispute over the proper conduct of pedagogy that cannot be subsumed under the outline of educational issues provided by *Emile* and on which Rousseau had a clear view of how to proceed properly.

In our times, we do not necessarily agree with Rousseau's *conclusions.* Rather, we conduct our debates within the terms he set. We agree that education must be based on the child's development, but we debate the nature of that development. We agree that the child's immediate environment is crucial to his learning but we debate how and to what degree to structure and control that environment. We agree that education should be liberal and liberating, but we cannot agree on what those terms mean: "Liberal" as opposed to what? Liberated from what? Above all, we agree that education must be built upon the teacher-student relationship. Some may argue for lower student-teacher ratios in the classroom; others may insist on home schooling. No one imagines an education that does not take for granted the caring relationship between teacher and student at its center.

As the author of our modern educational assumptions, Rousseau made pedagogy seem promising. But in creating this pedagogical promise, he created a paradox. At the same time that he framed for us the promise of pedagogy, Rousseau immersed us in the paradox of trying to teach freedom. Rousseau was the first to see his proposals as an unfortunate compromise with history. He knew that no one could return to a blissful state of nature and he concluded that society was the cause of human evil. That did not deter him from thinking carefully about the possibilities of education. But writing about the possibilities did not blind him to the likely impossibility of his own project. We begin, then, at the beginning of our modern understanding of pedagogy.

A Personal Pedagogy

Philosophers from Plato to Dewey, when they reflect on education, usually begin by remarking on the *social* functions of education. "Education, in its broadest sense, is the means of this social continuity of life," says Dewey on the opening pages of *Democracy and Education*.[2] He points out that "society exists through a process of transmission";[3] the immaturity of the newly born members of the human group, the eventual heirs to society, make this process of social transmission a necessity if the social group is to have any continuity, if it is to have a life longer than one generation. Scarcely any claim could be more obvious or less controversial than this one, and it thus seems to make a solid starting point for any philosophy of education.

How surprised we are, then, when we read in Rousseau's *Emile* that the entire success of his proposed education rests on *removing his pupil from society!* For Rousseau, society is the source of corruption; education's job is to avoid that unavoidable corruption while raising a child. Rousseau must, therefore, remove his charge, Emile, to the country, far from Paris, and isolate him from all the corrupting influences of urban social life. But the isolation must be far more extreme than this. Emile must be allowed to associate with virtually no one but Jean-Jacques—his governor and tutor.[4] It is perhaps impossible to prevent him from mingling with the servants, but they will be under Jean-Jacques's strict supervision; Emile certainly must not be allowed to see or speak to other children—not until he is ready. He need not fear being lonely, however. His tutor, Jean-Jacques, will be his constant companion. He will be Emile's playmate, his parent, his teacher, his friend—all rolled into one.

From these initial conditions—conditions Rousseau insists upon before he is willing even to contemplate raising Emile—we can see the four distinctive features of Rousseau's pedagogy: (1) a reliance on a conception of the child's natural development; (2) the removal of the pupil from society; (3) a strict supervision of the pupil's environment; and finally, the crucible within which the education will take place: (4) a deep and close personal relationship between pupil and teacher. Behind these critical features lies the foundation and the inspiration Rousseau will rely on in raising Emile: Nature. Emile's tutor will rely on his knowledge of a child's "natural" development. But he will also, eventually, imbue his charge with the sense that the modern human condition has the same force of necessity that Nature had originally. Jean-Jacques's task is to "create a new, artificial man, a 'social' man,"[5] a man whose education respects Nature but is also in tune with the nature of human affairs in a corrupting society. The essential spirit of Rousseau's project is to ground Emile's education in Nature and to aim it toward freedom, a freedom to enter with others into social and civic association.

A Personal Relationship

At the heart of this education lies the personal relationship between the student and his teacher. Only within the frame of this one-to-one relationship, this friendship, could a development that preserved much of Nature's influence be nourished. Though Emile's education is designed to protect him from the evils of early social influences, we cannot really call this education antisocial, or even asocial, because from the start it is centered on a relationship with a fellow human being. That is, it is centered on a social relationship, a fact that separates Emile from Rousseau's "savage man" (or "natural man").[6] So much rests on this social relationship that Rousseau goes to elaborate lengths to show how the relationship must be strengthened and protected at every turn. Jean-Jacques isolates himself with his pupil in the country. No other social relationships, accidental or intended, must enter into Emile's life. Any one would have the potential to dilute the primary relationship with the tutor, to weaken it, to set up currents running against it, or to sabotage it in some insidious way.

If we put our minds for a moment into a traditional cast, we can appreciate some of the shock inherent in Rousseau's insistence on the importance of a personal relationship. At the time of *Emile*'s composition, an educator was usually a "preceptor." His job was to instruct pupils by means of precepts—rational, moral statements whose internalization would shape a disciplined, obedient character. Education emerged out of a religious setting, and its job was to promote virtue and tame "fallen" human nature, particularly its infantile expression in children. It mattered little whether the teacher had one pupil or many; the master's posture toward his pupils would be the same—distant, stern, authoritative, an embodiment of reason, morality, and the adult world. His job was to transmit the culture and to shape the child so that he could take his place within that culture. Education's task was to replace the merely human with the moral and the good.

The old preceptorship was a relationship of authority imposed upon the child for his own good. Neither party to this relationship could imagine that "they are going to spend their lives together." It would hardly occur to either to "make himself loved by the other." Such attitudes would undermine the necessary structure of authority within which education took place. No "common lot" could be envisaged, nor was there any "fruit" for the teacher to anticipate harvesting.

Into this tradition comes Rousseau suggesting we abandon this inhumane approach to education and create instead a personal, loving bond between student and teacher. This bond will be the bedrock, the indispensable prerequisite, for any real education at all. And Rousseau was willing to go further in cultivating this bond than anyone before or since: The tutor takes as his sole job the raising of *one child* from infancy to adulthood. He lives with his pupil day and night during this whole period. He dedicates his entire life to one child's education. "One would wish that the governor had already educated someone. That is too much to wish for; *the same man can only give one education.* If two were required in order to succeed, by what right would one undertake the first?" (51; emphasis added).

Even to modern ears, such a venture sounds ludicrous. Rousseau's book is not a practical proposal; it is a "thought experiment" designed to highlight essential features of a good education. In this thought experiment, an exclusive and well-protected intimate relationship between teacher and pupil is the sine qua non of education.

Natural Development

Rousseau's pedagogy is thoroughly developmental. Nature dictates a sequence of development for children. At each successive stage, the child knows the world differently, and better, than at the previous stage.

A child can only progress when he is *ready:* "A child knows that he is made to become a man; all the ideas he can have of a man's estate are opportunities of instruction for him; but he must remain in absolute ignorance of ideas of that estate which are not within his reach. My whole book is only a constant proof of this principle of education" (178). Readiness cannot be rushed, even by the best tutor. For Rousseau, the scale along which development progressed is inscribed by Nature in every human being. Nature reveals when the pupil is ready to progress and Nature points out the direction of development. The tutor must take his cues only from Nature. He must always remember he is "the minister of nature" (317) and that attending closely to Nature's way is the teacher's first obligation, since "everything that is not nature is against nature" (405).

Rousseau sees human beings as moving through qualitatively distinct stages of development. He organizes his book around these stages. Each of the five Books in *Emile* deals with a distinct stage of Emile's development.[7] Each stage has its own objective—the potential it must realize—and each has its own accompanying set of dangers. The stages do not represent an immutable lock-step plan for growth. Instead, these stages represent the way human potentials and capacities are organized; they represent the natural fact that certain capacities rely on others, that certain strengths must be more fully developed before other strengths can even begin to develop. "Each age, each condition of life, has its suitable perfection, a sort of maturity proper to it" (158). These stages of natural development have to be respected: "Nature wants children to be children before being men. If we want to pervert this order, we shall produce pernicious fruits which will be immature and insipid and will not be long in rotting. . . . Childhood has its ways of seeing, thinking, and feeling which are proper to it" (90). Just as Piaget, much later, would think of development in terms of greater differentiation of cognitive activity accompanied by an integration and consolidation of the differentiated cognitive structures, Rousseau urged teachers to give their pupils time to consolidate all developmental gains: "In the career of moral ideas one cannot advance too slowly nor consolidate oneself too well at each step" (99). Each stage in its own time, is Rousseau's overarching admonition.

With each developmental opportunity comes dangers. Successful development provides a ground of solid and irreversible achievements. But missed opportunities, "premature" development, or false consolidations of developments only tentatively achieved can do irreparable harm since future developments will rest on a shaky or absent foundation. "With each lesson that one wants to put into their heads before its proper time, a vice is planted in the depth of their hearts" (92). The pupil must always be ready for the next educational movement and the teacher must ensure that developmental opportunities present themselves only when the child is ready to take advantage of them.

Rousseau's thoroughgoing developmental point of view leads him to make educational pronouncements that seem counterintuitive, even shocking. For example, during the "second period of life," the period of childhood to age twelve, Rousseau says, "Dare I expose the greatest, the most important, the most useful rule of all education? It is not to gain time but to lose it" (93). During this period, before the onset of reason, it is the child's senses and not his intellect that must be developed. Efforts to develop reason would run counter to the plan of Nature, which intends for reason to be developed between ages twelve and fifteen. Attempting to teach a child to be "rational" before his "readiness" for rationality develops would be one example of the socially imposed tendency to "force one soil to nourish the products of another, one tree to bear the fruit of another" (37). Since the aim of the second stage is the "education of the senses," and since most of this education will result from the free and spontaneous play of the child in a rich and variegated environment, the teacher has to do very little if any "teaching" during this stage. The biggest danger, in fact, is premature teaching. "Nature's instruction is late and slow; men's is almost always premature" (215). That is why Rousseau advises the teacher to "lose time," not to gain it.

Rousseau's justification for losing time reveals in detail how completely developmental is his perspective:

> The most dangerous period of human life is that from birth to the age of twelve. This is the time when errors and vices germinate without one's yet having any instrument for destroying them; and by the time the instrument comes, the roots are so deep that it is too late to rip them out. If children jumped all at once from the breast to the age of reason, the education they are given might be suitable for them. But, according to natural progress, they need an entirely contrary one. They ought to do nothing with their soul until all of its faculties have been developed, because while the soul is yet blind, it cannot perceive the torch you are presenting to it or follow the path reason maps out across the vast plain of ideas, a path which is so faint even to the best of eyes. (93)

The nature of development is decisively qualitative. One does not teach a child to be rational through one long, continuous, incremental sequence of instruction in rationality. One teaches rationality by fostering the nonrational development of the senses upon which rationality depends. Only when *that* development is complete—that is, only when there is the proper convergence of experience and physiological maturation—can a teacher attempt to open his pupil's eyes to reason. As Rousseau summarizes this point, "The masterpiece of a good education is to make a reasonable man, and they claim they raise a child by reason! This is to begin with the end, to want to make the product the instrument" (89). In these two sentences is compressed an entire developmental pedagogy.

At all stages of life, the good educator proceeds by paying close attention to the natural inclinations of his individual pupils, regardless of what is natural to any stage. In the preface to *Emile,* Rousseau writes, "Begin, then, by studying your pupils better. For most assuredly you do not know them at all" (34). Instead of adopting the traditional preceptor's interest in truth, Jean-Jacques must adopt an interest in Emile. Even from birth, natural inclinations must be respected. So, babies must be allowed to move and should not be bundled, clothed, or capped. "It seems that we are afraid lest he appear to be alive" (43), Rousseau says of the swaddled infant. At later stages, with the rising of the passions, care must be taken to channel the passions well, but nothing must be done to attenuate them or cut them off. The task of the good teacher is to read Nature and enable it to realize itself in every child. One does not reason with Nature; one tries to follow it. "I therefore closed all the books," says Rousseau's Savoyard Vicar. "There is one open to all eyes: it is the book of nature. It is from this great and sublime book that I learn to serve and worship its divine Author" (306—7). But this attention to Nature does not keep a good educator's eyes only on God in heaven; his attention must be directed to the nature of his particular, individual pupil: "One must know well the particular genius of the child in order to know what moral diet suits him. Each mind has its own form, according to which it needs to be governed; the success of one's care depends on governing it by this form and not by another. Prudent man, spy out nature for a long time; observe your pupil well before saying the first word to him" (94). Such a demand would still be considered rigorous even in the most "child-centered" schools, but Rousseau was an extremist: "I would prefer to follow the established practice in everything than to follow a good one halfway" (34).

Removal from Society

The traditional preceptor battled "fallen" human nature. Rousseau secularized the problem of education. Human beings had fallen, but for him they had fallen from a state of nature, not from a state of grace. Humans had "fallen" into society, which becomes the educator's antagonist. Jean-Jacques battles all of that which lies outside Nature, that which "mixes and confuses the climates, the elements, the seasons," that which "mutilates [the] dog, [the] horse, [the] slave," that which "turns everything upside down," "disfigures everything," that which "loves deformity [and] monsters" (37). His sworn enemy is human beings acting in and influenced by society—in a word, society itself. Society is the source of all the influences that lead educators and parents to try to induce premature development in youngsters. It is society that requires Emile know his right hand from his left at an early age. It is society that demands Emile learn to add and subtract, read and write, sit still, and have good manners—all prematurely.

Good education requires finding an environment in which the project of respecting a child's natural development can be carried out. Ideally, this environment is outside society. In his extremism, Rousseau goes as far as he can to establish the proper conditions for Jean-Jacques's education of Emile. He will take the "orphaned" Emile away from parents, siblings, and any future playmates, and remove him to the country. Emile must be isolated and protected not only from Paris and its wicked temptations, but from all other people, since it is people who carry social norms within them, and it is people who discipline others to those norms.

However, Emile must not be separated from *all* people. He needs his tutor. He needs him for three important pedagogical reasons. First, total isolation from society is impossible, so the tutor becomes a constant safeguard, someone to be vigilant about social contacts wherever they might crop up, someone to ward them off, and someone to palliate their influences when they occur. Second, left to himself, Emile's interactions with a natural surrounding would be random. The tutor can steer and guide Emile; he can artfully arrange for interactions that have great educational potential and he can help Emile learn from his experiences by helping him reflect on them once he has had them. Third, even though Emile is to be raised away from society, he is not being educated to be a "natural man." Emile is destined eventually to take his place in society, so he must be made fit to live in the social world. His tutor will become indispensable in the later stages of education as the person who carefully prepares Emile to enter and survive within society. All three of these functions point to the last important feature in Rousseau's pedagogy: the teacher's role in supervising the student's environment.

Supervision of the Environment

Rousseau may have characterized the pedagogical art he is preaching as the "difficult art . . . of governing without precepts and doing everything by doing nothing" (119), but he makes Jean-Jacques more active than this espousal of "negative" education might suggest. For Rousseau's ideal teacher to "do nothing," he must do, in fact, quite a lot. This seeming contradiction results in a pedagogy of indirection. In the context of his time, we can appreciate why Rousseau says he is "doing nothing." Unlike preceptors, Jean-Jacques will not positively teach his pupil anything: He will not tell him what is true, he will not tell him what to think, he will not tell him what to do. But he will be active in shaping Emile's *environment*. Emile's main teacher is the environment he interacts with. His constraints are set by *its* necessity, not by the arbitrary authority of a teacher. Emile does what he wants within the limits of what his natural environment will permit. But Jean-Jacques is not above tinkering with that environment, so that the constraints it sets serve pedagogical purposes. To be the supervisor of the child's environment is one of the teacher's main pedagogical functions:

> In the first place, you should be well aware that it is rarely up to you to suggest to him what he ought to learn. It is up to him to desire it, to seek it, to find it. It is up to you to put it within his reach, skillfully to give birth to this desire and to furnish him with the means of satisfying it. It follows, therefore, that your questions should be infrequent but well chosen. (179)

Rousseau was the first in our tradition to articulate the educational commonplace, "Present interest—that is the great mover, the only one which leads surely and far" (117). A teacher asks few, but well-chosen questions because the natural environment he artificially constructs engages his student and teaches everything.

But what if Emile does not turn out to be immediately interested in those things Jean-Jacques knows may be powerfully educational for him at his current stage of development? Then the tutor must engage in artifice. The tutor puts the object of interest "within [Emile's] reach," and "skillfully give[s] birth" to Emile's interest in the object. After that, the tutor must capitalize on Emile's nascent interest by providing the means necessary for Emile to learn from his encounter with the object. Rousseau advises the aspiring teacher: "Be satisfied, therefore, with presenting him with objects opportunely. Then, when you see his curiosity sufficiently involved, put to him some laconic question which sets him on the way to answering it" (169). "Giving birth to interest" and making the pupil's present interest "the great mover" imply that the tutor must never be the one who satisfies his charge's interest. Emile's curiosity must always be active ("to feed his curiosity, never hurry to satisfy it" [168]), and he alone must be the one to find answers to its questions.

Rousseau presents us with several examples of how Jean-Jacques fulfills this supervisory function with Emile. An astronomy lesson (169ff.) starts with their observing the rising sun. The following paragraph, which introduces this example, shows how well Jean-Jacques follows not only the letter but also the spirit of the advice to present "objects opportunely" and to follow up with "some laconic questions":

> On this occasion, after having contemplated the rising sun with him, after having made him notice the mountains and the other neighboring objects in that direction, after having let him chat about it at his ease, keep quiet for a few moments like a man who dreams, and then say to him, "I was thinking that yesterday evening the sun set here and that this morning it rose there. How is that possible?" Add nothing more. If he asks you questions, do not respond to them. Talk about something else. Leave him to himself, and be sure that he will think about it. (169)

From this beginning a lengthy but leisurely inquiry begins. Emile and Jean-Jacques hammer stakes into the ground to mark the placements of the setting and rising sun on different days and in different seasons. From the pattern of the stakes, Emile eventually works out the course of the earth's and sun's relative movements.

In a second example, Jean-Jacques discusses with Emile the fact that a straight stick appears bent if partially submerged in water:

> If, for example, he is deceived about the appearance of the broken stick, and to show him his error you are in a hurry to pull the stick out of the water, you will perhaps undeceive him. But what will you teach him? Nothing but what he would soon have learned by himself. Oh, it is not that

> which has to be done! The goal is less to teach him a truth than to show him how he must always go about discovering the truth. In order to instruct him better, you must not undeceive him so soon. (205)

Rousseau then develops this example, proceeding step by step with systematic observations, experimentation, and the inevitable "laconic questions." Jean-Jacques and Emile walk around the stick, observing it bend as they move. Then they look down the stick from its top end. Then they stir up the water around the stick. Finally, they let the water gradually flow out, observing the stick as more and more of it emerges into the air. From all these steps, Emile, learns much more than that the stick is not bent. He learns a method of active inquiry. He learns to think.

These examples show that the teacher has a great deal to do to accomplish his "negative" goals. Jean-Jacques is not imparting knowledge or precepts, and he is not telling Emile what to believe. But, by indirect means and artifice, he *is* teaching Emile. He acts as a stage manager, an engineer of Emile's environment. The tutor sharpens the pedagogical impact of the natural environment: he focuses it, brings its features to the fore, and slows down the pace of his student's spontaneous exploration of it so his student has time to draw conclusions from what he observes.

Raising Emile naturally does not mean Emile will become only a natural scientist. His environment has its social elements and so his inquiries must venture into the social realm. The difference between Emile and other children is that Emile's encounters with the social world will be as carefully controlled as his encounters with the course of the sun or with the stick in its bucket. In one such encounter, Jean-Jacques conspires with the gardener, Robert, to hatch a "lesson" on the meaning of "property." In this case, Jean-Jacques encourages Emile to plant and tend some beans on land that, as Emile learns only later, belongs to Robert. When Emile, one day, comes to find his carefully nurtured bean plot upturned and destroyed, he faces a social puzzle not unlike the puzzle of the bent stick. Robert has destroyed Emile's beans and, when confronted with this fact, Robert tells Emile and Jean-Jacques that, in fact, they had destroyed *his* garden on *his* property where he had planted some irreplaceable "exquisite melons." A new element in this encounter is that this puzzling situation not only provokes Emile's interests, it also provokes his anguish. "Tears flow in streams. The grieving child fills the air with moans and cries" (99). This lesson in the concept of "property" makes it plain that Jean-Jacques will not ignore society in his tutoring of Emile. On the contrary, he will make Emile ready for his inevitable, painful socialization. Jean-Jacques will plant many social "seeds" in Emile so that, when it comes, the final shock of encountering society face to face is not too great for his charge.

Rousseau repeatedly emphasizes that the child must learn from his own experiences with his environment and not from the words imparted by his social companion, the tutor. "Do not give your pupil any kind of verbal lessons; he ought to receive them only from experience" (92). Emile must learn only from necessity and natural "force," never from social authority. "Let him see this necessity in things, never in the caprice of men. Let the bridle that restrains him be force and not authority" (91). "Keep the child in dependence only on things" (85). Nevertheless, the tutor has a major role to play in supervising the environment. Rousseau complements his negative approach to teaching with a positive one, based on the "opportune" presentation of objects and the "laconic" presentation of questions. This positive approach is no less vigorous for being indirect.

In sum, Rousseau's principles lead him to an education that respects nature's developmental plan, that does not confuse the end of development with its instruments but allows each developmental step its time, and that worries constantly about the attempt to develop capacities prematurely. Rousseau's pedagogy also respects society's fierce powers to warp and mutilate natural development. Hence it protects and isolates the student from society. His pedagogy sees development and learning as emerging from interaction with an environment. It thus directs the teacher not to the child, but to the child's environment: the environment is the locus of pedagogical intervention. The tutor's role is thus negative much of the time, and indirect all of the time.

Nevertheless, the teacher is central in this pedagogy because his personal relationship with his pupil creates the entire context within which the pupil's development is fostered. Paradoxically, this pedagogy places the tutor in *direct* emotional relationship with his pupil, while insisting he remain in *indirect* cognitive relationship to him. A developmental pedagogy *requires* a personal, emotional relationship at the heart of it. All the teacher's artfulness, cleverness, and vigilance as a pedagogue will come to naught if he does not establish a direct personal relationship with his pupil as the framework within which development can be guided. That is why Rousseau asserts from the start that Jean-Jacques and Emile are to be inseparable—"never [to] be taken from one another without [their] consent" (53). Rousseau's pedagogy, then, is "natural," developmental, indirect, and above all, personal.

The Promise of a Personal Pedagogy

The Power of Rousseau's Personal Pedagogy

To place the personal relationship between student and teacher at the center of education, as Rousseau did, is to acknowledge, or to rediscover, some powerful features of education. In this section, we discuss four of them.

The first feature is the power of education to shape human character. Rousseau adheres to the ancient view that education *should* aim to shape the character of the student. Teaching "marketable skills" or "building a competitive work force" are antithetical to "building character." And "enhancing self esteem," "educating for independent judgment," and "developing responsibility and commitment" are weak caricatures of this goal. Rousseau had a strong program in mind: Emile would be shaped, in mind, body, and spirit, to meet the vicissitudes of social life. Emile would be, simply, a well-equipped human being: "The goal is less to teach him a truth than to show him how he must go about discovering a truth" (204). Emile's education is "rich in facts and sparing in judgment" (342). Its purpose is, however, to build Emile's judgment. A man whose knowledge is not located "in his memory" but whose knowledge "will be in his judgment" (327) has the kind of character Rousseau would seek to build by means of education.

Rousseau's emphasis on personal relationship recognizes that human character is less influenced by words than by interaction with other "characters." The development of reason and the building of character are not merely intellectual endeavors. As Rousseau put it:

> One of the errors of our age is to use reason in too unadorned a form, as if men were all mind. In neglecting the language of signs that speak to the imagination, the most energetic of languages has been lost. The impression of the word is always weak, and one speaks to the heart far better through the eyes than through the ears. . . . Reason alone is not active. It sometimes restrains, it arouses rarely, and it has never done anything great. Always to reason is the mania of small minds. Strong souls have quite another language. It is with this language that one persuades and makes others act. (321)

Human interaction, especially between intimates, is intellectual *and* emotional in a way that brooks no separation. A teacher divests himself of most of his power to influence if he only engages students intellectually. To be potent, the relationship between teacher and pupil must be as emotionally rich as it is intellectually substantive. A joke, a smile, a failure to smile when expected, an encouraging word, an omitted encouraging word, any of these at the right moment with the right person may do more to shape character than the delivery of a moral precept or a properly reasoned argument.

The second feature of education that derives from Rousseau's insistence on the personal pedagogical relationship is the necessary relational character of *all* education. Humans are inherently relational animals, and human pupils are going to "have" a relationship with their teacher regardless of what that teacher does or how he conceives his pedagogy. If a relationship is not cultivated in some intentional, self-conscious way, one will emerge unintentionally and unconsciously. Using the Piagetian idiom, we may say that the pupil will assimilate the teacher to some pattern of human relating he has already established. He will "make" his teacher into his father, mother, brother, priest, or friend. Given the inevitability of a "relationship," a relationship that will shape and constrain all interactions between the two, it would seem sensible to become self-conscious about student-teacher relationships. A smart teacher will try to cultivate the kind of relationship that will best promote the educational aims he has for his student.

Self-consciousness about the nature of the teacher-student relationship implies an openness to changing the relationship at appropriate moments in the developmental course. For example, as Emile passes into the later stages of childhood, Jean-Jacques notes, "the time is approaching when our relations are going to change, when the master's severity must succeed the comrade's compliance" (175). As the age of reason gives way to the age of passion, "it remains for us, in order to complete the man, only to make him a loving and feeling being—that is to say, to perfect reason by sentiment" (203). This development requires Jean-Jacques to change from a playmate and comrade into a rigorous teacher. Later, as adulthood approaches, the master's severity will give way, in its turn, to a new posture that opens the door to friendship. The teacher must see everything in advance and adjust his relationship to the pupil as each step of the pupil's development dictates.

The third feature that a personal pedagogy forces to our attention is the importance of *trust* between student and teacher. Education necessarily involves the student in taking risks. To think a new thought, to write, to experiment, to make an attempt at something one has not mastered, all are risky ventures. To make it more likely that students will engage in necessary risks, their educational environment must feel safe, secure, and protective. The student must trust his teacher. He must believe that the teacher really cares about his welfare, and is capable of protecting him. Trust is not something that can be guaranteed, imposed on, or required in a relationship. Trust is cultivated in relationship and it is tested and retested there. Trust is central to the process of education, to the capacity of the teacher to lead the student out of developmental immaturity and dependence. Although Rousseau does not use the word "trust" in this passage, trust is what he is describing: "If, therefore, gratitude is a natural sentiment, and you do not destroy its effect by your errors, rest assured that your pupil, as he begins to see the value of your care, will be appreciative of it—provided that you yourself have not put a price on it—and that this will give you an authority in his heart that nothing can destroy" (234).

Trust gives students the courage to take risks, but their efforts need an aim. The fourth potent feature of a personal pedagogy is that pedagogy must have an embodied direction to it. This sense of direction will not only help students decide which risks are worth taking, but will make the entire venture of taking risks seem worthwhile. A student will pursue many specific aims in the course of his education, but he needs to feel a more general, single sense of direction to motivate the entire educational project. The student needs to sense that he is on a path of development that leads somewhere. What will provide this sense of direction? The most ready source of direction is what modern psychology calls the "ego ideal." The pupil gains a sense of direction by identifying with a more mature human being, someone he not only admires and looks up to, but someone he can hope to be like. The intimate, personal bond between the student and his teacher provides the needed sense of continuity between the unfulfilled state of the student and the longed-for "developed" state of the teacher. Thus, to acknowledge the centrality of the personal relationship in education in the manner Rousseau does is to recognize the importance of the "ego ideal" in education, the importance of the personal, trustworthy embodiment of one version of the "educated" state of being.

Rousseau had a powerful insight into the promise of education. By emphasizing the personal and relational nature of the context within which the specifics of education take place, he has shown that a great deal more is entailed in education than merely listening to the words of a preceptor or imitating those words in speech or writing. He saw that education is ultimately a matter of human development, and that human development must take place in the matrix of human relationship. Separately, these two insights may seem trivial; taken together they represent the beginning of a modern and progressive tradition in education. We can see their impact in almost any progressive educator of the twentieth century. George Dennison, for instance, in one of the most articulate and sensitive books on the education of children, *The Lives of Children,* emphasizes what was distinct about "The First Street School": ". . . our reversal of conventional structure, for where the public school conceives of itself merely as a place of instruction, and puts severe restraints on the relationships between persons, we conceived of ourselves as an environment for growth, and accepted *the relationships between the children and ourselves as being the very heart of the school.*"[8] Dennison leans directly and heavily on Dewey, A. S. Neill, and Tolstoy—all writers in the liberal, progressive tradition whose roots may be traced to Rousseau. And it was Rousseau who first placed the fully cultivated personal relationship at the center of education and made it bear the greatest weight.

The Limits of Rousseau's Liberal Education

Much of the liberal tradition in modern education traces its roots to Rousseau. Society is, in this tradition, the principal corrupting influence in a life of freedom. What truth there is to be found, Emile will find by pursuing his "well-regulated freedom."[9] (Recall Rorty: leftists believe "if you take care of freedom, . . . truth will take care of itself."[10]) That is why Emile must be taken away from society and educated, developmentally and "naturally" (within the artificial constraints imposed by his tutor). But Emile will return to society and will live there. He will live more or less well because the freedom he spends his life pursuing is not an imperialistic Freedom, and the truth he will find through this pursuit is not an imperialistic Truth. It is a truth that has its limits and a freedom that will allow Emile to appreciate his own limits. Emile will grow to be a man and will find his place in society, but he will not become a proprietor of truth—either of an essentialist truth of the right or of the derivative and learned truth of the left with which and by which he will sally forth in an effort to reform or remake society. His concerns will always be local, immediate, and human.

Most ideas behind educational reform can be traced back in one form or another to the wealth of ideas in Plato's *Republic,* a book Rousseau calls "the most beautiful educational treatise ever written" (40). Plato's treatise is also distinctive for the way in which it reveals the impulse within philosophy of education to create utopias. Plato goes to elaborate lengths (including blunt deception) to ensure that his properly educated philosophers will maintain themselves as society's rulers. Even the ideas of the democratic John Dewey can become imperialistic and utopian once they get into the hands of a "Progressive Education movement." And Rorty, too, ends up proposing a "liberal utopia" based on the notion that liberals are a " 'we' . . . dedicated to enlarging itself, to creating an ever larger and more variegated *ethnos*."[11] The image of a creeping "we-ness" that emerges from this kind of language gives one pause. Educational thinkers, even of the most liberal persuasion, find it hard to avoid ideas that eventually lead to social planning, political programs, and utopian hopes. But Rousseau is different; he does not fall into this trap. His pedagogy is self-limiting.

Rousseau's educational position rests on one moral precept: "The only lesson of morality appropriate to childhood, and the most important for every age, is never to harm anyone" (104), and later, "So soon as Emile knows what life is, my first care will be to teach him to preserve it" (194). Rousseau offers no good reason for never harming anyone; it is simply something that must not be done. But this precept does not become the basis of a planned society, or an ever-enlarging sentiment of we-ness. It remains merely a mark of what constitutes right action by a good, well-educated individual. In fact, Rousseau immediately says that one cannot follow this precept in society because society is, in effect, a zero-sum game: "The precept of never hurting another carries with it that of being attached to human society as little as possible, for in the social state the good of one necessarily constitutes the harm of another. This relation is the essence of the thing, and nothing can change it. On the basis of this principle, let one investigate who is better: the social man or the solitary man" (105).

Rousseau's pedagogy seems to have an end that, to modern ears, is peculiar, but it is an end that respects the ultimate limit of human experience: the death of the individual. At the end of the age of coming into reason we are told of Emile, "With respect to death, he does not yet know well what it is; but since he is accustomed to submitting to the law of necessity without resistance, when he has to die, he will die without moaning and without struggling. This is all that nature permits at this most abhorred of all moments. To live free and depend little on human things is the best means for learning how to die" (208). For Rousseau, the soul may live on for a while beyond that "most abhorred of all moments," but there is nothing beyond death for which life must prepare or in the name of which society must be refashioned. A liberally educated person's truth is limited by the limits of the person. The Savoyard Vicar tells us, "My limited understanding conceives of nothing without limits. All that is called infinite escapes me. What can I deny or affirm, what argument can I make about that which I cannot conceive?" (283). Emile's education derives from the nature of its locale and its orientation is local. Rousseau's pedagogy demands respect for the limits of knowledge and insists on quiet ignorance as the mark of a well-educated person. Again, the Savoyard Vicar: "We want to penetrate everything, to know everything. The only thing we do not know is how to be ignorant of what we cannot know" (268). Emile is destined to live his life as any life must be lived, alone and always aware of life's natural limits in the realms of biology and knowledge.

Emile will return to society, but he will never be at home in society. At most, he will be at home with just a few friends. The ideal setting for sociality would be a moderately endowed farmyard and house: "There I would gather a society that was select rather than large, composed of friends who love pleasure and know something about it" (351). This select group would be chosen only according to "mutual attachment, agreement of tastes, suitableness of characters" (348). And among people who are "chosen . . . carefully," Emile will grow to think "well of those who live with him" at the same time he is taught "to know the world so well that he thinks ill of all that takes place in it" (236—7). For Rousseau, there is no basis for developing any encompassing, expanding, creeping notions of we-ness. His liberalism is resolute: "If a return to nature is impossible and if society proves incorrigible, then the man who sees clearly how things are is condemned to solitude."[12]

Rousseau's pedagogy is liberal in the old sense that it enables an "emancipation from the here and now of current engagements."[13] Emile will be suspicious of and hostile toward society and any attempt to socialize others not only because of the harm society always does to some, but also because of the immutable demand of society that its participants concern themselves with the here and now of modern life. Emile knows that life is not limited to the here and now; he knows that life offers a rich multitude of pleasures beyond the present instance. Emile looks beyond the limits of his immediate circumstances not with the eyes of a real estate developer or a "citizen of the world," but only in order to be liberated "from servitude to the current dominant feelings, emotions, images, ideas, beliefs and even skills."[14] Rousseau portrays modern people "as beings who have, indeed, lost the sense of living in ourselves, . . . who know how to live only mirrored in the opinions of others."[15] But he holds out the promise that through education one can see himself more wholely in the "mirror of his inheritance," so that he can understand himself more fully. This self-limiting objective frees him from the demands of convention and from the poverty of human experience, and provides whatever justification is necessary for a liberal education.

The Paradox of a Personal Pedagogy

Natural, developmental, personal, and humane, Rousseau's pedagogy offers great promise. A pedagogy grounded in a personally cultivated relationship with the individual student makes a liberal and liberating education seem possible and desirable. Yet embedded in Rousseau's promising pedagogy lies a paradox.

Rousseau bemoans the fact that teaching usually employs "all the most dangerous passions"—"emulation, jealousy, envy, vanity, avidity, and vile fear"—as part of its methods of instruction. He concludes, "All the instruments have been tried save one, the only one precisely that can succeed: *well-regulated freedom*" (92). This one phrase contains the paradox of pedagogy. The paradox of pedagogy is the paradox of inducing and regulating freedom for another person in that person's interest. As one scholar has put it,

> Emile is able to live freely only in relation to his Tutor, by identifying with the rule which the Tutor has established. . . . Emile internalizes the Tutor's rule. . . . This internalization is and must be induced. We may even say that it is forced, and this is indeed what Rousseau intends, when he reminds us in *Contrat social* that we may be forced to be free. He does not suppose that we can be physically constrained to be free. In tracing his argument, what we have found is that liberty demands spiritual constraint—the shaping of passion, opinion, and will. We have found that in the citizen both dependence and freedom are perfected, and in their perfection, made one.[16]

The beauty and brilliance of *Emile* arise from Rousseau's not trying to escape from paradox. Eventually, he found a way personally to elude the paradox of pedagogy, but he was willing to stick with its seeming contradictions for a long while. He appeals, "Common reader, pardon me my paradoxes. When one reflects, they are necessary and, whatever you may say, I prefer to be a paradoxical man than a prejudiced one" (93).

The paradoxical nature of Emile's education is manifested in four aspects of Rousseau's pedagogy. Each of these aspects corresponds to one of the four critical features of Rousseau's personal pedagogy. (1) Rousseau's reliance on a conception of the child's *natural* development grounds his entire pedagogy on the mystical, mystifying, always-contested notion of "Nature." (2) Rousseau's insistence that the tutor remove himself and his pupil from society constitutes an impossible demand. (3) The necessity for the tutor to supervise strictly his pupil's environment requires the tutor to be manipulative. Can anyone create a free person through deception and manipulation? (4) Finally, the intimate, personal relationship with the teacher, into which and then out of which the pupil must grow, constitutes a deeply paradoxical setting for a liberating education. How will the pupil ever get free from his teacher—"the friend he is going to have when he is grown"? (53)

Supervising the Environment or Manipulating the Child?

The most disturbing aspect—to people who would be modern and humane educators—of Jean-Jacques's teaching method lies in his continual and cheerful willingness to be manipulative, so we take up the third paradox first. Jean-Jacques goes to elaborate lengths to deceive Emile, always, so is the rationale, to set the stage properly so Emile can learn from his interactions with his environment. Rousseau is frank about the tutor's need to control and manipulate his pupil:

> Let him always believe he is the master, and let it always be you who are. There is no subjection so perfect as that which keeps the appearance of freedom. . . . Doubtless he ought to do only what he wants; but he ought to want only what you want him to do. He ought not to make a step

> without your having foreseen it; he ought not to open his mouth without your knowing what he is going to say. (120)

Deception in the name of development is a ground of Emile's instruction: "Although Emile is not directly dependent on the will of his Tutor, and recognizes no connection between the consequences of what he does and what is subject to the Tutor's will, yet he is indirectly dependent, in that the Tutor wills the entire framework within which Emile's actions "naturally" have the consequences the Tutor intends."[17]

The most elaborate deception in *Emile* involves a conspiracy between Jean-Jacques and a magician from a local fair. Jean-Jacques helps Emile discover that one of the magician's tricks works by means of a hidden magnet. Emile tries to expose the magician's trick. A complex plot has been formulated between tutor and magician whereby Emile is eventually humiliated in public; then the magician comes to Emile's home, discusses the incident with Jean-Jacques and his charge, excuses Emile's part in the affair since he is only a child, and chastises the tutor for allowing such prideful behavior by a child (172—75). It seems puzzling that a pedagogy grounded in Nature and aimed toward freedom should require such elaborate deception and artifice. Why can't Nature be counted on to show herself without Jean-Jacques's helping hand? Can one make a free person by deceiving and manipulating him? These are critical questions for all developmental pedagogies.

Developmentalism is often accused of being "elitist" because a developmental teacher must assume that she is at a higher level of development than her students. It is only by virtue of her more advanced level that she can guide her students upward through the stages of development. A developmental educator must make decisions about educational procedure that she can neither explain nor justify to her pupils, for her pupils are not sufficiently developed to understand the explanation or justification. The teacher may, like Jean-Jacques, have considerable foresight about where her students are heading, yet she will have to remain silent, since neither her foresight nor her predictions can help the student make progress. Indeed, announcing her views of where her students are headed may well hinder their progress. Students must achieve their own progress based on their own individual levels of understanding and functioning. The teacher can only place the student in unsettling, disequilibrating situations, situations out of which the student may develop.

Disequilibration can, of course, produce profound anxiety. Emile was distraught to find his carefully tended bean plot destroyed. Jean-Jacques's deception is an absolutely unavoidable, if unpleasant, part of Emile's intellectual development. In another instance, Jean-Jacques arranges for himself and Emile to get lost in a forest not far from his home. Again we have tears, this time "hot tears" (181). But the tears are a necessary part of the experience that is going to lead to Emile's learning the connection between the course of the sun, which he had studied previously, and how to get one's bearings on the earth's surface. The incident proceeds with a series of "laconic questions," and ends with Emile's discovering that he can use his knowledge of the sun's movements to discover his way out of the forest and back to his home. With this discovery, Emile "[claps] his hands and [lets] out a cry of joy" (181).

The modern developmentalist faces a moral dilemma. Rousseau's "well-regulated freedom" comes without such modern mitigating apparatuses as "informed consent." Even if the modern teacher tried to secure consent for the uncomfortable and upsetting situations he will have to lead his students into, such consent could never be "informed." The understanding necessary to "inform" the consent requires the disequilibrating experience before it can be attained! The alternative stance, which requires the teacher always to be honest and straightforward, always to obtain consent beforehand, is attractive for its straightforward openness and its lack of moral ambiguity. But the developmental teacher must reject such an approach because, though it will work for teaching facts and simple skills, he knows such an approach will not be effective in teaching conceptual or moral understanding. The developmentalist will have to commit himself instead to inflicting pedagogical deception and suffering his students have not requested and for which they are unable to give their permission.

Developmentalists ease themselves out of this dilemma (and out of the charges of "elitism") by appealing to a higher value than the values of honesty and openness. They argue that theirs is, in fact, education for liberty and for democracy, noting that it was the great American philosopher of democracy, John Dewey, who philosophically grounded the developmental point of view in education.[18] Lawrence Kohlberg defends developmentalism against the charge of elitism by pointing out that the developmental teacher "attempts to get all children to develop in the direction of recognizing the principles he holds,"[19] where the emphasis is on "*all* children." The teacher does start from a cognitively superior position compared to the child, but the teacher puts all his energies into launching the child on a path that will reduce and eventually eliminate the developmental differences between them. The goal is to have every child catch up to or surpass his teacher.

Even if developmentalism is democratic, is not getting children to develop "in the direction of recognizing the principles which [the teacher] holds" a form of indoctrination? Kohlberg says no: "Because the development of these principles is natural they are not imposed on the child—he chooses them himself. . . . These principles are not presented as formulae to be learned ready-made or as rote patterns grounded in authority. Rather, they are part of a process of reflection by the student and the teacher."[20] Since nobody can make someone else develop, and since the developing is done by the child himself, developmentalists argue that their pedagogy is noncoercive and non-elitist. The pedagogy is democratic because its aim is to render teacher and students finally equal.

The developmentalist's defense against the charges of elitism and indoctrination is grounded in a claim about the *naturalness* of the process of development. If our freely chosen development is to lead us all to a common end, it can only be because this development is grounded in our common nature. Even acknowledging that this view does not require us to venture into arguments about a preformed *human* nature,[21] it does force us to confront the problem of relying, ultimately, on any concept of Nature at all.

The Contested Concept of Nature

In these times of sophisticated cultural critique, it is very hard to convince anyone that anything is natural. Even the distinction between "natural" and "cultural" can easily be shown to be a construction of culture.

But the developmental educator still needs Nature. He orients his thinking about teaching and learning around the concept of development. He takes development to be the aim of education. He uses his conviction that development is qualitative, structural, sequential, logical, and fostered by disequilibrium in the organism's attempt to adapt itself to its environment to guide his every decision as a teacher. His whole orientation and rationale is grounded in an organizing concept that he takes to be natural. And then there is no good way to defend his central organizing device, Nature, against the suspicion that is spread whenever the claim of naturalness rears its head. What is he to do?

He may take some comfort from Rousseau's own parry to the problem of Nature. Near the beginning of *Discourse on Inequality,* Rousseau wrote, "For it is no light enterprise to separate that which is original from that which is artificial in man's present nature, and attain a solid knowledge of a state which no longer exists, *which perhaps never existed,* and which will probably never exist, yet of which it is necessary to have sound ideas if we are to judge our present state satisfactorily."[22] Rousseau's concept of nature is really a weapon in a war of persuasion. It might be thought of as a concept with no center but with very sharp edges. Nature can be used effectively to develop some critical distance on Culture, even if it can tell us nothing factual about human nature sans culture. In the Second Discourse, Rousseau paints us a picture of "savage man" in a "state of nature" that is unlikely to be true, and that one need not believe. Yet despite our lack of belief in his "state of nature," the picture Rousseau paints makes us look at present culture in a new light. Rousseau's imagined savage shows us fundamental flaws in civilization, flaws we might be driven to do something about. This is the same tactic Allan Bloom recently used to try to persuade others to join anew in "the rational quest for the good life according to nature."[23] Nature becomes a measuring stick against which to compare any proposal for reforming a society that is corrupt.

In *Emile,* Rousseau imagines doing something about some of those flaws in present society through pedagogy. When he says, for instance, that "all wickedness comes from weakness. The child is wicked only because he is weak. Make him strong; he will be good" (67), he is not really telling us something factual. He is rather appealing to us to see that we could be living a better life and finding more happiness if we cultivated ourselves differently in the course of our childhood. There is always something that culture misses, always something that culture suppresses, ignores, deforms, or inhibits. Talk about Nature gives us a way to talk about what is lost in society. A concept of Nature gives a way to bring out the fact that culture does violence to us.

The developmentalist's reliance on a naturalistic pedagogy puts him out of step with the times and thrusts him into an untenable philosophical position. Nevertheless, like Rousseau, he will continue to follow his convictions about Nature without shrinking from the critique that his criticism was not necessarily based in anything historical, real, or even attainable. As with Rousseau, the stakes are too high to abandon good work simply because it is mired in conceptual paradox.

Removal from Society?

From the beginning, Rousseau insists that Jean-Jacques withdraw with Emile from society. This condition is crucial to protecting and giving full power to the personal relationship he intends to form with Emile, and upon which his entire pedagogy will rest. Yet this aspect of his pedagogy—this fundamental strategy—is also problematic. Upon reflection it appears virtually impossible.

Especially in our times, forming a complete relationship like the one Rousseau imagined between Jean-Jacques and Emile is impractical. Today's "tutors" teach in schools of one sort of another, and schools are social institutions. Even though schooling defers most students' responsibility for earning a living through work in society, much of the explicit curriculum, and virtually all of the hidden curriculum, is devoted to socializing and preparing students for the discipline of the work world. We can scarcely call entry into a contemporary school a withdrawal from society.

The modern Rousseauian teacher again faces a dilemma. He cannot remove his pupil from society but he cannot afford to abandon the idea of doing so. He may strive to make his classroom into a "country retreat," even though it be located in an urban center with teeming city streets or in a suburban area where schools and malls enter into easy symbiosis. He cannot withdraw from society, but perhaps he can create a "space" where he and his students together can gain some distance from society. Perhaps he can create an artificial community, with somewhat different norms and expectations, a place where development that runs counter to society's aims can be fostered.

But to do so is a dangerous enterprise. Society well knows how dependent it is on educational transmission; it knows how much its survival in its present form depends on the "proper education of the young." It does not treat lightly those who would steer education toward other aims, nor does it treat lightly those who are the products of such alternative educations. As with Plato's philosopher returning from daylight to the cave, the developmental teacher must engage in the single effort of making life dangerous and difficult for his students even as he strives to promote what he believes will make them wise and happy. He must engage in the paradoxical effort of protecting students from society in the very heart of a social institution.

Pedagogical Intimacy

In Rousseau's pedagogy, the carefully cultivated, intimate relationship between tutor and pupil constitutes the crucible within which Emile's education takes place. The personal relationship is the matrix of the education; developmental pedagogy scarcely seems possible without it. But even beyond the practical constraints of finding a haven for this relationship discussed above, the personal relationship required by Rousseau is double-edged and problematic in its own right.

As the traditional "preceptor" knew only too well, there are dangers and difficulties that invariably arise once a personal relationship is created, one in which the pupil and the governor "regard themselves as so inseparable that the lot of each in life is always a common object to them," one in which "it is important for each to make himself loved by the other." A relationship of this sort is difficult to leave, both for teacher and student. If the aim of education is development, and if the teacher's goal is to promote the development of autonomy and independence, then his pedagogy must aim toward eventual equality of teacher and student. The original intimate pedagogical relationship in which a student is dependent on his teacher will inevitably curtail the development that pushes the student to a new status with respect to his teacher.

Just as children are not permitted to marry their parents and remain in their original families but are pushed out of the family and required to start new families with their peers, so too must teachers push their students to sever their relationships with them and to go "back to society" to put to use what they have learned in the original relationship. Just as there is a perceived danger of incest in families, there is a danger of incest in teaching too. There is, in teaching, an incestuous urge toward perfecting the all-important relationship that has been the foundation and indispensable framework for the student's education and for the teacher's vocation. Both teacher and student have a strong motive to make the relationship more and more satisfying. Pedagogical incest can be as tempting as any other form.

Rousseau reveals the shape of these urges at the end of *Emile.* At the end of this long story, a girl, Sophie, is chosen, properly educated, and prepared to be Emile's wife. Emile and Sophie marry and have a child. But then, staggeringly, Jean-Jacques continues to live with them! The relationship between Jean-Jacques and Emile, so carefully nurtured for so many years, cannot be ended. Educated to independence and now a father and the head of his own family, Emile remains dependent on his old tutor. In the final paragraph, Emile takes for himself the responsibility for rearing his own child, but immediately begs Jean-Jacques to "remain the master of the young masters." "Advise us and govern us," he says. "We shall be docile. As long as I live, I shall need you. I need you more than ever now that my functions as a man begin" (480).

So this is what Rousseau meant when, in the opening pages, he referred to "the fruit [the tutor] is going to harvest." We see why Rousseau says that "whatever merits [Jean-Jacques] imparts to his pupil is an investment he makes for his old age." Jean-Jacques will live with his pupil and his pupil's wife in a ménage à trois. This is the sinister side of the tenet that "the same man can only give one education." If he is never prepared to leave his student, if he rears a student who is not capable of leaving him, then of course he can only give one education. If his whole life is dedicated to providing but one education, then naturally he will find it hard to leave his pupil.

This pedagogical incest is only one manifestation of an impulse to perfection that runs throughout *Emile.* Despite the place accorded to chance in what Emile will become, Rousseau suggests that pedagogy can perfect the man. Jean-Jacques, for example, displays an attitude of possessive creativity toward Emile: "I am Emile's true father; I made him a man. I would have refused to raise him if I had not been the master of marrying him to the woman of his choice—that is, of my choice" (407). At the end of the book, Jean-Jacques is inclined to think of the couple as his personal work of art. He grows giddy with the pride of craftsmanship: "How many times, as I contemplate my work in them, I feel myself seized by a rapture that makes my heart palpitate!" (480). This is too much pleasure in the results of teaching. Yet this reaction is but an exaggeration of the feelings all teachers are tempted to feel with respect to their "best" students. Even if we are willing to let them go, we still want to claim a bit of their souls as our own.

Despite his profession that Emile is to be hardened by his encounters with Nature, Rousseau nonetheless implies that students are fragile, unformed, and merely await the perfecting pedagogy of their masters in order to mature properly. The notion that one mistake by the teacher may cause his good work to come to naught ("A single proved lie told by the master to the child would ruin forever the whole fruit of the education" [216]), or that every detail of the teacher's method is crucial ("Everything must be foreseen, and everything must be foreseen very far ahead of time" [175]) betrays an attitude that the teacher, in fact, is the anchor of the educational encounter. This attitude comes from an overestimation of the teacher's power to influence and from an underestimation of the student's ability to interact robustly with his teacher. It intimates, though the general gist of Rousseau's advice runs to the contrary, that the student's achievements are fragile and his development reversible. It does not allow that the student brings his own judgment to the interaction with his teacher or that he responds selectively and judiciously to what the teacher says or does with regard to him. Again, we are presented with an implicit image of the all-powerful artist whose one slip of the chisel will forever damage his sculpture. To create a perfect product, one must be very powerful. If one is very powerful, one must be very careful. Only so can one ever successfully complete the perfect student.

Teachers, of course, can never create the perfect student. Every term of the sentence is problematic. They are not *creating* students in the first place. They are not trying to do anything *perfectly.* And they are not trying to make *students,* but rather educated adults like themselves. But for teachers the temptations represented by these terms will never be far from hand. The temptation to perfection will not be far from teaching grounded in the carefully nurtured, close, personal relationship between teacher and student.

This, then, is the ultimate paradox of Rousseau's pedagogy. Rousseau carefully creates what he is not willing to destroy and yet what must be destroyed: Jean-Jacques's loving relationship with Emile. Any developmental teacher knows he needs a "good relationship" with his student if he is to practice his pedagogy, and yet the more successful he is in creating it, the more dangerous and difficult will be the necessary ending of this relationship. He courts disaster in his work even as he courts success. He will have to hope, as he pursues his ambiguous and paradoxical pedagogy, that he can find a way to leave his work unfinished, unperfected, partial, and open-ended. He cannot be an artist nor can he hope to harvest any fruit. He will have to be satisfied with weeding and watering in a garden that belongs to someone else.

Eluding the Paradox: Rousseau as Writer

Rousseau was a solitary walker, a writer of confessions, a political philosopher, the author of a near-novel on education. He was not a teacher. In *Emile,* he presents us with the promise and the paradox of modern pedagogy, but as a writer he eludes the paradox associated with the hope he holds out for us. We will do well to pay attention to what Rousseau does in his effort not to do what he says must be done in regard to teaching.

We find in the *character* of Rousseau's writing, more than in the content of that writing, something instructive about education. Instead of telling his readers directly how to educate, Rousseau invites them into a conversation about education, a conversation from which they may profit or not, out of which some educational effort may develop or not. Rousseau eludes the paradox of pedagogy by rejecting the role of pedagogue, and by adopting instead the posture of a conversationalist.

The written conversation about education into which Rousseau invites us is striking for the way it engages us. It is engaging both because of Rousseau's writing voice and because of its penchant toward narrative. Rousseau's voice is at once sympathetic, witty, and authoritative. A superb stylist, he fashions his sentences with clarity and flourish. He is a master of the well-crafted aphorism. As a result of his engaging style, we readers find ourselves attached to Rousseau the writer and eager to talk with him.

This attachment is further strengthened by Rousseau's tendency to write narrative fiction. In imagining a pupil and naming him, and then casting himself as the pupil's tutor, Rousseau has chosen a most effective device to elaborate his philosophy of education. This narrative format allows him to move back and forth easily between didactic discourse and concrete narration. However, the tendency to write narrative prose gradually overtakes the author, so that by the lengthy and concluding Book 5, on Sophie's education and Emile's marriage to her, the book has become almost a novel.

Rousseau's engaging writing creates a relationship with his reader that parallels the personal relationship cultivated by Jean-Jacques with Emile. Readers feel drawn to Rousseau. His humor and generosity of spirit make us like him; his wit makes us admire him; his authority makes us respect him. We want to converse with him. Out of this conversation may come, perhaps, developments in our own thinking that will help us become better teachers.

Yet the warm and witty embrace of the reader that makes this conversation so inviting threatens to make it didactic. It is all too easy, when reading his book, to treat Rousseau as the master and to follow where he leads. To counter this tendency in his readers, to avoid adopting the authorial role of pedagogue, Rousseau does two things. First, he impresses on us that his educational project is both practically and theoretically impossible. Second, he recurrently reminds us that it is we readers who are the teachers—he is only a dreamer.

By making his proposal so extreme, Rousseau forces on his readers the awareness that Emile's education is impossible. We are supposed to devote our entire professional life to teaching one child? We are supposed to give up any kind of private life in order to live constantly with this child? We are supposed to retire from society for the better part of the duration to accomplish this education? It is, in fact, worse than that. The good master would himself have to have been raised by a good master, and so on back through time:

> It would be necessary that the governor had been raised for his pupil, that the pupil's domestics had been raised for their master, that all those who have contact with him had received the impressions that they ought to communicate to him. It would be necessary to go from education to education back to I know not where. How is it possible that a child be well raised by one who was not well raised himself? (50)

The whole educational project would have to be preformed or else it could not proceed.

Rousseau's project, by his own analysis, is even theoretically impossible. He does not wish to side with those like John Dewey who see education as the means for forming participants in a specific social and political community. Nor does he wish to side with "individualists" who see education as promoting an entirely personal happiness. He insists on the rigorous separation of individual and social aims and argues that education must never confuse these two ends, or combine them in any proportion: "Forced to combat nature or the social institutions, one must choose between making a man or a citizen, *for one cannot make both at the same time*" (39; emphasis added). One must choose between rearing a natural man, entirely for himself, or a social man, entirely for the community. The two are so fundamentally different that the creation of each would require an entirely different education. To try to create a natural man who must live within the civil order is to create a monster, or worse: a bourgeois:

> He who in the civil order wants to preserve the primacy of the sentiments of nature does not know what he wants. Always in contradiction with himself, always floating between his inclinations and his duties, he will never be either a man or a citizen. He will be good neither for himself nor for others. He will be one of these men of our days: a Frenchman, an Englishman, a bourgeois. He will be nothing. (40)

Yet we may wonder, what is this education we have just read about? What has Emile's education been if not the raising of a natural man destined for the civil order? Indeed, before the introductory passage is over, Rousseau announces to us that he *is* going to try to produce "the double object" he declares to be either impossible or undesirable ("a bourgeois," a "nothing"):

> There remains, finally, domestic education or the education of nature. But what will a man raised uniquely for himself become for others? If perchance the double object we set for ourselves could be joined in a single one by removing the contradictions of man, a great obstacle to his happiness would be removed. In order to judge of this, he would have to be seen wholly formed: his inclinations would have to have been observed, his progress seen, his development followed. In a word, the natural man would have to be known. I believe that one will have made a few steps in these researches when one has read this writing. (41)

And later, Rousseau affirms his educational objective: "There is a great difference between the natural man living in the state of nature and the natural man living in the state of society. Emile is not a savage to be relegated to the desert. He is a savage made to inhabit cities" (205). So, although Rousseau's own analysis tells us his educational project is doomed, he is going to attempt it anyway. Why?

Rousseau is going to attempt the impossible because in writing his book he *attempts* nothing. He succeeds absolutely at what he does, which is to write a near-novel that invites the reader into a conversation. Rousseau spells out his educational ideas not by becoming a real pedagogue with real students, but by telling us a rambling story about vivid characters, filled with detours and digressions. The form of Rousseau's writing suggests that his educational ideas must not be taken as a systematic program, or even as a viable individual project.

The second way Rousseau avoids the role of pedagogue and counters the warm attachment of his reader is by suggesting, occasionally but insistently, that despite all the advice he is showering on us, he can really do very little to help us. He reminds us that we are the teachers. By implication, he is but a dreamer. He suggests that our own intelligence, not his, will have to bear the main burden of our becoming good teachers: "If you have to be told everything, do not read me" (137); "The reader does not expect me to despise him so much as to give him an example of every kind of study" (182); "But, on the other hand, how many times have I declared that I did not write for people who have to be told everything?" (487 n. 6). Rousseau reminds the reader that it is he, not Rousseau, who, in the end, must do the hard work of teaching.

In the final analysis, Rousseau can do little to help teachers because he is *not* a teacher. He is a thinker and a writer, and thus, more concerned with perfecting his project than with making it practical. In his preface he tells us that he is not going to "propose what *can* be done" (34; emphasis added), for that would entail proposing "some good that can be allied with the existing evil," a project he has no interest in whatsoever. Rather he is going to propose what *should* be done. Rousseau is explicit about *not* solving the problem of implementing an education based on his principles for us:

> The greater or lesser facility of execution depends on countless circumstances that are impossible to determine otherwise than in a particular application of the method to this or that country, to this or that station. Now all these particular applications, not being essential to my subject, do not enter into my plan. Other men will be able to concern themselves with them, if they wish, each for the country or estate he may have in view. (35)

This prefatory warning sounds a deep note. It reminds us that we are the ones who must live our lives as teachers. Rousseau would make no compromise with his actual social circumstances, which he viewed as evil, nor would he suggest a return to a state of nature, which he knew was impossible. Rousseau lived his life as a philosopher, a writer, and a dreamer. We can enter into a conversation with him. We may even feel that we have "learned something" from our time with him. Eventually, though, *our* time must come when we go away and choose a life of our own, in teaching or out, doing as we see fit on our own.

"If you have to be told everything, do not read me." In the harshness of this statement, there is a kindness. It is the kindness of the educator who knows that the educational relationship must contain its own destruction, that eventually the best of pupils must leave the best of teachers. Rousseau, the writer, establishes a good pedagogical relationship with his readers, and then he invites them to experience, as any good pupil must, the wrenching trauma of this brutal fact of development.

But Jean-Jacques the tutor stays. He lives out his life with Emile, Sophie, and their child. Emile does not grow up to live on his own. His teacher does not depart. In this final paradoxical moment of his book, Rousseau confronts us with what we think is the inevitable trap of any modern personal pedagogy.

2

THE PARADOX OF A PERSONAL PEDAGOGY: FREUD'S CONCEPT OF TRANSFERENCE

> Nobody said not to, so I jumped aboard . . . , a capable boy of learning, and I see now capable of adoring worshipping that rudeness of power of which he was a greater student than anybody, oh and that menace of him where it might be all over for anyone in his sight from one instant to the next, that was what it all turned on, it was why I was there, it was why I was thrilled to be judged by him as a capable boy, the danger that he really was a maniac. . . .
>
> So I knew everything, and everything brings with it an exacting discretion, I went back to school to stay.
>
> —E. L. Doctorow, *Billy Bathgate*

ROUSSEAU ELUDED THE paradox of pedagogy by not being a pedagogue. He was a writer who left us a tantalizing book. We have taken *Emile* as a promissory note. If we are to judge by the modern investment in the educational enterprise, the note is a valuable one, worth much effort and trouble.

Into this scene of at least modest hopefulness comes another figure to say, "Rip up the note; Rousseau's marker is no good." Sigmund Freud's psychoanalysis suggests that pedagogy in practice is a form of human relationship destined to provoke unending dependency, the messy continuing demand for relatedness, the knotty entanglement that Rousseau's final paragraph (in which Jean-Jacques consents to remain with Emile and Sophie) can only tentatively anticipate. Freud's concept of *transference* casts a dark shadow over whatever hopefulness we may find in Rousseau's promise. Instead of leading to freedom, a personal and humane pedagogy may seduce the student into an enslavement to his past. Liberation through pedagogy may be a paradoxically paralyzing project.

Rousseau's pedagogy is grounded in a critique of modern society, a critique expressed by means of an appeal to Nature. Freud also provides a critique of modern society, and his critique, too, is advanced in an appeal to Nature (via his notion of "instinct"). Whereas Rousseau disguised his pessimism and implied that the lot of humans might be improved by education, Freud is brutal about not offering any obvious route of escape from society. What he offers instead is a deep inquiry into the brutality of modern forms of relating to one another. At the heart of every comforting, socially useful, productive relationship is a kernel of violence directed at the self or at others.[1] The notion of *transference* throws a wrench into virtually every effort undertaken in modern society to get people together for personal or social improvement. Pedagogy, the relationship through which we imagine ourselves equipping future generations, does not escape the glare of this severe critique.

Rousseau and every good teacher of our time think that students profit if teacher and student take an interest in one another, get to know each other on more than a purely intellectual basis, "become dear to one another." Rousseau put the personal relationship at the center of progressive pedagogy where it has remained ever since. Freud's concept of transference corrodes this hope of modern education. Like an acid, transference eats away at the promise of a personal pedagogy. As Janet Malcolm, one of the most acute commentators on the contemporary psychoanalytic scene, puts it,

> The concept of transference at once destroys faith in personal relations and explains why they are tragic: we cannot know one another. We must grope around for each other through a dense thicket of absent others. We cannot see each other plain. A horrible kind of predestination hovers over each new attachment we form. "Only connect," E. M. Forster proposed. "Only we can't," the psychoanalyst knows.[2]

The "horrible predestination" is that every personal relationship will always be ultimately unsatisfying. We are condemned by desire to search for a completion of the self, and we are predestined always to be disappointed. The concept of the transference tells us that we will repeat this cycle of searching and failure endlessly through life. In the educational idiom, we will always be students looking for the perfect teacher, or teachers in search of a few good students. We will also always be failures, and the brutality left in the wake of our efforts will not deter us from continuing on roughly the same course throughout our lives. Like Billy Bathgate, we all usually go "back to school to stay."

Freud's concept of transference provides a framework for understanding why a pedagogy whose fundamental condition is the development of a personal relationship between student and teacher must remain forever ambiguous and paradoxical. It reminds us that in the imagined kindness of an imaginably liberatory pedagogical encounter, there is a brutality that binds. In the previous chapter, we identified the need to rely on a concept of Nature, the imperative to remove the child from society, the tutor's manipulativeness, and the impulse to complete or perfect the personal pedagogical relationship as four problematic aspects of Rousseau's pedagogy. Freud shows us how all problems of pedagogy are subsumed under the final problem. The modern teacher must create what we must finally call, if we are honest, a loving relationship between himself and his student. There can be no pedagogy without love. Yet love poses, Freud shows us, a grave threat to pedagogy. Teaching may always require love, but love always seeks to undermine teaching. Freud's discussion of "the transference" will help us understand why.

The Transference

What is transference? Psychoanalysis tells us that transference is many things: Love. Hostility. A neurosis. The basis of cure from unresolved intrapsychic conflicts. A resistance to cure. A tactic. A strategy. The basis of every personal relationship.

Transference as Neurosis

Freud originally used the term "transference" as part of the more specific concept of a "transference neurosis." In the transference neurosis, the patient suddenly began to manifest either strong feelings of love or strong feelings of hostility, or both, toward the figure of the analyst. Freud called these affects "neurotic" because they were inconsistent with the situation in which they were felt and expressed. As Freud put it, "The patient has transferred on to the doctor intense feelings of affection which are justified neither by the doctor's behavior nor by the situation that has developed during the treatment."[3] Because the analyst introduced only the smallest elements of his personality into the psychoanalytic encounter, he did nothing to create a basis for genuine love or hate.

Psychoanalysis was designed to proceed by rather strict rules, and the figure of the analyst had to remain shadowy, marginal, out of sight behind the patient's head, seldom heard from. He was not to give advice. His interventions were to be tediously focused on breaking down resistances to following the fundamental rule of psychoanalysis ("to report to us whatever internal perceptions [the patient] is able to make . . . in the order in which they occur to him . . . to leave aside any criticism of what he finds, whatever shape that criticism may take"[4]). Occasionally the analyst provided interpretations for the patient to consider. Over the long run, the analyst was under the imperative to remain neutral, blank, and "generalized." In this way he made himself into a screen onto which patients could project feelings that arose originally in response to persons significant in the genesis of their emotional lives. Affects originally experienced with parents, a significant sibling, an uncle, or a caretaker would be, under these rigorous conditions, unconsciously *transferred* in analysis from the original object onto the blank screen of the analyst.

Transference is a neurosis, then, because it is an instance in which present behavior is maladaptively driven by repressed infantile feelings. The overpowering love, or hate, for the analyst derives from a long-"forgotten," now unconscious, feeling for a parent-figure, a person not present in the room with patient and analyst, but dictating the experience transpiring between them.

Transference as Re-experience

The transference is indispensable to the patient's discovering the conflicts and repressed emotions that lie at the root of his symptoms. The transference allows the patient to rediscover in the present the repressed emotional conflicts from the past that would otherwise remain difficult to recover because they have been, in fact, "forgotten." Even if evidence of old conflicts surfaced in dreams or fantasies or slips that could be subjected to interpretation during analysis, the understanding of such interpretations can easily remain merely intellectual and hence ineffective. It is only through the transference neurosis that the patient can *re-experience* in the present old patterns of emotional reaction. Freud said,

> The decisive part of the work is achieved by creating in the patient's relation to the doctor—in the "transference"—new editions of the old conflicts; in these the patient would like to behave in the same way as he did in the past, while we, by summoning up every available mental force [in the patient], compel him to come to a fresh decision. Thus the transference becomes the battlefield on which all the mutually struggling forces should meet one another.[5]

The recognition that comes through finding oneself in the very act of feeling and experiencing old conflicts, of finding oneself on an actual, immediate "battlefield," is of a different order than the results of interpreting dreams, behaviors, or associative links. There is a shock of recognition, the shock of staring a piece of evidence in the face, that cannot be dismissed as can an analyst's suggested meaning of a dream. Transference involves the patient in emotional discovery, and discovery that has an emotional component is, according to Freud, the only kind of discovery that can lead to genuine change.

Transference as Resistance

Change is never easy, however. The battlefield of the transference is, ideally, a place for the patient to observe for the first time in the cooler light of rationality those emotional conflicts, those narcissistic wounds, that have driven him throughout his life. Given this representation of the analytic scene, it is easy to focus on the words "conflict" and "wound" and to imagine that a patient would do all he could to change, that he would gladly have his wounds healed and his conflicts resolved. It is easy to imagine that, once begun, the process of change would proceed apace. But psychoanalysis shifts the emphasis in this representation to the fact that it is on the basis of his wounds that a patient is *driven throughout life*. Repressed emotional conflicts condition the manner in which a person relates to all others all his life. They establish patterns of relationships that, over the long run in life, have been more or less successful:

> Each person, through the combined operation of his innate disposition and the influences brought to bear on him during the early years, has acquired a specific method of his own in his conduct of his erotic life—that is, in the preconditions to falling in love which he lays down, in the instincts he satisfies and the aims he sets himself in the course of it. This produces what might be described as a stereotype plate (or several such), which is constantly repeated—constantly reprinted afresh—in the course of the person's life.[6]

Change is difficult because it requires one to give up long-established patterns of behavior that, regardless of their painful side effects, have "worked." To change, the patient must give up his very ways of being.

To account for the fact that patients will not readily give up their "more or less successful" patterns of neurotic behavior, psychoanalysis posits that there is a "secondary gain" obtained even from debilitating symptoms. Secondary gain is the reward one gets from entering what sociologists call the "sick role." Symptoms may be somewhat debilitating to the person, but they bring with them certain social privileges that have a pleasurable component. The transference is a reenactment of past patterns of relationships that have had a component of pleasure to them, even though they arose out of painfully conflicted feelings. In the transference, the patient employs in relation to the therapist his entire repertoire of behaviors toward others. It is very hard to change this repertoire since, in a real sense, it is all that one is for others.

This conceptualization leads to a curious conclusion. The transference is at once the basis for discovering unconscious material and making it conscious—the basis for cure—*and*, simultaneously, a resistance to cure. Freud discovered that even the most debilitated patients in analysis will muster all their resources to resist getting better. He made the word "resistance" into a technical term to refer to the myriad ways in which patients fight to remain unchanged and to keep unconscious what has been repressed: "The resistance accompanies the treatment step by step. Every single association, every act of the person under treatment must reckon with the resistance and represents a compromise between the forces that are striving towards the recovery and the opposing ones which I have described."[7]

Resistance can take the most surprising forms, including falling in love with the analyst. In Freud's words, "The transference is . . . preeminently suitable as a weapon of resistance,"[8] and "the transference in analysis confront[s] us as resistance."[9] Freud considered the transference to be *"the most powerful resistance* to the treatment."[10] So, although the transference might be, ideally, a place for the patient to observe, coolly and rationally, the emotional conflicts that have conditioned his emotional responses and the patterns of all his relationships, it is, in practice, a battlefield on which the patient struggles with the analyst over the value of keeping repressed material unconscious, over the right to remain debilitated. The analyst tries to break down resistances while the patient strives to keep them in place. Freud said, "The patient brings out of the armory of the past the weapons with which he defends himself against the progress of treatment—weapons which we must wrest from him one by one."[11] In this armory of weapons by which patients resist cure, the love of the transference is the biggest gun.

Transference as Love

In its most typical form, transference involves the patient in a deep love for the analyst. But it is not as simple as that may sound.

Freud said that one could sometimes recognize the resistance of the transference by the odd fact that the patient's symptoms disappear. In the transference, a patient "gives up her symptoms or pays no attention to them; indeed, she declares that she is well. There is a complete change of scene; it is as though some piece of make-believe had been stopped by the sudden irruption of reality."[12] That is, the "make-believe" that is the patient's illness has been suspended by the "reality" of her love for the analyst. Jacques Lacan called the transference the "closing down of the unconscious."[13] All of the unconscious material that had been poking its way through the defenses is suddenly bottled up. The patient experiences no more symptoms and reports no more interpretable slips or dreams. All avenues for the relatively incoherent expressions of the unconscious slam shut, save one. The energies of the unconscious become coherent and articulated with laserlike intensity through one route, the affects projected onto the analyst. "All the libido, as well as everything opposing it, is made to converge solely on the relation with the doctor," as Freud put it.[14]

The transference occurs inevitably at a precise point in treatment. It occurs just when treatment has gained access to a fundamental conflict, exactly at the point when treatment has exposed the raw nerve of an old wound, at the moment "the treatment has obtained mastery over the patient."[15] The "change of scene" that occurs with an outburst of love (or hostility) "quite regularly occurs precisely at a point when one is having to try to bring [the patient] to admit or remember some particularly distressing and heavily repressed piece of her life-history."[16] So just as the treatment has made it possible for the patient to gain access to the sources of those old, still active wounds—just as it has become possible for cure to begin—the old conflicts muster themselves in their old practiced forms to resist cure and they do so by momentarily forsaking all symptoms, by declaring a state of health and by focusing all energy behind expressions of love for the analyst.

To psychoanalysis, then, the patient's love has to be seen as a tactical maneuver in the battle over cure. It is a tactic designed to bring the analyst into the battle on the patient's terms. The transference is the patient's tactic designed to make the analyst, who must remain a "blank screen," present in the relationship that the patient is so desperately trying to create during the analytic hour. Put as forcefully as possible by Freud, the transference is a strategy "to destroy the doctor's authority by bringing him down to the level of a lover."[17] A lover would never tweak the raw nerves of old wounds. A lover would never ask the other to examine her expressions of love to discover their source in her infantile past. In response to an outright declaration of love, a lover would never say, "And what does *that* bring to mind?" In response to the patient's expression of love, the psychoanalyst has a binary choice: release the patient from patienthood by reciprocating (or by spurning) the patient's love *or* remain a doctor and, following the rules of psychoanalytic method, pursue the resistance that the patient's love is. Love—or hostility—is, for psychoanalysis, a tactic in a battle that the patient desperately tries to make the analyst party to. If she succeeds, by that very fact she has won the battle, and with it the right to avoid treatment and remain ill.

Counter-Transference

Into this somewhat confusing, tactic-ridden, but, from a psychoanalytic point of view, utterly predictable scene, we must add one more crucial element: *counter-transference.* In the same way that a patient "falls in love" with an analyst by projecting the outcomes of repressed conflicts onto the doctor whom she knows not at all well, the doctor inevitably "falls in love" with his patient by projecting the outcomes of his repressed conflicts onto the patient whom he knows not at all well. Freud had little to say about counter-transference per se. He did admonish analysts not even to experiment with letting oneself "go a little way in tender feelings for the patient." He added, "Our control over ourselves is not so complete that we may not suddenly one day go further than we had intended. In my opinion, therefore, we ought not to give up the neutrality towards the patient, which we have acquired through keeping the counter-transference in check."[18] Freud did not have to say much about counter-transference beyond this practical advice because exactly the same dynamics operate on both sides in the analytic encounter. Transference is transference, whether experienced by the doctor or by the patient.

Just as inevitably as the patient experiences the transference, the analyst will experience a counter-transference. Both occur always because in psychoanalysis the contact made through an exchange of words is fundamentally a contact between one unconscious and another. As Freud described good analytic technique, "To put it in a formula: [the doctor] must turn his own unconscious like a receptive organ towards the transmitting unconscious of the patient. He must adjust himself to the patient as a telephone receiver is adjusted to the transmitting microphone."[19] The single difference between the analyst and the patient is that the analyst will more readily recognize his "tender feelings" toward the patient for what they *really are:* misplaced emotions acting to resist the progress of the analysis. It is the duty of the analyst to recognize and deal with (on his own time) his resistances to providing the analysis that may help the patient improve. An analyst must do battle with both the patient's resistance to cure and with his own resistance to providing good care. So that the latter is less of a problem than the former, Freud enjoins the analyst to recognize his counter-transference and to "become aware of those complexes of his own which would be apt to interfere with his grasp of what the patient tells him."[20] Out of this injunction comes the one critical element in all modern psychoanalytic training, the training analysis. All analysts must be analyzed themselves, so that they are equipped to identify and then keep in check their counter-transferential reactions.

Love as Transference

Transference encompasses more than the precisely timed outbursts of affect in the analytic encounter. Freud believed that transference is the root of all personal relationships. At first it seemed that transference was a mimicry of love, but in the end, Freud held it to be the very root of love:

> It is true that the love [the transference] consists of new editions of old traits and that it repeats infantile reactions. *But this is the essential character of every state of being in love.* There is no such state which does not reproduce infantile prototypes. It is precisely from this infantile determination that it receives its compulsive character, verging as it does on the pathological. Transference-love has perhaps a degree less of freedom than the love which appears in ordinary life and is called normal; it displays its dependence on the infantile pattern more clearly and is less adaptable and capable of modification; but that is all, and not what is essential.[21]

All personal relationships are the effects of transferential appropriations of two people one by the other. This is a radical insight. Whenever there is personal relationship, one person is going to behave and feel toward the other person in some respects and in some ways that have nothing to do with who that other person is or how she has acted. Some significant portion of my feelings, thoughts, and actions toward you will not come into being as a response to *you*, but rather will come into being as coded expressions of my conflicted feelings about some emotionally important figure from my infantile past, and neither you nor I will be aware of the origin and true meaning of my actions and feelings toward you. The feelings associated with my transference reactions are conscious, but the source of those feelings is unconscious. At the very same time, the other person in this relationship, you, will be having transference reactions of your own toward me. You will be manifesting feelings toward me that are conditioned by your unconscious conflicted feelings toward another person from your infantile past. Consequently, in every personal relationship there are at least four "people" present: not just you and I, but also your transference object (or objects) and my transference object (or objects). We may wish to be alone in our loving relationship, but privacy is not possible. The private space of any intimate relationship is always a crowded room.

"Curing" the Transference

The resistance that is the transference is as crucial at the end of psychoanalytic treatment as it is as a mark of the beginning of any treatment. The transference constitutes the pure, distilled essence of the patient's wounds, the wounds that have brought him to therapy. Out of that essence the patient fights to build a personal relationship with the therapist. In the patient's mind (but in a successful analysis, *only and strictly* in the patient's mind), she succeeds. Then, odd as it may sound, psychoanalysis aims to *treat* (one might say, *cure*) *the personal relationship* that lies at the heart of the therapy. Freud notes that in other forms of therapy the tender feelings and the surrender into dependency that are parts of the transference are preserved as an ally of the therapist. But "in analysis [the transference] is itself subjected to treatment and is dissected in all the shapes in which it appears. At the end of an analytic treatment the transference must itself be cleared away."[22]

Freud devotes a considerable amount of attention to the "management" of the transference, management that has the eventual aim of "dissolving" the transference. The emotional discovery of who from the past really is the basis for one's strong feelings of love and hate allows the patient to release the analyst from the spell of the patient's feelings. The analyst can finally be experienced as the person he really is, a professional helper who is also a relative stranger. Resolving the transference is usually a sign that an analysis has been successfully completed, for the patient will only be capable of such resolution once he has recovered to consciousness ("remembered") the unconscious emotional conflict that is the source of the symptoms that brought him to therapy, which is at the same time the conflict at the source of "the transference neurosis." It is for these reasons that Freud placed so much importance on the transference, did all he could to cultivate it, and wrote a number of papers counseling analysts on how to "manage" it so that it would not defeat the therapy and so that it could eventually be dissolved:[23]

> Every beginner in psycho-analysis probably feels alarmed at first at the difficulties in store for him when he comes to interpret the patient's associations and to deal with the reproduction of the repressed. When the time comes, however, he soon learns to look upon these difficulties as insignificant, and instead becomes convinced that the only really serious difficulties he has to meet lie in the management of the transference.[24]

What the analyst must manage is the patient's love, the loving relationship between patient and doctor that the transference is. This is not something that can be done in a coldly calculating way (though there is an element of calculation in therapy) or in a viciously brutalizing way (though there is some brutality involved). Freud warned that analytic treatment had its dangers not unlike surgery. Handling a patient's love is a *very* delicate operation. Julia Kristeva makes it clear that what drives a patient to analysis is a "want of love," the continuing experience of the pain from old wounds, rooted in childhood, of the absence or absenting of the love one expected always to be present. And, according to Kristeva, the good analyst will use the transference to show the patient the enduring value of love and her capacity for it. No bombast about "love is resistance" or pretty speeches about battles and tactics have a place in the analytic space.

Ultimately, however, after cultivating the transference, the trump card of analysis must be played and love must be revealed for what it is, a neurotic search for stability, for completion, and for an integrated identity that is all illusory. Love, including the love experienced in the transference, must be shown to be a tactic that tries, always with a mixture of success and failure, to make any given other complete the self, to use the other to provide what the self lacks. Kristeva conceives of analysis this way: "It is want of love that sends the subject into analysis, which proceeds by first restoring confidence in, and capacity for, love through the transference, and then enabling the subject to distance himself or herself from the analyst."[25] One is enabled to take this final step of distancing because analysis shows that love is something directed "to an impossible other—always unsatisfactory, transitory, incapable of meeting my wants and desires." The patient's reexperiencing of love in analysis "is ultimately shaken by the discovery that the other is fleeing me, that I will never possess him or even touch him as my desires imagined him, ideally satisfying."[26] In the discovery that one can never possess the other as one once wanted to possess one's parents, and as one has wanted to appropriate all other love objects since, lies a more shocking discovery about the self: "This discovery reveals that I myself, at the deepest level of my wants and desires, am unsure, centerless, and divided."[27]

The horror of the intimate relationship, according to psychoanalysis, is that it is, first, not intimate at all since the space of the relationship is crowded with figures from each person's past and, second, that it is not a relationship at all except in the tragic (and neurotic) sense that Janet Malcolm formulated it at the beginning of this chapter ("we cannot know one another. . . . We cannot see each other plain."). If the transference is resolved, as psychoanalysis seeks for it to be, the crowded room of the intimate relationship is revealed to be, finally, a lonely place.

But we must add one final paradoxical note to this twisted paradox that psychoanalysis puts before us. It is not clear that even Freud finally believed in the possibility of resolving the transference. Neurosis may not be curable. In his late and pessimistic musing on the question, he continues to maintain that "resolving the transference" is the critical criterion for terminating an analysis, but he seems to conclude that using this criterion will mean that analysis is essentially interminable.[28] For the transference is so deeply embedded in the unconscious and draws on such powerful instinctual forces that there is no prospect for the relatively weak ego ever to resolve it fully. As Annie Reich put it in 1950,

> Even after the transference has been well analyzed and its important infantile sexual elements have been overcome, even after the neurotic symptoms have been given up, the relationship to the analyst is still not completely a mature one. We have to state that the transference is not completely resolved. The analyst is still an important object for the patient, and is still the object of fantasy expectations. . . . In nearly all cases which I have analyzed, there remained a wish to be loved by the analyst, to keep in contact with him, to build up a friendship. . . . The analyst is still seen as a person endowed with special power, special intelligence and wisdom. In short, to a certain degree he is still seen as partaking in the omnipotence which the child attributes to the parents.[29]

So psychoanalysis leaves us with the suspicion, if not the flat-out assertion, that once love (in whatever form) has inserted itself into a relationship between two people, a knot is tied between them that can never be undone. This knot is the transference, the introduction of other emotion-laden figures out of one's past into the loneliness of the present relationship, the domination of the present relationship by past relationships that have failed to satisfy.

The heaping of paradox upon paradox that emerges from an inquiry into the transference led Freud to term psychoanalysis an " 'impossible' profession," one that he lumped with two others: "It almost looks as if analysis were the third of those 'impossible' professions in which one can be sure beforehand of achieving unsatisfying results. The other two, which have been known much longer, are education and government."[30] We are now in a position to use an understanding of transference in psychoanalysis to appreciate more fully what we called the problematic aspects of Rousseau's approach to liberal and liberating pedagogy, the approach to which we still appeal, albeit in modern and sometimes less rigorous forms, today.

Pedagogy and the Transference

Our examination of Rousseau's *Emile* led us to focus on the modern idea that any worthwhile education is built on a personal relationship between teacher and student. We have glimpsed the power of the perspective that can be developed once a teacher makes the personal relationship the framework within which her pedagogy will unfold. We followed Rousseau to a pedagogy that is natural, developmental, personal, and humane. Now it is time to follow Freud to appreciate the depth of the ambiguities and difficulties resident in such a pedagogy—to appreciate the shadow side of teaching.

Rousseau and Freud

A casual reading of Freud spots some important similarities to Rousseau. It is instructive to see how far they walk together before parting company.

For example, Freud seems to parallel Rousseau in his thinking about the role of a teacher. From his theoretical statements and from his actual teaching, we see that he eschewed the role of mentor per se and seemed to want to be an educator in the mold of Jean-Jacques. Of his encounters with patients, he said, "There is nothing we would rather bring about than that the patient should make his decisions for himself."[31] This attitude recurs in his lectures. He brackets his two-year course of *Introductory Lectures on Psychoanalysis* with a warning that echoes Rousseau's dictum, "If you have to be told everything, do not read me." In the first lecture, Freud tells his audience that everything in their past educations will predispose them to be opponents of psychoanalysis. He tells them that if any one of them is truly interested in learning about psychoanalysis, he will have to do so via the one-on-one, paradoxically intimate encounter of psychoanalysis itself, and he adds, "This excellent method is, of course, applicable only to a single person and never to a whole lecture-room of students together."[32] Near the end of the course, just as he is introducing the concept of transference, and after admitting that his students have an "indisputable right" to learn "in the most general way the method by which psycho-analytic therapy operates," he concludes flatly, "I shall not, however, tell it [to] you but shall insist on your discovering it for yourselves."[33] "If you have to be told everything. . . ."

Freud parallels Rousseau in another way. He insists the learning that counts is not entirely cognitive. Sensibility and the strong language of emotions are crucial to the kind of learning that can lead to emotional development. In several places, Freud urges against intellectualizing the immediate situation for patients. At one point, he entertains the thought that, perhaps, if a patient is told about possible future emotional conflicts, if he is aroused to anticipate them, if he is told of the possibility of new symptoms arising from old conflicts, the patient may be more immune to their effects than if he were not so forewarned. But Freud rejects this idea: "But this time experience speaks with no uncertain voice. The expected result does not come about. The patient hears our message, but there is no response. He may think to himself: 'This is very interesting, but I feel no trace of it.' We have increased his knowledge, but altered nothing in him."[34] Like Rousseau, Freud relies on a notion of "readiness" in learning. The strength of a logical argument is no substitute for an experience occurring on appropriately prepared emotional ground. The loving bond must be cultivated; the seeds of relief that are planted there will grow in their own time.

Freud's formulation of the psychoanalytic analogue of the learning situation parts company from Rousseau's theoretical formulation of the educational encounter in one essential regard. Freud makes no appeal to Nature as the basis for whatever "learning" or "development" might occur as a result of a patient's psychoanalysis. Freud relies on a concept of Nature in his meta-psychology, which is expressed through his theory of the instincts, but in his psychology proper there is no recourse to Nature. Although Freud always stressed the importance of constitutional (innate) factors in mental illness, he never attempted to inquire into them. They remained outside the scope of his discourse. In fact, in his early writing Freud is explicit about this omission. In a footnote to his first paper on "The Dynamics of Transference," Freud says that although innate or constitutional factors certainly play a role in illness, his focus is on the effects of "infantile impressions" that occur by chance. Freud, the master rhetorician, engages the skeptic by beginning, "We refuse to posit any contrast in principle between the two sets of aetiological factors; on the contrary, we assume that the two sets regularly act jointly in bringing about the observed result. [Endowment and chance] determine a man's fate—rarely or never one of these powers alone." And then, in a typically Freudian twist, he concludes the note with, "Incidentally, one might venture to regard constitution itself as a precipitate from the accidental effects produced on the endlessly long chain of our ancestors."[35] Individual learning, for Freud, seems to mean learning about those random events in one's life to which one has, by chance, attributed considerable significance and thereby afforded them the place of, literally, a driving force in life.

Rousseau's interest in Nature justified the pedagogue's protecting his charge from the corrupting effects of society. Because the analyst cannot *prevent* social corruption, but must take on the job of trying to *undo*, partially, the effects of society, Freud's view points the would-be pedagogue in a different direction. It points the pedagogue toward a deep, incisive inquiry into an individual's peculiar social history. For the psychoanalytically inclined, it is the little chance events of life, events to which the individual has attributed special meaning, on which the pedagogue must take aim. The individual cannot, following Freud, avoid social corruption and, at the same time, the analyst cannot realistically anticipate a completely satisfactory outcome to his interventions. Learning simply implies coming to understand those aspects of one's character formed in social interactions that have limited one's freedom. Freud often likened psychoanalysis to surgery and conceived of it as a radical and dangerous intervention, but he developed no analogue to the "health" toward which surgery supposedly aims. The outcome toward which psychoanalysis aims is, at best, ambiguous. Freud is clear about not making "a recommendation to the patient to 'live a full life' sexually" and, at the same time, not advocating a life of asceticism.[36] In the famous parable about the starving horse with which Freud closed his five Clark University lectures, Freud tries to strike a middle position, but his parable, in the end, is ambiguous and leaves the question unsettled.[37] Freud parts company from Rousseau in not finding a way for a faith in Nature to ground any optimism for the pedagogue. If there is to be a trustworthy guide to good learning, Freud finds it in history (in the sense of personal history), not in Nature.

Transference between Student and Teacher

Though the opportunities for learning and rational understanding psychoanalysis offers the individual patient are striking and novel, ultimately we must conclude that Freud adopts a weak pedagogical stance. His writing informs us of strictly governed circumstances (those surrounding the analytic session) that might effect limited change (learning) in a person. But, taken as a whole, his writing is much more compelling as a critique of any form of teaching and learning that bases itself in a personal relationship. The cautionary, paradoxical, critical perspective offered by the concept of transference extends to circumstances beyond the analytic encounter. "It is not a fact," writes Freud, "that transference emerges with greater intensity and lack of restraint during psycho-analysis than outside it."[38] One can expect to find irrational feelings and fantasies between patient and medical doctor, legal client and lawyer, audience member and performer, citizen and political leader, and, of course, student and teacher. Transference reactions arise in any situation that invites one person to become unilaterally trusting and dependent on another. What usually happens in such relationships is that one gets another chance to rehearse old patterns of behavior that have been, in life, "more or less successful." In all these relations, the dependent person remains, during certain moments, a hopeless victim of his repressed patterns of response to his parents. Transference is a concept that must heighten our suspicions whenever we are told that entering into a relationship with some "helper" is only "for our own good."

There is scarcely a relationship outside of psychoanalysis more ripe for understanding via the concept of transference than the relationship of student to teacher. The requisite inequalities in knowledge, experience, authority, power, and, usually, maturity, are all present. These inequalities are more than sufficient to invite unilateral trusting and dependency on the part of the student. Any pedagogical relationship is going to be suffused with transference reactions. This means that the love the student bears for his teacher will be out of proportion to what the pedagogical situation warrants. One need not go to the extremes of a Jean-Jacques, who makes himself parent, guardian, caretaker, and sole friend, as well as tutor, to his student. A student's love for his teacher will grow in the student's breast and that love will have little to do with the teacher and almost everything to do with the pedagogical setting. Similarly, the fear the student feels toward his teacher, and the hate he sometimes bears for him, will be out of proportion to what the actual situation warrants.

In the emotional framework created by the pedagogical relationship, all students are, like Emile, orphans. Every student has been given over by his biological parents to a teacher, who becomes the new surrogate parent. As the new parent, the teacher must now promote the development of his charge. This mandate and the ambition it fosters bring with them the need to assist nature in its job of development, the need to control the student and supervise his environment, the need to protect the student from society and its corrosive influence, and the need to nurture the precious relationship student and teacher have together. The student gets the chance to find what every human wants: the chance to make a new beginning and to make it better this time. And the teacher gets the chance to provide this opportunity.

"Making it better" can mean many things, but inevitably, if we follow Freud, it will mean restoring the lost object of one's total love. It will mean repairing the split caused by the separation between parent and child. It will mean having one's (new) parent entirely to oneself, receiving the love one deserved but never got, and so on. The teaching/learning encounter is an arena for trying, once again, the impossible: to perfect and complete the self through a critical, intimate relationship. Put another way, the teaching/learning encounter is another opportunity to try to freeze and preserve a completely satisfying relationship in its original, perfect, if also fantastic, form. The notion of "pedagogical incest" is scarcely a metaphor. Since the transference guarantees that the student will not want to leave the teacher, and the counter-transference guarantees that the teacher will not want to leave the student, we must not be surprised to find Jean-Jacques finishing out his years in residence with Emile and Sophie.

"The Subject Who Is Supposed to Know"

Jacques Lacan has framed the transference in terms that link it directly to the aims of most educational efforts.[39] Lacan's idealized rendering of "transference" says that at the beginning of an analysis the patient approaches the doctor as the "subject who is supposed to know." The doctor is the one who is supposed (by the patient) to know what the patient needs to do to solve his problems, to fulfill his desires, to heal his wounds. The patient thus invests the doctor with enormous trust and is ready to surrender to the doctor, if only he will speak the words that will release the needed knowledge to the patient. As analysis proceeds, the patient comes to suspect, and then to know for certain, that the doctor is withholding the knowledge that he, the patient, needs to know. The patient comes to this conclusion "logically," since the doctor is the "subject who is supposed to know" and he is telling the patient none of his knowledge that the patient knows would be helpful. Thus, the transference becomes a battle of tactics by which the ignorant patient tries to extract knowledge from the one who is "supposed to know."

We should pause here, because this is the point at which most relationships of unilateral trusting dependence, which are not mandated to aim for a resolution of the transference, stall. The attribute of being the one who is supposed to know, an attribute that is posited in analysis by the patient, is easily assumed by those in roles that carry the social obligation that anyone filling the role truly *is* supposed to know. Teachers readily make this assumption. Those people who have been socialized to understand that they possess valuable knowledge easily slide into the activity of fulfilling the demands for knowledge from their patientlike supplicants in search of knowledge. The student who invests a teacher with the moniker "the subject who is supposed to know" will rarely be disappointed by the ensuing performance of the teacher, even if the teacher has openly or secretly wondered to herself about the adequacy of her knowledge. The old joke has it that teachers can talk for fifty minutes on any given topic. But who would not talk when faced with so many eager students so evidently enthralled by the knowledge that one is supposed (by them) to have? If one is supposed to have knowledge, one will have it; if one gives the least indication that one is not up to the title of "the subject who is supposed to know," if the mask slips the least bit and suggests that it disguises a fraud, the teacher risks losing the love of his students, which, for a teacher cut from the mold of Jean-Jacques, is everything.

The concept of the transference, however, insists that the relationship between teacher and student, based on the supposition of knowledge, is only a relationship of constructed artifice. It insists, if one follows psychoanalysis to *its* end, that the relationship not become stalled at the point of finally (from the teacher's perspective) "being able to teach them something," or finally (from the student's perspective) "having learned something valuable (which I knew that she knew)." The transference exists, from a psychoanalytic perspective, only to be dissolved and, if that happens, the patient goes away, according to Lacan, "knowing something." The patient goes away knowing *not* what she is supposed to know, for there is no "supposed to" except in the neurotic, fantastic constructions of the patient; *not* what is valuable to know, for value is an ascription that comes from the collective fantastic constructions of society. The patient goes away *knowing something,* utterly unspecified and unspecifiable.

From a psychoanalytic perspective, an educational encounter that frames its ends in terms of the student's having specifiable knowledge or specifiable capabilities is a corrupt enterprise. Such an encounter is an unending one. From a psychoanalytic perspective, the teacher who believes that there is something to be known or something worth knowing (or some method for acquiring knowledge that should be known) is issuing an invitation to incest. From a psychoanalytic perspective, the only worthwhile encounter is one that does constant battle with itself and with the temptations that the encounter itself contains. The concept of transference points the thoughtful pedagogue toward an educational encounter that fights against the transmission of knowledge so that the student may come to "know something."

"Finding One's Voice"

Now, given that most education succumbs quickly and thoughtlessly to the temptation to form "loving" pedagogical relationships, it is perhaps ironic that Lacan's state of knowing something corresponds closely to an end valued in contemporary educational discourse. Educators say that they listen for the student to begin speaking "in her own voice," not simply mimicking the voices of her mentors. François Roustang writes from a Lacanian perspective, "Neurosis is always an inability to speak, to fantasize, to desire on one's own, . . . it is also a longing, the deep-rooted longing to be an echo or a mirror of what others say or think."[40] The cure of neurosis, then, implies that one finally gains the capacity to speak in one's own voice, to desire one's own desires, to live one's own life, which is precisely what many liberal, progressive educators say they want their students to become "empowered" to do.

What most educators are unwilling to face is the complement to this aim. In order for the student to come to speak in her own voice, "this other [the analyst/teacher] must become inexistent, the other who makes me desire must become nobody, or pure contingency. This occurs through the collapse of every object of desire, be it the one who is supposed to know or anyone else."[41] Roustang says that at the end of analysis, the analysand will say to himself, "I am the one who knows something; the analyst's knowledge no longer interests me."[42]

Teachers who mouth the words that they are trying to get their students to speak in their own voices should note well: It is not that the teacher's knowledge, once discovered or learned by the student, is seen as needing improvement, refinement, or modification (a response that every teacher appreciates because it indicates "growth" on the part of the student); it is not that the teacher's knowledge comes to be considered wrong (a response that indicates independence and, perhaps, feistiness in a student); it is not that the teacher's knowledge is unreasoned (a response that indicates a student's underlying commitment to reason itself); but it is that the teacher's knowledge *no longer interests.* The threat for the liberal, progressive, developmental teacher that transference puts into relief is that his students will regard him as uninteresting, that they will regard him with indifference, that he will become for them "inexistent."

The love between student and teacher is necessary to a developmental pedagogy for all the reasons we discussed in the preceding chapter. Yet the love between student and teacher also subverts and resists developmental pedagogy. If the student's task is to develop, then his task is gradually to learn how to stop being a student. He must progressively outgrow the teacher. Yet the loving relationship between student and teacher demands that he remain a student, for his being a student is the entire basis for the relationship.

Just as it is easy to imagine a patient embracing change to alleviate her suffering, it is easy to imagine the student eagerly anticipating the end of his studenthood. We should not be fooled. Recall that at the bottom of the transference reaction is the amazing fact that the patient does not want to get better. He would rather go on being a patient. He would rather go on being loved and nourished. The same is true for the student. The presence of the teacher has given him a second chance. Giving up his new parent may not be quite as painful as separating from his original parent, but this separation is certainly not going to be easy. This bind is beautifully expressed in Emile's final plea to his tutor on the last page of *Emile*, "Remain the master of the young masters." Emile, like any good student, wants and needs to have it both ways—to be a master and yet still to have a master. In one breath Emile says, "God forbid that I let you also raise the son after having raised the father," and in the next he says, "As long as I live, I shall need you. I need you more than ever now that my functions as a man begin."[43] The student demands that he be allowed to remain, forever, a student.

The good teacher finds it equally difficult to leave the educational encounter. The very identity of "teacher," like "husband" or "wife," is a contingent identity. It rests on the continued presence of an other, a "student." The terror every teacher faces is contained in a variation on a joke from another arena of battles: "What if you gave a course and nobody came?" If the student ceases to be a student, or even threatens to cease being a student, how can the teacher go on being a teacher? Whereas a student might anticipate no longer being a student, a teacher finds it hard even to conceive giving up being a teacher. Unlike Jean-Jacques, most teachers do give up being the teacher of a specific student, but they simply replace their departing students with new ones. All that this process does is repeat the emotional problem over and over endlessly; it does not resolve it.

Roustang paints the following picture, worth quoting at length, of the dynamic that ensues:

> [A disciple or pupil must] think his own thoughts through the thoughts of the master, or else speak for himself while strictly matching his words to those of the master, or quite simply speak without repetition when it would be time to remain silent. The pupil has the right to speak only in order to utter stupidities, stupidities that would then be picked up and castigated by the master. To everything the pupil might say—and he must speak, for otherwise the master's word would have no echo, and therefore no influence—the master is expected to reply, and this is what the pupil waits for: You have understood nothing; That is not at all what I meant to say; I am distressed to see the results of my teaching; and so on; the effect of which is either to silence the pupils, or to drive them to speak elsewhere (as in the case of dissidents). Then comes a second series of pupils, who once again repeat stupidities before falling silent, and so on it goes. Thus the master is able to continue his work, tirelessly consuming generations of disciples. If all the pupils were to fall silent at the same time, the master would be forced to abandon teaching.

Summarizing this paradoxical situation, Roustang says, "For the institution, based on the master's word, can survive only through fidelity to this injunction: Make them speak in order to make them silent."[44]

The intimate pedagogical relationship is not just paradoxical. It is vicious. It involves a battle for existence between two foes locked in a loving relationship.

The Tension of the Transference

Psychoanalysts are required to undergo a training analysis, in part, so they can experience and understand first-hand the dynamics of the transference. Without this deep, personal understanding they would not be capable of "managing" the transferences of their patients and they would not be able to recognize, acknowledge to themselves, and "manage" their own counter-transference reactions. They would become unwitting allies with their patients in promoting the transference and thus in sustaining their patienthoods.

Because of the parallels between psychoanalysis and education, an obvious question arises: Could we not make an important step in resolving the knotty problem of teachers' keeping their students students by giving teachers, too, a proper education about transference? We need not dwell on the fact that the required education would be too long, costly, and specialized ever to be practicable in any but the most unusual cases. No matter how much he knew about psychoanalysis, the teacher could not make it his job to make the student aware of his own transference reactions. To do so would be, ipso facto, to convert education into psychoanalysis. Being aware of one's own counter-transference reactions and knowing how to interpret (to one's self) students' transference reactions would certainly aid the teacher in avoiding many of the emotional traps and pitfalls that arise in the relationship between him and his students.[45] But a teacher cannot make "resolving the transference" an *educational* objective.

Knowledge of the transference can only help us appreciate how all the problems of any developmental pedagogy based on the personal relationship between student and teacher are subsumed under that final problem, the impulse to completion or totality in a relationship of trusting dependence. We can review the problems of Rousseau's pedagogy anew with an understanding of transference in hand.

The manipulativeness that developmental education requires is often expressed as a technical or as an ethical problem. Technically, there is a question of whether teachers need intervene in students' lives at all. The skeptical developmentalist rhetorically asks: Won't a student's spontaneous encounters with the environment eventually provide the developmental challenges that everyone needs to progress educationally? If the teacher does decide to intervene actively in the name of education, he is confronted with an ethical question: How much distress caused by my disequilibrating interventions is ethically acceptable? When does the developmental teacher cross the line between education and torture?

On the question of manipulativeness, Freud and his concept of the transference are not so much reassuring to the developmental educator as they are confounding. On the one hand, Freud might argue that the patterns of response in any intimate relationship, the pedagogical relationship included, are set down early in life and will remain relatively unaffected by any interventions an educator might undertake. The stereotypical plates, the limited repertoire of reactions, persist throughout life. But on the other hand, Freud has shown us that manipulativeness lies at the heart of every relationship. *Mutual* manipulativeness. Every relationship is a battleground on which each party uses tactics and maneuvers to try to turn the other party into what he desires. Every relationship involves manipulation aimed by both parties at completing the self, at gaining, finally, the satisfaction that imaginably comes when the other is made into one's complement. So to those who trouble themselves on technical or ethical grounds over the manipulativeness that they think good education requires of them, Freud would probably say something like, "Worry if you must; understand if you can." Understanding would require an appreciation of the paradoxical and, to Freud, tragic nature of the manipulations toward which an impulse to complete the self forces everyone.

Freud's perspective provokes a similar response to the problematic reliance on a concept of Nature. Freud's last works suggest that every action, including the loving pedagogical relationship, is the result of two opposing forces of nature: the impulse to come together, build, and unite (Eros, or the life instinct) and the impulse to destroy (Thanatos, or the death instinct).[46] To rely, as the developmentalist does, on a belief that Nature aims to build whole persons composed of more differentiated, more integrated cognitive systems is fine, but only half right. Nature also seeks, simultaneously, to disintegrate, homogenize, and level living systems. So at the heart of nature, whether the educator "relies" on it or not, is an inexorable, conflicted process that proceeds partly through our actions, but regardless of our conscious intentions, and that seems to call only for our understanding, not for our using it to some educationally beneficial end.

Finally, developmentalists worry about the "contaminating" effects of society. Again, Freud might wonder why educators would ever hope to resolve a fundamentally paradoxical situation. Any intimate relationship is social. People entering into such relationships bring all previous relationships with them and simply try, as they are condemned to do, to repeat them. Every relationship, as we said, takes place in a crowded room. Jean-Jacques and Emile could never hope to escape society by moving to the country. Even orphans bring society with them, if they bring their tutors along. Roustang says of psychoanalysis, "If we consider [psychoanalysis's] rigorous aims, if psychoanalysis exists to undo repression, then it should include no social formations, except as elements to be expelled."[47] So Jean-Jacques and Emile could have spent their time in their socially crowded country retreat trying to "expel" the society they brought with them, but then Rousseau's book would have to have been subtitled "On Psychoanalysis," not "On Education." Once again, the developmental educator is confronted with paradox.

Psychoanalysis provides us with a lens through which to view the progressive and developmental practice of pedagogy. Like pedagogy, psychoanalysis is a helping profession in which the knowledge, experience, and skill of the helper is brought to bear in order to help an "incomplete" client. Like pedagogy, psychoanalysis is built around a two-person relationship between the helper and the helped, and this relationship provides the emotional matrix within which all the action transpires. And, as in Rousseau's developmental pedagogy, in psychoanalysis the "guiding" activities of the helper (countering resistance so that unconscious material may surface) are indirect, whereas the emotional relationship is very direct. It is no wonder, then, that Freud had occasion to refer to psychoanalysis as an "after-education."[48]

For us, the language of the transference (with its accompanying strong terms like "love," "hostility," and "pedagogical incest") is a useful way to understand some facts of contemporary institutional life in schools. Others may prefer to discuss something like "the problem of authority in the classroom." For us, this cool, technical language severs the connections between the grand passions of life and the passion that is pedagogy. We find in the language of the transference a useful way to talk about the progressive educator's axiom that "the relationships between the children and ourselves [are at] the very heart of the school."[49]

There is relative safety in a technical conception of education. If the problems of education can be cast as technical problems in search of technical solutions, then we can all securely undertake an endless effort to "solve the educational crisis" or some such venture. For us, such a conception of the problems of modern education avoids the inherently problematic character of the educational encounter itself. Pedagogy has not had its Freud. It has no modern figure to warn us of the fundamentally paradoxical nature of education. Instead, our technical approach to education gives us a constant barrage of educational debates, exhortations, teaching methods, model institutions, model programs, white papers, policy councils, research, more exhortations, more methods, more research, ad nauseam. What we have avoided in our search for solutions is any considered, patient discussion about what we are undertaking when we undertake to educate. We have had no one ask: What kind of relationship are you inviting a student to enter into when you undertake to educate him? What will be the long-term effects of this relationship on him? Will he ever escape that relationship and its effects? What gives a teacher the right to educate someone else anyway? These questions become more complex and serious once we begin to sound the depth of the waters a student enters when he takes the plunge into "the pedagogical relationship" with his teacher. Is the teacher quite prepared to take on someone who may have the impulse to stay with him forever? Is he quite prepared to invite someone into his heart who will express to him and elicit from him the extremes of love and hate that we have come to recognize as the inevitable reactions accompanying transference?

These are questions that require slowing down, taking stock, cultivating humility. Instead, the discourse on education is rushed and urgent; it always has been a discourse about national emergency. Freud's lens helps us pause. It makes us look at some fundamental questions surrounding a dimension of pedagogy that, since Rousseau, have been taken for granted. Perhaps the next time a humane and progressive educator mouths the cliché that education is a lifelong affair, we may think at least twice.

That the lens of the transference reveals education to be problematic, even dangerous, and at times vicious, does not mean that education is bad. We would not be so foolish as to suggest that society do away with education. We only wish to ask whether it is possible to educate and also to permit people to develop freely? Can we imagine a pedagogy that is progressive, humane, and developmental, yet that does not put the two-person relationship between student and teacher at its heart? What might such a pedagogy look like? Would it be liberatory? Would it liberate the student from the snares of thralldom? Might it do the same for the teacher? Might it possibly provide a means to realize the developmental dream—the attainment of genuine equality between student and teacher? Can there be the non-oppressive, democratic pedagogy that John Dewey dreamed of? Is there a resolution to the paradox of pedagogy?

3

THE PROMISE OF A SOCIAL PEDAGOGY: PAULO FREIRE'S CULTURE CIRCLES

> Thus the educator's role is fundamentally to enter into dialogue with the illiterate about concrete situations and simply to offer him the instruments with which he can teach himself to read and write. This teaching cannot be done from the top down, but only from the inside out, by the illiterate himself, with the collaboration of the educator.
>
> —Paulo Freire, "Education as the Practice of Freedom"

> The thinking Subject cannot think alone. In the act of thinking about the object s/he cannot think without the co-participation of another Subject. There is no longer an "I think" but "we think." It is the "we think" which establishes the "I think" and not the contrary.
>
> —Paulo Freire, "Extension or Communication"

ROUSSEAU'S PEDAGOGY was based on a personal relationship between the pupil and his tutor. The personal nature of the bond between student and teacher lay at the heart of this pedagogy and was the secret to its great promise, for the intimate and slowly cultivated relationship between adult and child created a protected space, a haven in which the natural processes of development could take place without being deformed and defiled by corrupting social influences. Freud showed this carefully constructed, protected space to be the fiction it was. No personal relationship could keep out the influence of the social. On the contrary, a personal relationship between student and teacher is in some ways the ideal spawning ground for the reproduction of society, and thus hardly allows for an education designed to liberate the student from social deformation.

But Rousseau understood the paradox of his proposal. Some educators may read *Emile* as a how-to book, but that would miss an essential point: the impossibility of Rousseau's project. A richer reading of Rousseau would have to recognize that any response to the paradox of pedagogy would have to be social. "How may [the] new freedom [implied by Rousseau] be brought about?" one scholar asks. "Only an irruption into history can effect the transformation needed if human beings are to be united in true community."[1] Or according to another interpretation, "As history plunges toward its nadir, it is just possible that social upheaval and revolution result in a government that is 'closer' to 'the legitimate institution.' . . . The return to legitimate government . . . is a glimmer of hope in an age of barbarism."[2]

The Brazilian educator Paulo Freire comes at the task of liberatory education with a revolutionary program mounted as a "glimmer of hope." His education is an "irruption into history" that proceeds "from the inside out." It is based in the possibility of a social "we think" that is the basis for a "true community." From the start he abandons two pillars of Rousseau's pedagogy: the intimate two-person relationship and the retreat from society. The experiences on which Freire based his educational reflections were with illiterate peasants—adults, not children. Freire's students were long past the possibility of tutorial protection from society's blows, yet he found he could open a door that led to a new educational beginning for them. By setting up the right conditions, he could help illiterate peasants quickly begin to learn not just how to read and write, but how to think critically about their world and their place in it. They appeared to Freire to have retained their fundamentally human capacities to reflect on their own situations after lives of educational and financial impoverishment.

So Freire sees no need to retreat from society. Instead, he gets his students to disengage themselves from their immediate enmeshment in their own worlds. Education means overcoming "submersion." This disengagement requires not separation from society but an opening of one's eyes to the social and cultural realities that are always immediately present. But the ordinary, everyday present must be reexperienced as something extraordinary so it can be reflected on and judged, so it will no longer simply be taken for granted. To do this, student and teacher must remain together in society, not retreat from it.

For Freire, student and teacher are *equally* victims of social structuring (despite their obvious differences). Therefore Freire makes the social group, not the two-person student-teacher relationship, the basic building block of his pedagogy. This grouping of students and teachers together into a "culture circle" means that the individual student is no longer the conceptual object of educational theorizing. Instead, a social group becomes the *subject* of education. Moreover, the educator is obliged to define himself as a member of this group, however difficult that may be. The "students" in this new form of education thus become not "you" singular, not even "you" plural, but rather part of a "we." "There is no longer an 'I think' but 'we think.'" The first person plural must take precedence, for in a society based on domination, we are all under the imperative to think critically and act freely to try to create a more just and fully human society.

Freire is aware of the unconscious tendency of the oppressed to identify with those in authority, and thus for the liberated to reproduce conditions of oppression once they become the authorities. He believes he has circumvented this problem of social reproduction by basing his pedagogy on the study of the common social reality of both student and teacher and by creating a social grouping in which student and teacher can find a common ground to replace the traditional imbalance of the two-person student-teacher bond. Whether this shift is successful and whether Freire's pedagogy represents a resolution of the paradox of pedagogy remain to be seen.

Education for Oppression

Freire formulates his "pedagogy of the oppressed" in sharp opposition to conventional pedagogy. His pedagogy takes off from a critique of what he characterizes as the "banking concept" of education, an education designed for oppression.

The banking concept of education begins with a thinking Subject, the teacher, and a knowable object, the curricular material. The knowing Subject manifests his ownership of the cognizable object by articulating the truth of that object. The "chlorophyll-infused cells" seen through the microscope literally *belong* to the biologist who is solely capable of pointing to them and saying their true name. The third element in the banking conception of education is the student or educatee in whom the teacher attempts to deposit his knowledge of the object. The student must file away the "communiqués" issued by the Subject of knowledge, his teacher. Educatees could never hope to own those cells as their biologist-teacher does. Even if they moved beyond seeing "green globs with black stripes and spots" to the point where they could repeat the words from their teacher's communiqué, "chlorophyll-infused cells," the words and therefore the object of knowledge would never belong to them. They could never hope to appropriate the object of knowledge from the biologist; at best, they could only hope to "get it right," that is, to repeat the words of the Subject at the correct time and under the correct circumstances. They could only hope to withdraw what had previously been deposited in their bank. They could only hope to pass the test.

In his most popular book, *Pedagogy of the Oppressed,* Freire summarizes the features of the banking approach to education this way:

> (a) the teacher teaches and the students are taught;
> (b) the teacher knows everything and the students know nothing;
> (c) the teacher thinks and the students are thought about;
> (d) the teacher talks and the students listen—meekly;
> (e) the teacher disciplines and the students are disciplined;
> (f) the teacher chooses and enforces his choice, and the students comply;
> (g) the teacher acts and the students have the illusion of acting through the action of the teacher;
> (h) the teacher chooses the program content, and the students (who were not consulted) adapt to it;
> (i) the teacher confuses the authority of knowledge with his own professional authority, which he sets in opposition to the freedom of the students;
> (j) the teacher is the Subject of the learning process, while the pupils are mere objects.[3]

In general, the teacher *deposits* all necessary knowledge *into* his students and takes all other actions *on* the students that are necessary to make the deposits stick.

Under a banking approach to education, students are made into objects not unlike those "chlorophyll-infused cells." They are thought about, worried about, agonized over, joked about, planned for, anticipated, and in general, known by the only actively knowledgeable person, the teacher. Just as the cells on a microscope slide are suspended in time and space, ripped from their social and historical context by the acts of a knowing Subject, so too are the students suspended by the teacher's knowledge of them. Students become abstracted knowable objects created by the educator's acts of educational theorizing.

"Theory," in its classical sense, was a double-edged concept. The *theoros* was a representative of the Greek city-states sent to "look on," through *theoria,* at religious festivals. The *theoros,* then, was an embodiment of the power of the state. However, he also, through the process of "looking on," abandoned himself to the religious scene and transformed himself as the situation demanded.[4] In the modern era we have lost this reflective, self-transformative aspect of "theory" and retained only the stately power associated with the act of "looking on" and discovering the true structure of the world into which all objects must be made to fit. Students not only become objects of a teacher's concerned "looking on"; they also experience themselves as objects ready to accommodate themselves to the structure of the world as it is known through their teachers' theories. In this way education helps students come to experience themselves as *part* of the world, inextricably tied to it, unable to gain the sense of separateness across which an act of consciousness might operate.

Freire says that a banking approach to education is always violently invasive. Education of this sort is cultural invasion. Speaking of Brazilian agricultural "extension agents," Freire painted this picture:

> The relationships between invader and invaded are situated at opposite poles. They are relationships of authority. The invader acts, the invaded are under the illusion that they are acting through the action of the other; the invader has his say; the invaded, who are forbidden this, listen to what

> the invader says. The invader thinks, at most, *about* the invaded, never *with* them; the latter have their thinking done for them. . . . Thus, any cultural invasion presupposes conquest, manipulation, and messianism on the part of the invader. It presupposes propaganda which domesticates rather than liberates.[5]

The extension of technical, agricultural knowledge to those who "need" it is not the politically neutral act the experts would make it out to be. By substituting their form of knowledge for the knowledge of the peasants, or worse, by assuming that the peasants have no knowledge of their own about their everyday experience and practices, expert-teachers dehumanize their students. In the names of education and assistance, they become cultural invaders who contribute to the oppression of their "clients."

Depositing knowledge into students or extending knowledge into the peasantry is almost always done in the name of being "humane," of being "helpful," of "assisting those in need." Freire says that this attitude contributes to the objectification of students. To think that another "needs" the knowledge that one has or owns is to put the educatee in an inferior position from the outset. To begin from the assertion that one has what another does not have and that, by gift or contract, one will extend necessary knowledge to the ignorant is to silence the educatee by trivializing, from the outset, whatever knowledge and experience he has. By trying to make a student fit for her world, one thereby asserts that it is exclusively the student, not the world, that is in need of adjustment.

A curious dynamic of identification of the oppressed with their oppressors is set in motion by the banking concept of education. A student sees in her teacher a person obviously well fitted to the world. Her education, she comes to understand, holds the promise of fitness for her if she will but receive the word as it is spoken by those fit to speak. Students trying to adjust themselves to become fit lose their capacity to act on the world to change it. People come to know themselves only to the degree they are part of that which oppresses them. Even rebellions, Freire suggests, often result in the simple inversion of oppressor and oppressed because rebellious, oppressed people cannot think beyond becoming the oppressor of their former oppressors, so firm are the bonds of identification between the two.

The banking approach to education does not reveal reality to educatees as it claims to do. The abstractions of theory and of technical language obscure and hide reality. Banking education fragments reality and makes it disjointed and rigid. Who, after all, would make a connection between those "chlorophyll-infused cells" and anything else in human life? A biologist might make connections, but those connections would not be made by anyone not rigidly disciplined to understand certain, disciplinarily given connections. All connections would have to be made in the abstracted language of the discipline of biology. One function of banking education, Freire reminds us, is to numb students with a barrage of verbalisms. It "anesthetizes and inhibits creative power." It "attempts to maintain the *submersion* of consciousness."[6]

The aim of banking education is *control*. It begins with the educator's controlling "the way the world 'enters into' the students."[7] Those cells enter the student's eyes in a tightly controlled situation called the "microscopic examination." The words "chlorophyll-infused cells" enter the student's ears only when the teacher is assured his students are looking at "the right thing." The banking approach to education ends with students being controlled. Students "meekly" speak true names of known objects and hope they are pointing to the right things as the watchful teacher passes by.

Freire quotes Fromm to note that the passion for control that suffuses the banking approach to education is, in fact, a passion for death. The educator who relies on the banking approach is "necrophilous":

> The necrophilous person is driven by the desire to transform the organic into the inorganic, to approach life mechanically, as if all living persons were things. . . . Memory, rather than experience; having, rather than being, is what counts. The necrophilous person can relate to an object—a flower or a person—only if he possesses it; . . . if he loses possession he loses contact with the world. . . . He loves control, and in the act of controlling he kills life.[8]

The cells, cut off from all that supports them so they can be subjected to a microscopic examination, must die. The students, cut off from alternative supportive social relationships so they can be examined for their knowledge in the mechanistic teacher-student relationship, are as good as dead. Freire says that the banking approach to education and all those who would employ it are necessarily necrophilous: "Based on a mechanistic, static, naturalistic, spatialized view of consciousness, it transforms students into receiving objects. It attempts to control thinking and action, leads men to adjust to the world, and inhibits their creative power."[9]

So Human an Animal

Freire constructed his liberatory pedagogy in response to his understanding of education conducted under the banking concept. But his pedagogy is not merely reactive. It is built also on his conception of human beings. It is only when the truly *reflective,* the truly *transforming,* the truly *social,* and the truly *historical* nature of humans is brought to light that we can see how ill-suited conventional education is to our species. More than ill-suited, it is deforming, isolating, and stupefying—in a word, oppressive.

Other animals live a life submerged in nature, submerged in their immediate natural environment. Humans, according to Freire, are distinguished by their ability to pull themselves out of a life of immediacy, to create some distance between themselves and their environment, and, as a result, to reflect on their situations and create meanings.

Animals live "'submerged' in a world to which they can give no meaning," says Freire.[10] They live in response to a series of stimulations that the world provides them through their contacts with their environment. They have no capacity to reflect upon those contacts or the stimulations they provide and, thus, they can never attribute meaning to anything. What happens to them simply happens and they move on through their environments until they die. Animals have no history and no future since these are inventions that arise from the reflective ordering of events into causal or narrative chains and from attributed meanings. Animals may act in their environments and may actually make things in that environment—shelters for themselves or tools for getting or operating on food, for example—but their actions are not purposeful acts chosen reflectively from a field of alternatives, each of which has a different value attached to it. Their actions are mere responses to the environment that presses on them. Animals may act with others of their kind, but such collaborative actions are not actions out of relationships and do not involve "communication," as Freire wants to use that term. Their actions together are simply compulsive repetitions of behaviors that the animals' bodies make them perform. An animal's reality consists entirely of the contacts it makes with everything else, including other bodies, in nature. An animal is simply a being in nature that experiences but that cannot know.

Human beings are capable of being more than natural animals. Freire begins his essay, "Education as the Practice of Freedom," by making this distinction between humans and animals:

> To be human is to engage in relationships with others and with the world. It is to experience that world as an objective reality, independent of oneself, capable of being known. Animals, submerged within reality, cannot relate to it; they are creatures of mere *contacts*. But man's separateness from and openness to the world distinguishes him as a being of *relationships*. Men, unlike animals, are not only *in* the world but *with* the world.[11]

In other words, humans can develop enough distance from their world to experience all aspects of it, including themselves in it, as objective entities available for naming, judging, and manipulating. By deciding to name an object one name and not another, humans determine how that thing will be treated. Thus, the decision to select one particular name and not another transforms the object under consideration. So one's hand can be, in one set of circumstances, a "tool," in another an "instrument of comfort," in another an "instrument of war." Every name, with its associated values, remakes one's hand into something else. From the imaginable range of names, humans can decide what a thing, in its truth, is, and through that act of deciding on a truth the thing is transformed. Unlike animals, human beings do not have to accept the press of the world as it presents itself to them. They can actively transform and remake it.

Humans do not engage in the reflective transformation of the world independently and individually, according to Freire. It is only as members of a community and a culture that they can perform the reflection necessary to cognize their world: "Intersubjectivity, or intercommunication, is the primordial characteristic of this cultural and historical world. The [cognitive] function cannot be reduced to a simple relation between a Subject that knows and a knowable object. Without a relation of communication between Subjects that know, with reference to a knowable object, the act of knowing would disappear."[12] For Freire, the very act of knowing is a social act. He reverses the normal way we think of knowing, maintaining that social knowing precedes and makes possible individual knowledge. Thus, the social nature of humans is crucial to their capacities as active, reflective transformers of their world. It is only in culture that human beings can realize their humanity. Acting in, through, and on culture, people rise above the natural to become fully human.

As social and cultural beings, humans are necessarily historical beings as well. The relationships one has with the world are conditioned by history. Freire says, "Human beings are not just what they are, but also what they were."[13] So one is never faced with the task of constructing the world de novo. One exists always in relationships to the past that one, in the present, actively "takes on," as Freire puts it.[14] One "takes on" the previously attributed meaning as a set of constraints, and then one "takes on" those constraints combatitively in an act of freedom. Through one's relationships in the present, one can become an active collaborator in the transformation of this reality that one has "taken on."

Freire rejects both an idealistic and a mechanistic conception of history. He insists that to be human is to be aware of oneself as a historically active being:

> [We] cannot view men and women isolated from the world (creating it in their consciousness) nor the world without men and women (incapable of transforming it). . . . [In history] one does not find only a mechanistic process in which human beings are incidental to facts. Nor does one find the result of the ideas of a few human beings which have been developed in their consciousness. History, as a period in human events, is made by humans beings at the same time they "make" themselves in history.[15]

People are collective actors working with others in the making of a new future.

To bring about change, one does not simply act. Thoughtless action usually commits one more deeply to a dominating present. Human action must grow out of a reflective consciousness of one's own situation. This reflective consciousness starts with the dawning awareness that humans are more than natural creatures, that *all* humans, not just the "cultured" classes, have a culture: "The first dimension of our . . . program . . . would be the anthropological concept of culture—that is, the distinction between the world of nature and the world of culture; the active role of men *in* and *with* their reality; . . . culture as an addition made by men to a world they did not make; culture as the result of men's labor, of their efforts to create and re-create."[16] If culture is the result of human labor, it can be changed by people acting conscientiously. Language and history lead people to develop a consciousness that "the world is theirs, and their work is not the price they pay for being men but rather a way of loving—and of helping the world be a better place."[17]

Freire's view of the human is not a description of the way all human beings are in all human situations. Freire's view of "the human" serves the same critical purpose as Rousseau's view of "the natural." It is a yardstick by which to measure changes in the human condition. Indeed, most of the time in most situations most people experience themselves as objects acted upon by the forces of the world. Instead of searching for ways "of *becoming more* fully human," most people exist in a "state of being [that] is almost a state of *non-being*."[18] Many people are little more than animals in their day-to-day existence: "They come so close to the natural world that they feel more *part* of this world than the transformers of the world. There exists between them and their natural world (and obviously their cultural world) a strong 'umbilical cord' which binds them,"[19] that makes it impossible for them to achieve the sense of separateness that is essential for the development of awareness and consciousness: "The oppressed feel like 'things' owned by the oppressor. For the latter, *to be* is *to have*, almost always at the expense of those who have nothing. For the oppressed, at a certain point in their existential experience, *to be* is not to resemble the oppressor, but *to be under* him, to depend on him."[20] Under circumstances of domination a person comes to understand himself in terms of relationships about which he must be silent, not through the relatedness in and through which he might engage in dialogue, communication, and action.

In more "advanced" societies, the only thing that is truly advanced is the sophistication of one's alienation. We live, Freire says,

> the alienation of routine, of repeating things bureaucratically, of doing the same thing every day at ten o'clock, for example, because "it has to be done" and we never question why. . . .
>
> In these complex societies we sometimes find ourselves living very much submerged in time, without critical and dynamic appreciation of history, as if history were flying over us, commanding and relentlessly regulating our lives. This is a fatalism that immobilizes, suffocates, and eventually kills us.[21]

There is a poverty to the situation that most know as "life." That which perpetuates this poverty is the education system that "helps" us to know only what society needs us to know about the world and about ourselves. Banking education suppresses the reflective, transformative, social, and historical nature of human beings. It turns us into the kind of creature for which a banking concept *would* be appropriate: a passive, impulsive, nonreflective herd animal. To become fully human, we need an education that is liberating, one that will reverse the process of submersion and enable us to become critically conscious of our situation and able to act on it in order to transform it.

Freire's Liberatory Pedagogy

The starting point of Freire's liberatory education is the everyday, concrete, real-life situations of the parties to the educational encounter. The goals are "conscientization," the development of a critical consciousness of one's situation and, based on that consciousness, a capacity to transform the world and remake one's situation in it. The method is "problematization," making problematic the taken-for-granted aspects of real-life situations. By making problematic aspects of life that students have taken for granted, the teacher begins the process of detaching them from submersion in their lives. In the space gained through this detachment, the processes of critical thinking can begin.

So far, Freire sounds like a good developmental educator, in the spirit of Piaget, Kohlberg, or Rousseau. Just as Jean-Jacques made problematic the bean-patch in which Emile planted his beans, so Freire will isolate aspects of the typical environment of his students—a well, a bow and arrow, or a potter's wheel—and, through questions and discussion provoke his students to think about these ordinary objects in ways that transcend the ordinary. Dewey's conviction that intellectual development takes place only through reflecting on one's own experience appears to express the guiding spirit of Rousseau and Freire equally well. Because each believes that humans learn through the active use of their own inquiring intelligences, and because each assumes that such inquiry proceeds best when motivated by "present interest" (to use Rousseau's phrase), we should not be surprised to find them engaged in similar pedagogical practices.

But Freire parts company from Rousseau and his developmental followers in his disavowal of the single-student/single-teacher pair as the organizing unit of education. The scene of the pedagogical encounter shifts from the person-to-person, teacher-student relationship to the social situation in which teacher and student must find a common ground and become, in Freire's terms, educator-educatee and educatee-educator. These terms respectively designate two people who are co-present with each other in a historical world that it is their common project to understand and transform. Freire replaces the two-person encounter complete with "ego ideal" (the teacher) and less developed person (the student) with that of a study circle (or "culture circle," as he terms it) in which everyone is fundamentally equal.

The banking approach to education begins in the solitude of the scholar/Subject's study or lab as he contemplates his objects of knowledge. Liberatory education begins in the situation of the students, the everyday arena in which students live their more or less common lives. The libertory educator does not stride from his study with a curriculum in hand. Freire says, "The point of departure of the dialogue [between teacher and student] is the quest for curriculum."[22] Ira Shor, one of Freire's most ardent disciples and advocates for the applicability of a critical pedagogy in industrially advanced societies, explains what it means for pedagogy to be *situated*. He writes,

> This goal asks teachers to situate learning in the students' culture—their literacy, their present cognitive and affective levels, their aspirations, their daily lives. The goal is to integrate experiential materials with conceptual methods and academic subjects. Grounding economics or nursing or engineering or mathematics or biology in student life and literacy will insert these courses in the *subjectivity* of the students. . . . By turning to subjectivity, the situated course will not only connect experience with critical thought, but will also demonstrate that intellectual work has a tangible purpose in our lives. . . . Further, only situated pedagogy can bring critical study to bear on the concrete circumstances of living, the immediate conditions of life that critical learning may help recreate.[23]

Instead of a curriculum coming full-blown from the head of the teacher or from the head of the administration, curriculum must be emergent. Finding together the objects of study, how they are to be approached, and what is to be "made" of them (in the several senses that word may take on in the classroom) are the common tasks of teacher *and* student in liberatory pedagogy.

For both parties to education to be able to find their curriculum, their course of study and their objects of inquiry, they must be able to experience themselves as separable from their world as well as integral to it. This is what Freire has in mind when he stresses that people must be "with" the world as well as "in" it. Education, for Freire, requires "confrontation with the world as the true source of knowledge."[24] Objects in the world cannot be, simply, "things to be known"; they must become mediators of communication if one is to embark on a liberatory course. Objects stand between an educator-educatee and an educatee-educator as a mark of their commonality. Instead of "objects of knowledge," they become "objects of dialogue."

Ira Shor says that by changing an "object of knowledge" into an "object of dialogue," one comes to "extraordinarily re-experience the ordinary." Objects common to one's world must be forcefully removed from their taken-for-granted everyday context and subjected to a scrutiny that their usual embeddedness in reality makes impossible. Shor recalls how in one class of community college students he bought a hamburger at the college's grill and brought it to class with him:

> What better way to extraordinarily re-experience the ordinary? The burger is the nexus of so many daily realities. It's not only the king of fast foods, the lunch/snack/dinner quickie meal, but it's also the source of wages for many students who work in the burger chains. In addition, the spread of fast food franchises is tied into the suburban dispersal of the American city. This dispersal is further connected to the automobilization of American life. The car, the suburbs, and the burger thus connect central themes of everyday life. So, I was able to hold in my hand a weighty interstice of mass experience. My students have eaten, cooked and sold countless numbers of hamburgers, but they have never reflected on all this activity. I brought a burger to class and interfered with a major uncritical flow of mass culture. It was a lucky break, played out on a hunch.[25]

He had his students each examine the hamburger and write a detailed description of it, not something one usually does with this piece of taken-for-granted reality. "Close up, on reflection, many of the students found the hamburger repulsive."[26] They began to talk *about* this object, which, if it is allowed to remain in its usual context of the fast-food grill, is normally by-passed by conversation. The hamburger became for *both* the students and for Shor a medium for thinking about their common situation, their situation in a community college, in an environment of "junk food," in a world economy that produces and distributes such products, and so on. In a seminar on Shor's book at the authors' public college at which a visitor from Dartmouth College described the luxury of her college's "dining hall" with its salad bars, freely open ice cream machines, hot tables, and extended lunches over which students lingered, consideration of Shor's little event became an object lesson in the class-based nature of American education as our students reflected on the lunches they were about to purchase from a Marriott concession and through which they were about to rush in a crowded, noisy "activities building."

In our own attempt to encourage students to extraordinarily reexperience the ordinary we brought "pocket-sized" packets of Kleenex to class. Students and faculty in groups of seven to ten closely examined these objects that had been suddenly extracted from the "flow of reality" and placed before them as something in common to be discussed.

One of the first discoveries of this group of one hundred or so people was how much knowledge about this piece of our common reality was resident in our group. One person remembered that an original advertising slogan for Kleenex, in its battle against its only competitor, the pocket handkerchief, was, "Don't carry a cold in your pocket." The person said, "It seems *that* battle has been won," since the slogan was no longer on the packaging. Another used the packet to discuss the way in which a quarter, the cost of a single packet of Kleenex, has become the new "lowest unit of monetary value." It has replaced, this person noted, the penny, as in "penny candy," and the nickel and the dime, as in "five and ten cent store," as the least one could pay for something of value. She came to this point by noting that the packages we actually had brought to class cost less than fifteen cents each since they were bought in bulk, but if she were to buy *one* package in the college bookstore it would cost twenty-five cents. Others talked about the nationwide manufacturing and distribution system that would be necessary to get these things from Wisconsin (where the packaging said they somehow "originated") to us in Washington. Others reflected on what they called the "corporate appropriation of language" (N.B.: this was the *students' term,* their name for this aspect of their lives) by noting that we offer people a "Kleenex," a registered brand name as the label reminded us, instead of a "tissue" or a "paper hanky." Finally, by having some members of the class display their red, patterned "farmer's" handkerchiefs and others their linen or lace ones, discussion turned again to social class and the different ways in which class is marked (or, at least, was marked) in our society. By coming together around a common object and making it an "object of dialogue," students came to appreciate one another's knowledge and came to trust more their own capacities to understand their world, a world that usually seems "beyond them," in part because it is so close to them that they never see it.

Through liberatory education, one comes to "enter into" objects in the world instead of having objects enter into one's life in a manner controlled by those knowledgeable in the "proper" use of those objects. Rather than following the well-worn path to the grill and eating their hamburgers, that is, having this object enter them as it "should," Shor's students literally inserted themselves into the hamburger in order to describe it. They took it apart. They looked deeply into it; they examined all of its various surfaces. They felt it, smelled it, and eyed it, as if for the first time. Our students entered into the Kleenex packets on their own terms, not on the terms they are taught that dictate the proper use and disposal of Kleenex. Almost everyone in our class carefully pulled each "facial tissue" from the package and reflected on the rather considerable pile of stuff this activity created in front of them. Some groups named this material, now, "waste." Some students chose to chew part of the object before them and considered the question of why it had to have such incredible absorbency. Liberatory education must interrupt the flow of reality that presses on one's body so that the body may regain its human posture toward the world that humans have made and, by implication, can remake. One must enter the world and must stand against all attempts of objects in the world to enter one's self unbidden.

By "entering into" objects in the world, inquirers "open up" a world that would otherwise remain closed to them:

> Entering into the world, [people] perceive the old themes and grasp the tasks of their time. . . . This is the point at which hopelessness begins to be replaced by hope. . . . Society now reveals itself as something unfinished, not as something inexorably given; it has become a challenge rather than a hopeless limitation. . . . During the phase of the closed society, the people are *submerged* in reality. As society breaks open, they *emerge*. No longer *mere spectators*, they uncross their arms, renounce expectancy, and demand intervention.[27]

By entering on their own terms a pocket-sized packet of Kleenex, our students opened for themselves a world of logging (an industry in its death throes just one county south of their college), of chemical processing of paper (the bleach for which is one of the contaminants of the water that laps on their college's beach), of product marketing and distribution, of the copyrighting of words on the packet (a fact of modern life that, even though they had read copyrighted books, some of them had not reflected on before), of the relationships between the market and varying conceptions of health, and so on.

"Entering into" objects causes the inquirer-student to experience herself as an *intentional* creature. Being intentional contrasts with being controlled. A student's intention with regard to objects of knowledge in a teacher-controlled, banking-inspired pedagogical scene is, at best, irrelevant, at worst, a nuisance. Under a liberatory pedagogy, it is not the case that control shifts from the teacher to the student. That would be an inversion and therefore a reproduction of an education for oppression. Instead, control becomes a non-issue. In the investigation of everyday objects stripped from their everyday contexts, it is not so much that students "control" their inquiry as that they experience themselves as intentional beings with regard to the object. They can "enter into" an object intentionally; they can intend to do something about it. Through their intentions they can transform objects before them. Some of Shor's students left their exploration of the hamburger intending to learn more about nutrition. Others left intending to cooperatize the college grill. Control is replaced under a liberatory scheme by a *co-intentionality* on the part of both teacher and student toward their objects of dialogue. "A revolutionary leadership," which is how Freire conceives of liberatory educators, "must . . . practice *co-intentional* education. Teachers and students (leadership and people), co-intent on reality, are both Subjects, not only in the task of unveiling that reality, and thereby coming to know it critically, but in the task of re-creating that knowledge."[28]

Intentionality toward a common reality leads to action and reflection as one unified whole, a whole Freire terms *praxis*. To live "authentically" both poles of praxis must be present. Theory must always be integrated with action. Action must always be undertaken reflectively and thoughtfully. Without one or the other pole, praxis degenerates into either "activism," action for its own sake, or "verbalism," words without meaning (the meaning that comes from a matrix of activities): "When a word is deprived of its dimension of action, reflection automatically suffers as well; and the word is changed into idle chatter, into *verbalism*, into an alienated and alienating 'blah.'"[29] One cannot merely intend reflectively toward reality or merely act; to be human means, for Freire, to undertake an intimately integrated thought-action, to engage in praxis.

Central to praxis is the thought-action of *naming*, speaking the true word. Freire says, "To speak a true word is to transform the world."[30] Naming is Freire's linchpin of the conceptual network of "dialogue," "communication," "praxis," and "education." In contrast to the relative silence in which an education centered on a transference-like relation between student and teacher is conducted, critical liberatory education must occur in a community of people actively naming the world. Silence is, for Freire, a sign of adjustment and accommodation to the world and an indication that human beings have been distracted from their "ontological and historical vocation" of transforming the world. It is through praxis, and in particular through the act of naming, that humans open their world for the emergence of people who, through their actions, are capable of becoming more fully human. "Men are not built in silence, but in word, in work, in action-reflection."[31] To declare, through common discussion with a group of colleagues, a pile of stuff from a pocket-sized packet of Kleenex to be "waste" is a first step in considering ways to make the world a better place.

Naming is, obviously, at the heart of dialogue. But to enter into dialogue there must be considerable *trust* among participants. By trusting them from the outset, Freire makes it possible for participants eventually to trust one another. Freire's pedagogy rests on the faith in groups of people to come to appreciate the knowledge the group has of its common situation.

A Fulbright scholar teaching college-preparatory English (English 016–06) to Bahamian women tried to use Freire's approach to literacy. After she got the students past writing essays designed to "please the teacher," she had them talk about their situation as women in the Bahamas. They wrote about the advantages and disadvantages of marriage. Fairly quickly they moved beyond anecdotal accounts of "my marriage" to more general, abstract accounts of "typical marriages." These reports were based on class dialogues, on the common knowledge of the collective group of students, and on published information the group was able to accumulate. Freire's approach, which Nan Elsasser followed in this instance, is to foster dialogue among participants in a common inquiry in the sure knowledge that dialogue will foster the trust that is necessary for people to engage together in the transformative acts that they come to deem necessary. The class of Bahamian women eventually published an open letter to the men of the Bahamas titled "Bahamian Women Deserve a Change." It appeared in the two newspapers there. It described the deteriorating circumstances of women and concluded with recommendations on how to change the situation of both men and women in Bahamian society. Their suggestions ranged from the demand that men participate in child care, housework, and family worship to the suggestion that "men make more effort to sexually satisfy their wives." The women signed their letter "English 016–06." These women, who entered class expecting more instruction on pronouns and adverbs and expecting to receive more indications of their personal failure when grades were issued at the end of the term, came together around their common situation and took action on that situation through their writing.[32] As Freire summarizes, "It would be a contradiction in terms if dialogue . . . did not produce this climate of mutual trust, which leads the dialoguers into ever closer partnership in the naming of the world."[33]

Freire's ineradicably social vision of humans explains why he ultimately insists on *love* as an aspect of liberatory pedagogy. Although some revolutionary pedagogues might think it sufficient to insist that teachers exist in solidarity with their students, Freire goes further. He insists on love because in the final analysis education comes down to dialogue, and dialogue, fully understood, requires love as a condition of its existence:

> Dialogue cannot exist . . . in the absence of a profound love for the world and for men. The naming of the world, which is an act of creation and re-creation, is not possible if it is not infused with love. Love is at the same time the foundation of dialogue and dialogue itself. . . . Because love is an act of courage, not of fear, love is commitment to other men. No matter where the oppressed are found, the act of love is commitment to their cause—the cause of liberation. . . . Only by abolishing the situation of oppression is it possible to restore the love which that situation made impossible. If I do not love the world—if I do not love life—if I do not love men—I cannot enter into dialogue.[34]

The Liberatory Educator

Freire's lovers of the world and of men are liberatory educators. They are revolutionary leaders necessary to guide others through historical changes that will lead to liberation. Freire posits a sequence of stages of social development through which societies must pass on the way to freedom. These stages are rough and schematic, but they show Freire's Marxian conviction that education to promote individual development cannot be envisaged while ignoring the crucially determining social and historical context the world supplies. Freire's schema involves three stages. The movement from the first to the third stage (from "semi-intransitive consciousness" to "transitive consciousness") defines the nature of the hoped-for development, and the second stage ("naive transitivity") shows why liberatory educators are required.

Freire uses the phrase "intransitive consciousness" to describe the state of complete immediacy in which animals exist. "Semi-intransitive consciousness" is the stage of submersion in which illiterate peasants and many other people live. It is a state lacking in critical awareness, one in which humans take social forms as "natural," and in which all human effort centers on survival:

> Men of semi-intransitive consciousness cannot apprehend problems situated outside their sphere of biological necessity. Their interests center almost totally around survival, and they lack a sense of life on a more historic plane. . . . Semi-intransitive consciousness means that [man's] sphere of perception is limited, that he is impermeable to challenges situated outside the sphere of biological necessity. . . . In this state, discernment is difficult. Men confuse their perceptions of the objects and challenges of the environment, and fall prey to magical explanations because they cannot apprehend true causality.[35]

Relying on magical explanations leads people to orient themselves toward some "super-reality" or directs them inward. Either movement diverts their attention away from the objective circumstances that oppress them. "It is not hard to trace here the origin of the fatalistic positions men assume in certain situations."[36]

"Transitive consciousness" is Freire's way of describing the end point of a social development that allows humans to become fully human, that is, critical, reflective, fully conscious, acting beings who take collective responsibility for their world. The move from semi-intransitivity to transitivity is marked by an opening of the self to the world. One's bonds to the world loosen; one becomes separable from one's circumstances and therefore capable of reflecting on and acting on those circumstances. Opening oneself to the world and expanding one's arena of perception, actions that are possible once the press of society is attenuated, permits people to become transitive: "Transitivity of consciousness makes man 'permeable.' It leads him to replace disengagement from existence with almost total engagement. Existence is a dynamic concept, implying an eternal dialogue between man and man, between man and the world, between man and his Creator. It is this dialogue which makes of man an historical being."[37]

Between the beginning stage and the final stage, there exists a transitional stage, the stage of "naive transitivity." This stage is necessary in the historical development of a society's freedom, but it is also a moment of considerable danger.

The emergence into naive consciousness is enabled by "cracks" in the system of domination that has kept humans silent. These cracks appear "under the impact of infrastructural changes" like the abolition of slavery, the mobilization of a populace for war, fundamental economic shifts, and so on.[38] People can see through these cracks and can come to realize that their situation is the result of the historical actions of other people, not the result of a supernatural being or the result of their "natural" inadequacy. People break their silences and begin to sense that they have control over at least parts of their lives. Freire also calls this the stage of *popular consciousness*. The possibility for the development of critical consciousness opens.

During this stage popular leaders appear. People do not automatically see through and into their situation on their own. Popular leaders, *educators*, help them to do so and help people begin to formulate an historical and social understanding of their situation. This is the time of the emergence of revolutionary leadership. People in a state of naive transitivity can imagine themselves as actors in their social situations but they tend to act by mimesis and through an identification with leadership.

The danger at the stage of naive transitivity is that the populace will fall under the sway of slogans and become not a people but a mass. Consciousness can develop at this stage into *fanaticized consciousness* instead of critical consciousness. Becoming a fanatic, a part of a mass, opens each person to the possibility that "he will become even more disengaged from reality than in the semi-intransitive state."[39] People sometimes give their thinking over totally to the revolutionary leadership. In that case, they would move only from magical thought to *mythical* thought. Supernatural beings that used to be considered the causes of one's circumstances are replaced by humans-become-gods. The revolutionary leadership becomes a mythical class and "the possibility of dialogue diminishes markedly. Men are defeated and dominated, though they do not know it; they fear freedom, though they believe themselves to be free."[40] They are content to let others, who are obviously fit for the job (given their mythical characters), live their freedom for them.

The stage of naive transitivity is critical for social development and, hence, individual development. Everything hangs on what happens in this moment: "In short, naive transitive consciousness can evolve toward critical transitivity, characteristic of a legitimately democratic mentality, or it can be deflected toward the debased, clearly dehumanized, fanaticized consciousness characteristic of massification."[41] A society that is to take the path of democracy, humanization, and critical consciousness requires revolutionary leaders who are true educators. If the leaders succumb to the temptations of domination in this moment, true development is aborted. The revolutionary leadership merely replaces the displaced oppressors of the previous regime. True educators will seize the moment and enable the people to achieve the aim of their own development, a society in which it is possible to be always more fully human. True educators will renounce any invitation to power and will enable others to realize their collective freedom, which a transitive society makes available to everyone.

What then will these true educators look like? How will they operate? How will they conceive their work?

Since liberatory pedagogy is situated, the work of educators begins with the students in their daily lives. Educators must do research, find out how their would-be students live, what they do and think, what worries them, what and how they love. The first step is to do a careful investigation of the circumstances that, for most teachers, are only impediments to education but that, for the liberatory educator, become the very stuff of education itself. Shor's hamburger, the Bahamian women's lives in their marriages—these are the things around which students' lives revolve. These things must, therefore, become the mediators of the educational encounter.

Once the educator has identified salient aspects of the students' lives that will form the basis of their educations, "the task of the dialogical teacher in an interdisciplinary team working on the thematic universe revealed by their investigation is to 're-present' that universe to the people from whom he first received it—and 're-present' it not as a lecture, but as a problem."[42] The job of the educator is not to tell students about their lives but to problematize parts of their lives for them. Presenting everyday life as a problem and not as "everyday life" interrupts the flow of life in which people are submerged. In his literacy programs, Freire re-presents life to those who live it by selecting "generative words" and "generative themes," everyday words and concepts—"work," "sex," "family," "govern," "learn," and so on—that are highly political but that have become de-politicized by the course of history. Taking these words out of their everyday context allows students to investigate the extended network of meanings that form around them and thus apprehend their reality more fully.

Shor has his students describe and then *diagnose* objects like hamburgers or the uncomfortable chairs on which students always sit in their community college classes. The idea that one should "diagnose" an object implies directly that the object is a problem, not a "fact of life" as it is usually experienced. Indeed, a chair, a hamburger, a packet of Kleenex is a problem that students find is linked to a vast national, even international, arena of problems that they can come to appreciate through consideration of the simple object before them. By "cut[ting] a disruptive path across the domesticating flow of events,"[43] the liberatory teacher enables students to transform the givenness of their situation into a problem that then, they can imagine doing something about.

Problems seek solutions. Shor says that diagnosis leads easily to *reconstruction*. Students who are permitted to see parts of their lives as problematic will transform their life situations. After being helped to see college-classroom chairs as a problem,

> each person writes out her or his vision of the chair she or he wants. They come up with ideas for large, wooden chairs, for upholstered chairs with arms, for floor pillows, for big old used couches, for clay-like soft chairs, and more. In their thoughts and in their writing, they gain a clear image of

> what they would do to transform the classroom. The simple question of furniture has been turned into a politicizing issue.[44]

Writing is only one way students can begin to undertake the act of reconstruction. But writing is not the "goal" of the education. It is only because writing is particularly well suited to the task of reconstruction that the teacher might suggest that they all try it out.

Indeed, the liberatory educator does not have any specific goal in mind. Neither "writing" nor "learning" nor "social change" nor "thoughtfulness" can be a teacher's goal. The teacher must renounce all teacherly goals. As Shor puts it, "It was my responsibility to initiate the process and to keep it going, by setting problems for a critical excursion. I knew where we started from, and knew when we were moving, stagnating or regressing, but I rarely knew where we would wind up. Each class was a surprise, some happy, some not, a learning process itself in-process."[45] The dialogical educator must renounce all a priori goals to be open to anything because the nature of the reconstruction must not be prefigured or limited in any way.

It sounds strange to modern ears, but the liberatory educator cannot hold in mind any conception of what students *need*. Liberatory education *proscribes* any attempts to design curriculum based on an informed notion of student needs. Indeed, all "needs," especially educational "needs," must be seen as problematic. The dialogical educator must not be tempted to tell his students what they need, "if only they realized they need it"; he must not be tempted to coax them into trusting him to interpret their needs to them. Such action would terminate the dialogue and defer true development.

The only way to identify what needs to be done at any moment in the educational setting is to allow it to emerge from dialogue itself. Freire says that the agricultural extension agents often told him that "dialogue is not viable . . . because its results are slow, uncertain and long-drawn out" and that they, as experts, could not afford to waste their time on ignorant peasants who employ backward techniques and hold irrational beliefs about farming. Freire does not challenge their assertion that didactic teaching would be faster; instead, he questions the nature of such experts' commitments. Their assertions, to Freire, "express an unjustified lack of faith in people, an underestimation of their power of reflection, of their ability to take on the true role of seekers of knowledge: that of Subjects of this search."[46] Educators can be committed either to the knowledge they own or to the people they serve. For Freire, there is no middle ground, no compromise. And there is no question that the central issue is commitment:

> The work of the agronomist as educator is not confined, and should not be confined to the domain of techniques. For techniques do not exist without men and women, and men and women do not exist apart from history, apart from the reality they have to transform.
>
> The difficulty that hierarchical structures, to a greater or lesser degree, impose in the task of dialogue, do not justify anti-dialogue—of which cultural invasion is a direct consequence. However serious the difficulties, those who are committed to human beings, to their cause and to their liberation cannot indulge in anti-dialogue. These are the difficulties that cause agronomists—and not only agronomists—to talk of lost time or of time wasted in dialogue.[47]

Any excuse for not engaging in dialogue is due to a lack of commitment to people.

A commitment to people implies a trust in their own capacity to know what is essential to their educational development. That means that even the learning situation itself may be viewed by students as problematic. The liberatory educator must be open to this possibility and to the likelihood that he himself will be viewed as problematic: "In the act of problematizing the educatees, the educator is problematized too."[48] After all, the liberatory educator recognizes that the teaching-learning situation is one part of the students' everyday reality. Thus, it becomes available as an object of dialogue. A nonliberatory educator seeks to keep schooling separate from the experiences available for students' reflective thought. She would rather have her students think about her objects of knowledge, not about the fundamental problem of gaining any knowledge at all. In contrast to the typical situation in which the teacher is essential, Shor says, "one goal of liberatory learning is for the teacher to become expendable."[49] Freire suggests that it takes humility to be a liberatory educator and that the more humble one is, the more one will learn from whatever educational encounter the teacher finds himself in.

"Becoming expendable" and "learning with" the educatees are actually tame ways to describe what must happen to the liberatory educator. Freire relies on explicitly religious imagery to depict the radical action involved. Those who are oppressed undergo "a sort of Passover in which they will have to die as an oppressed class, in order to be reborn as a class that liberates itself."[50] For the revolutionary leadership—the true educators—the task is doubly difficult because that class consists usually of people who have left their roots in oppressed classes (or never had them in the first place) and have returned to help but who bear the stigma of the oppressor with whom they have been consorting. Ira Shor instructively opens the first edition of *Critical Teaching and Everyday Life* with an autobiographical note on his IQ-test-based transportation out of the working class and of his eventual return to it as a university teacher:

> I passed that test by twenty points and my life changed. They identified me as part of that fraction of worker-kids to be tracked on to the university. In their enveloping expectations, I was grateful. It meant that I wouldn't have to live forever on drab streets bordering a dismal swamp. The friends who failed that test faded from my life year by year. . . . The blows to [their] pride were repeated year after year, first in school and then on the job, until the great divisions we were born into had shaped the amorphous humanity of our new generation.
>
> In an ironic way, I returned to the people I grew up with. After a university education, I taught Open Admissions students for six years at Staten Island Community College, a unit of the City University of New York. I began there in 1971.[51]

Shor did not—could not—return as a mature version of the child he was. He left his childhood behind and returned suspect, tainted by what that retake of the IQ test allowed him to become. He could not return and announce, "I am like you, working class . . . ," for that would have been a lie (and his students would have known it). He had to return as who he was, a well-schooled member of the upper middle class employed as an agent of the state. Shor and Freire say that the true educator must commit "class suicide."[52] The intellectual returning from a university education to his birthplace in New York or the minister of education concerned about the re-Africanization of the institutions of a newly independent nation must undertake this act of self sacrifice to become one with his students in their collective education. This is not a simple task. It points to some paradoxical aspects of Freire's pedagogy, paradoxes Freire himself understands to some degree.

Paradoxes of Liberatory Pedagogy

For Rousseau, all people are born free. Convention enslaves them.[53] Humans, for Rousseau, seek their freedom by escaping the conventions of society and culture, by trying to find the signs of their God, who created them free, in the residuum of nature left in the wash of society, and by returning, in so far as it is possible, to the free existence with which everyone begins. In contrast to Rousseau, Freire thinks the creations of culture are the greatest signs of human freedom. Yes, convention enslaves. But the recognition of all conventions as human creations, with the implication that all made conventions can be unmade and remade, is the kernel of human freedom. Rousseau's free person seizes freedom by turning away from society. Freire's free person acts her freedom in society. Rousseau's free person begins her quest with an act of rejection of convention. Freire's free person begins her quest with a deep, sustained, critical confrontation with convention.

We came to understand Rousseau's pedagogy as deeply paradoxical by arguing that one can never get away from the compulsion of the social, no matter how radical the turn away from convention. Freire's pedagogy impresses us as paradoxical because we suspect one can never get away from the compulsion of the social even by using the social against itself, as Freire so brilliantly attempts to do.

The deeply paradoxical nature of Freire's view is revealed most clearly by considering the position in which it places the would-be liberatory educator. Consider first Freire's insistence on using the cumbersome term "educator-educatee" to denote the liberatory teacher, and its equally cumbersome complement, "educatee-educator," to denote the student. In his quest for precision, he thus gives us such monstrous-sounding sentences as: "With regard to the overcoming of the educator-educatee contradiction this produces:

there no longer exist the educator of the educatee nor the educatee of the educator but the educator-educatee and the educatee-educator."[54] His struggle with language here—one he is clearly not winning—betrays his struggle with the troubling problem of teacher-student equality. His insistence that dialogue lies at the heart of education requires him to insist on fundamental equality between teacher and student, but this equality is a problem of the highest order.

Freire insists on the teacher's equality with his students, but he will have no truck with educators of the so-called humanistic school who would reduce teachers to "facilitators" and deny the importance of the teacher's knowledge and experience. As he says in his "Letter to North-American Teachers," "There is, however, one dimension of every teacher's role that is independent of political choice, whether progressive or reactionary. This is the act of teaching subject matter or content. It is unthinkable for a teacher to be in charge of a class without providing students with material relevant to the discipline." And again: "[A progressive] teacher would never neglect course content simply to politicize students."[55]

So the teacher clearly has knowledge that the students do not have and is thus not equal to them with respect to that knowledge. Yet he must be nevertheless equal. He must be both equal and unequal, and thus we get the cumbersome terminology of "educator-educatee" that must have it both ways.

Freire tries to resolve this problem by arguing, first, that students also have knowledge that the teacher does not have (knowledge about their everyday lives, knowledge that pertains to the application of a teacher's specialized knowledge, etc.) and, second, that in teaching his students the educator necessarily must reconstruct his own knowledge and thus join his students in the role of educatee. Both of these are considerable claims, but they do not resolve the problem. Freire's equality between teacher and student is a semantic equality, an argued-for equality, an equality that the teacher needs to believe in, but that empirically does not describe the interactions between liberatory educators and their students—at least not at the start. Shor acknowledges this fact by advocating the "withering away of the teacher."[56] "Withering away" describes a process that, even in the best of circumstances, takes considerable time, and is probably only partial in the end. Freud's concept of transference has already shown us how difficult if not impossible such "withering away" might be, and even optimistic assessments of educational processes designed to bring the transference to light in students' experience suggest how arduous is the attainment of experienced equality *on the students' part.*[57]

Thus, Freire may claim he has eradicated the initial educational inequality that, even in the name of liberation, reproduces social domination, and he may adopt terminology to express this claim without falling into the trap of the "humanistic" schools, but he is finally not convincing. The fact that his educator performs research on the students' lives before commencing is an act of profound respect, and moves him miles away from the arrogant position of the conventional educator who knows what his students need before he meets them. But it is still the educator who is performing the research, and it is still on the students' lives that the research is being performed.

Once the research is completed, and the actual teaching begins, the same problem appears in a new guise. Here is how Freire frames the process in *Pedagogy of the Oppressed:*

> The problem-posing method does not dichotomize the activity of the teacher-student: he is not "cognitive" [discovering knowledge] at one point and "narrative" [telling knowledge] at another. He is always "cognitive," whether preparing a project or engaging in dialogue with the students. He does not regard cognizable objects as his private property, but as the object of reflection by himself and his students. In this way, the problem-posing educator constantly re-forms his reflections in the reflection of his students. The students—no longer docile listeners—are now critical co-investigators in dialogue with the teacher. The teacher presents the material to the students for their consideration, and re-considers his earlier considerations as the students express their own.[58]

The description makes it sound wonderful, but who is going to believe it? Freire, we think, underestimates the power of the developmental, problem-posing teacher to delude both his students and himself about the open ended nature of their "mutual" inquiry. He who poses the problems, he who arranges the environment, has the upper hand, as Rousseau so well understood. ("There is no subjection so perfect as that which keeps the appearance of freedom."[59]) It is true we didn't know exactly what the students would say when we brought packets of Kleenex into class, but we did spend considerable time selecting this particular object to bring in, and we were not entirely surprised at the general drift of the conversation it provoked. Nor do we think Shor was completely surprised by the results of his "hamburger" conversations. Delighted, yes. Surprised? Probably not.

Freire himself is forced to reveal the paradox inherent in his pedagogy most clearly when he tries to answer some deeply distressing questions about revolutionary leadership. His hedging in these responses reveals the tension we have been suggesting. Near the end of *Pedagogy of the Oppressed* Freire tries to reconcile his humanistic, humanizing, individually liberating pedagogy with the fact that liberation must come about through revolutions that often require inhumane practices. To achieve freedom one must often create conditions of unfreedom. To enter into dialogue one must often be severely antidialogical. Freire proffers Che Guevara as an exemplary revolutionary educator/leader. But Che's work shows there are some revolutionary requirements that are antidialogical, antipedagogical. For example, Che wrote, "Mistrust: at the beginning, do not trust your own shadow, never trust friendly peasants, informers, guides, or contact men. Do not trust anything or anybody until a zone is completely liberated."[60] Freire, who has emphasized to the liberatory educator the centrality of trust in the people, writes in response, "Although trust is basic to dialogue, it is not an *a priori* condition of the latter,"[61] a somewhat surprising statement. It would be generous to say that this is a chicken-or-the-egg problem. At what point does one begin to love and trust? Does that mean that love and trust are conditioned? But, if love and trust are conditioned, can they be revoked? Then, following Kierkegaard, was there ever love or trust at all?[62]

Freire also seems to agree with Guevara's notion that it may be necessary to punish those who desert the revolutionary cause by denouncing the leadership instead of their common situation.[63] In a curious note Freire acknowledges that dialogue with former oppressors is "impossible." He writes, "Once a popular revolution has come to power, the fact that the new power has the ethical duty to repress any attempt to restore the old oppressive power by no means signifies that the revolution is contradicting its dialogical character. Dialogue between the former oppressor and the oppressed as antagonistic classes was not possible before the revolution; it continues to be impossible afterward."[64] And those who would be liberated have to be ready to inhibit some actions of others.[65] We are left with the paradoxical conclusion that to become truly free, people must firmly band together. One achieves liberation only through unity and it is the task of the liberatory educator to effect this unity even at costs that seem extreme for one who is professedly humanistic, dialogical, trusting, and loving.

Freire justifies his acceptance of practices that appear inhumane by arguing that the oppressed live, even following the revolution, in a certain "ambiguity."[66] They love freedom but they fear it. They want to change their situation in life but the only change they can imagine—moving from being under another to being on top of others—is a change that is no change. Freire seems to be saying that the stage of naive transitivity is not just a dangerous diversion on the path to transitivity and conscientization but is rather an inevitable sticking point in any liberatory effort. He seems to be suggesting, in these justifications, that in the final analysis the educator indeed does know what is best for his students—a tenet that would undermine his whole philosophy of education. Freire's responses here highlight the paradoxical nature of the position that a liberatory educator/leader must fill.

Freire himself acknowledges the paradox. In an interview with Donaldo Macedo, Freire does not accept Macedo's premise that he, Freire, "operates outside the status quo," that his thinking represents a fundamental departure from "the system." Freire said,

> I have been trying to think and teach by keeping one foot inside the system and the other foot outside. Of course, I cannot be totally outside the system if the system continues to exist. I would be totally outside if the system itself were transformed. But it is not transformed because, in truth, it goes on transforming itself. Thus, to have an effect, I cannot live on the margins of the system. I have to be in it. Naturally, this generates a certain ambiguity, not just for me, but also for people like you, Giroux, Carnoy, and Berthoff. This is an ambiguity from which no one can escape, an ambiguity that is part of our existence as political beings.[67]

It is not a trivial matter that many of the experiments with Freire's pedagogy have paradoxically taken place in schools and have been conducted by certified educators, even educators of some note who have used their experiments to elevate themselves in their profession according to the very standards of their disciplinary professions. All liberatory educators may experience that ambiguity that no political being can escape, but with Freire's disciples there is often a question of how deeply embedded in the system their practices are. Ira Shor teaches and publishes on his teaching just as any professor is expected by the system to do. Bahamian women are taught writing by visiting scholars, sponsored by the Fulbright system, who return home and publish their own version of their students' story in professional journals. There is something deeply paradoxical about undertaking a self-proclaimed liberatory pedagogy in institutions that are, arguably, important foci in networks of social control. There is something deeply paradoxical about the way Freire's ideas have become "Freirean," about the way they have become programmatic, or as contemporary educators might put it, about the way his ideas have been mainstreamed.

Schools like Shor's community college or the Bahamian college preparatory school are disciplinary institutions. They regulate and discipline not only students but their faculty as well. Freire understands this, perhaps better than his disciples do. Of the ambiguity of keeping one foot outside the system he said, "This ambiguity is often risky. That's why many people keep both their feet squarely inside the system. I know people who sometimes slowly try to place their right foot outside, but they are immediately overcome by fear. They see other people who have stepped outside and are punished."[68] And speaking of an American professor, Henry Giroux, who tried to use Freire's scheme in American colleges, he said, "This is the case with Giroux, who was denied tenure because he had firmly stepped outside the system with his right foot. I don't doubt that many people, who were trying (and had even declared themselves) to be outside the system, ran back and plunked both feet inside after learning of Giroux's painful experience. These people have resolved their ambiguity."[69] Disciples are people who, in the Christian tradition in which Freire writes, often abandon the project at the last moment. And, in the tradition, institutions need to increase the fearfulness of their prospects only a little to have the seemingly strongest advocates flee the scenes of freedom.

To preserve the integrity of his scheme Freire has other conceptions of how educators should "resolve their ambiguity." He hopes for a "new Easter" after which the resolves of the disciples will be strengthened, as it was in the original tradition. He hopes, of course, that revolutionary leader/educators will not run in fear from their task but will, instead, be able to commit those acts of "class suicide" that will allow for true communion—Guevara's term—with the people he or she serves. He hopes for a new Passover where everyone will escape all disciplinary mechanisms and be born into a new order of their own making. This is how Freire saves his system.

We think Freire's approach to education is a social, developmental, humane alternative to the intimate one-on-one pedagogy of Rousseau over which Freud cast a shadow of suspicion. But we wonder if, perhaps, Freire has not underestimated the power of social disciplinary mechanisms? Is it possible to escape the power of the social by confronting and remaking it? Is it possible for the teacher to commit class suicide and become anything but what he already is? Is there an outside in which to plant even one's right foot?

4

THE PARADOX OF A SOCIAL PEDAGOGY: THE INSTITUTIONAL ANALYSES OF IVAN ILLICH AND MICHEL FOUCAULT

> The carceral network does not cast the unassimilable into a confused hell; there *is* no outside.
>
> —Michel Foucault, *Discipline and Punish*

ROUSSEAU CONCEIVED OF inequality as the source of all social ills—not natural inequality, which he found to be small in magnitude and inconsequential in effect, but socially constructed inequality, which he deemed monstrous.[1] But a carefully plotted, individual, developmental education could lead to equality between teacher and student.

Freud, however, made such equality seem almost impossible. His concept of transference turns the student's own psyche into the chief opponent of equality. No matter what the teacher does, the student unconsciously sustains his teacher as his teacher and makes himself always a dependent student. Rousseau's promise of equality fades.

Freire restored the hope of student-teacher equality by moving away from the two-person pedagogical relationship. By making the social group the unit of education, and by making the common cultural situation of the group the subject matter of education, he placed students and teachers in a virtual, if not actual, equality. The teacher can become one member of the group that is learning together. An education that is liberatory is both premised on and aims for equality of teacher and student.

Ivan Illich and Michel Foucault destroy Freire's dream. They do so, ironically, by accepting—by asserting even more strongly—the equality of teacher and student. They do not worry about whether students and teachers can eventually *attain* equality; they insist that both students and teachers *are* equal as a result of their common subordination to social institutions. The equality of students and teachers consists in the fact that everyone will operate according to the same axioms, the same unspoken assumptions, and therefore will be equally subject to the same social power. As long as they remain within social institutions—and it is virtually impossible to escape them—they will not be able to break the hold this power has on them. Illich holds no truck with educational reformers and Foucault offers no program of social change. If the teacher ever really possessed the power Freire works so hard to deprive him of, then there might be some hope that liberation could grow out of a pedagogical relationship. But if teachers are really equals to their students in and through their subordination before social power, how can a pedagogical relationship between them—no matter how carefully cultivated—ever result in the liberation of anyone? According to Foucault and Illich, it cannot. It can only produce the illusion of liberation—an illusion that in the end will be encouraged, nurtured, studied, measured, and finally programmed by the school system itself. And an illusion of liberation may be more dangerously deforming than outright oppression. The analyses of Foucault and Illich sound a hard caution in the face of Freire's faith in the revolutionary possibilities of liberatory education.

Illich's Schooled Society

In 1971, Ivan Illich published *Deschooling Society*[2] and became well known. Published amid a spate of books critical of the state of public education in America, Illich's book distinguished itself from the others by its penetrating social and historical analysis. *Deschooling Society* did not attack teaching methods, teacher apathy, or any of the specific arrangements within public schools that were so vigorously and intelligently attacked by the new generation of school critics. Instead, he focused on the way the school system functioned as a social *institution*, on the system's economic and cultural *utility*. He did not argue that schools were failing children and society; he proclaimed the obvious: schools do what they do very well. He argued that school reform would only make a harmful institution better at exacting its harm. Obdurately, he rejected reform in any guise; he insisted that schools had to be disestablished, that society had to be deschooled!

The School as a Sacred Cow

As a young priest in Puerto Rico, and a sometime resident of Mexico, Illich had witnessed the successful marketing of the proposition that universal, compulsory, "free" schooling was indispensable to the economic development of so-called developing nations. Illich found the consequences of accepting this proposition devastating. Making schooling compulsory enabled the state to subsidize entry into the middle class for the very small minority who could succeed at school and simultaneously to create "ignorance" and despair in the vast majority doomed to fail at school. In an essay called "The Futility of Schooling," Illich used an analogy with transportation to point out that the majority pays for the benefits "development" brought to the privileged few:

> Ownership of a car is now rapidly becoming the ideal in Latin America—at least among those who have a voice in formulating national goals. During the past twenty years, roads, parking facilities, and services for private automobiles have been immensely improved. These improvements benefit overwhelmingly those who have their own cars—that is, a tiny percentage. The bias of the budget allocated for transportation thus discriminates against the best transportation for the greatest number. . . . Opposition parties may challenge at times the need for superhighways. . . . But what man in his right mind would challenge the need to provide every child with a chance to go to high school?[3]

Schools could get away with the redistribution of privilege because they created a new culture based on the value of schooling. School became an "oppressive idol" that protected those who succeeded at school and degraded those who failed. But worse, schools made "the degraded accept [their] own submission."[4] In fact, Illich argued, one did not even have to attend school to get the message that the unschooled are less valuable and less deserving than the schooled:

> Half of the people in our world never set foot in school. . . . Yet they learn quite effectively the message that school teaches: that they should have school, and more and more of it. School instructs them in their inferiority through the tax collector who makes them pay for it, or through the demagogue who raises their expectations of it, or through their children once the latter are hooked on it.[5]

Illich called school "a sacred cow" and schooling a "cult" with its own rituals and myths. "The school," he said, "has become the established church of secular times."[6] And it is no small venture to attack an established church: "Today it is as dangerous in Latin America to question the myth of social salvation through schooling as it was three hundred years ago to question the divine rights of the Catholic kings."[7]

Education vs. Schooling

The success of the school system derives from the acceptance of the equation: education equals schooling. Illich is not opposed to education, but he insists on rigorously distinguishing education from schooling. Problems arise when everyone is schooled to accept that education can only occur in a school.

Illich defines schooling as "the age-specific, teacher-related process requiring full-time attendance at an obligatory curriculum."[8] By considering each of the terms of Illich's definition we can discover how schooling works its effects on society and also how far removed schooling is from education.

"Full-time Attendance": Diffusing Social Authority

The full-time attendance required by modern schooling has several effects. First, it depersonalizes authority. Full-time attendance removes the pupil from the family, one traditional locus of social authority for young people, for a significant portion of their lives.

Full-time attendance in schools makes it clear that social authority is now dispersed across several institutions and is located in "officers" other than parents.

Second, full-time attendance undermines the personal authority of any particular teacher. Schools do not operate on Rousseau's one-on-one-for-life teaching model. As children age, they move from having one teacher all day to having multiple teachers arrayed around a "home room" teacher to, finally, the smorgasbord of the university curriculum. Rarely do students in modern schools get the opportunity to enter into a critical dialogue with a "master" around a common text. Rarely do they get to live with an older person of genuine authority for a long enough time to develop some authority of their own. Modern students rarely get a chance to succeed at something of substance, for schools offer little of substance to succeed at. Instead, today's students accumulate credits.

Illich claims schools diffuse authority by schooling students "to confuse process and substance. . . . The pupil is . . . 'schooled' to confuse teaching with learning, grade advancement with education, a diploma with competence, and fluency with the ability to say something new."[9] Modern schools insinuate themselves into the lives of pupils. To the degree that schools are successful, a pupil will never experience herself as autonomously successful or authoritatively knowledgeable without institutional validation of that success or knowledge. The specific content of what schools teach is irrelevant. What matters is that they teach everyone the absolute need always to be taught and the need to have all legitimate knowledge institutionally produced. "School makes alienation preparatory for life," writes Illich: "School prepares for the alienating institutionalization of life by teaching the need to be taught. Once this lesson is learned, people lose their incentive to grow in independence . . . and close themselves off to the surprises which life offers when it is not predetermined by institutional definition."[10]

"Age-specific": Quantifying Selves

The age-specific structure of schools is but one aspect of their quantitative orientation. Illich reminds us that "childhood" itself is something produced by only the most modern of societies. The creation of distributions of capacities according to age is, following Philippe Ariès, an invention of the modernized West.[11] Age is, for Illich, the quantitative hook on which the entire mechanism of schooling hangs because paying social attention to differences in age permits age discrimination, and "only by segregating human beings in the category of childhood could we ever get them to submit to the authority of the schoolteacher."[12] But on this foundation of segregation is built the logic of schools that differentiates and segregates on the basis of many other quantifiable variables:

> In school we are taught that valuable learning is the result of attendance; that the value of learning increases with the amount of input; and, finally, that this value can be measured and documented by grades and certificates. . . . The institutionalized values school instills are quantified ones. School initiates young people into a world where everything can be measured, including their imaginations, and, indeed, man himself.[13]

The pupil in school who comes to understand everything of value in terms of quantified, assessable criteria applies these same criteria to the one thing most immediately available for judgment and manipulation, the self. Pupils in schools come to understand that their sole lifelong project is the shaping of their personal self along the reigning lines of "personal development" that society lays out for them. And they tackle this project with a vengeance because in schools there is literally nothing else to do. As Illich puts it,

> People who submit to the standard of others for the measure of their own personal growth soon apply the . . . ruler to themselves. They no longer have to be put in their place, but put themselves into their assigned slots, squeeze themselves into the niche which they have been taught to seek, and, in the very process, put their fellows into their places, too, until everybody and everything fits.[14]

"Obligatory Curriculum": Creating Inequality

Illich's inclusion of "obligatory curriculum" in his definition of school makes clear the school's function in creating inequality.

"Curriculum," Illich says, "has always been used to assign social rank," but that rank usually had something to do with the life history of the person whose job it was to run the "course" or work through the "curriculum." One's bloodline might put a person on one or another life track, or the way a person bore a rite of passage might be read as a sign of his character that, in turn, could influence the life course available to him. The curriculum of the institutionalized school, in contrast, "was meant to detach role assignment from personal life history."[15] The obligatory curriculum of schools was objectively designed to sort those who pass through it without regard to a person's circumstances or character. One function of schools is to propagate the idea that everyone is supposed to have an equal chance of passing the course. If some accident of nature or nurture leaves a modern school child incapacitated in some respect—sightless, without hearing, "developmentally impaired," without self esteem—the curriculum adjusts for that incapacity and permits the child to compete on roughly the same course as his age-mates. He is subjected to "special education" or to "mainstreaming"; both derive from the same logical mandate.

Modern institutions replace blood, family, and personal history with a public accounting of every person relative to "objective" criteria as the determining force in a person's life. Relationships based on personal or communal characteristics give way to relationships based on institutionally allowed, role-based identities. The differentiation effected in a society in which blood or personal history matters is a potent, symbolic differentiation according to the essences, alliances, and social lives of people. These relationships are historically grounded and make social sense. Differentiation effected by modern, objective criteria, such as the completion of obligatory curricula, is an abstracting differentiation. It acts independently of history, independently of any assumed essence, independently of community. Modern relationships are enabled through the public creation of institutionally based "roles" that have little to do with the people who occupy them.

Of course, this is precisely the justification of the meritocratic system schools support. Social station will no longer be determined by such accidents of birth as blood, personal contact, or personal history. They will be determined only by "merit." The problem is that merit gets defined as precisely those qualities that enable one person to pass successfully through the school's obligatory curriculum and that prevent another person from doing so. The school's self-justification is circular. And the circle is a vicious one, for the consequences to those who fail are dire:

> The belief in the ability of schools to label people correctly is already so strong that people accept their vocational and marital fate with a gambler's resignation. In cities, this faith in school-slotting is on the way to sprouting a more creditable meritocracy—a state of mind in which each citizen believes that he deserves the place assigned to him by school. A perfect meritocracy, in which there would be no excuses, is not yet upon us, and I believe it can be avoided. It must be avoided, since a perfect meritocracy would not only be hellish, it would be hell.[16]

"Teacher-related": Creating Delinquents

The only "relationship" that matters in modern schools is that between teacher and pupil. Illich calls school a "teacher-related process." Indeed, the first and final differentiation effected by "school" is that between pupil and teacher. To encounter the teacher, as the pupil must everyday, is to encounter one's superior, one who has obviously run the course of the curriculum successfully. The school is a teaching machine that constantly rehearses the message that only things taught through certified teachers are valuable. All that occurs outside of the pedagogical encounter, all that occurs outside of a teacher-related instructional milieu, does not count. Nothing learned outside of school, nothing learned on one's own or from friends, can truly count as education. This is the fundamental message schools promulgate.

For the student, the teacher is not a person of wisdom or even a person who has certain skills. Instead, the teacher becomes a person who fuses together what used to be three distinct social roles: custodian, moralist, and therapist. As custodian, the teacher is responsible for warehousing "children." As moralist, she indoctrinates the pupil about what is right and wrong; she substitutes "for parents, God, and the state." As therapist, she "feels authorized to delve into the personal life of [her] pupil in order to help him grow as a person."[17]

The result of this con-fusion, this merging of social functions, is that the teacher becomes for his pupils and their parents the center of a field of observation and assessment, the center of what Foucault would later call a "field of visibility." Instead of being a person to the pupil, the teacher becomes more like an eye:

> Under the authoritative eye of the teacher, several orders of value collapse into one. The distinctions between morality, legality, and personal worth are blurred and eventually eliminated. Each transgression is made to be felt as a multiple offense. The offender is expected to feel that he has broken a rule, that he has behaved immorally, and that he has let himself down. A pupil who adroitly obtains assistance on an exam is told that he is an outlaw, morally corrupt, and personally worthless.[18]

Every pupil is made into a potential delinquent. His ever-possible delinquency is effected by the ever-present watchfulness of the teacher. And the more personally concerned—the more patient, the more understanding, the more caring—the teacher is, the more severe is the attribution of delinquency, once made, and the more severe is the judgment the errant pupil imposes on himself.

The School as a Social Paradigm

The modern public school, then, serves many social functions, but it must not be suspected of educating. And certainly we should never think that teacher-based tutelage could ever be liberating. What would a public school look like if it were educational? Illich says:

> The basic purpose of public education should be to create a situation in which society obliges each individual to take stock of himself and his poverty. Education implies a growth of an independent sense of life and a relatedness which go hand in hand with increased access to, and use of, memories stored in the human community. . . . This presupposes a place within the society in which each of us is awakened by surprise; a place of encounter in which others surprise me with their liberty and make me aware of my own.[19]

That today's schools are not such a place needs no arguing. Teachers are the first to say so. Students go to school to get "empowered" and to develop "self-esteem," not to take stock of their poverty or to be surprised.

Schools, according to Illich, are paradigmatic of a vast array of modern institutions that operate according to a common scheme: (*a*) They create values that induce human needs; (*b*) they assign themselves the job of producing outcomes to satisfy those needs; (*c*) they fail to satiate public demands; and thereby (*d*) they create scarcity—and an addictive reliance on themselves to go on trying to satisfy the demand for their scarce product. Schooling creates the value associated with "education" by effecting an equivalence between "the educated person" and "the person who has been to school." Within such a logic, only schools can produce the educated person. Schooling creates the demand for more and better schooling, *even among those who fail*. There are always more courses, remedial programs, self-help seminars, workshops, and continuing education programs to take. No one is ever shut out from further schooling. Today we have reached the point where we all know that "education" is a lifelong affair. But it has become an obsessive addiction to more and better schooling, not a passion for finding some understanding.

Foucault's Disciplinary Power

Illich suggests schooling has become a part of life lived as an indeterminate sentence. This phrase evokes the social vision of Michel Foucault. For Foucault, the school room and the pedagogical encounter are, together, one among a swarm of modern institutions he characterizes as "disciplinary." School merits no special attention in his work and we are left to infer an understanding of schools from his understanding of other institutional forms. His social analysis extends and deepens the one provided by Illich. Foucault is even clearer than Illich in arguing that there is no outside ground onto which the educational reformer, even Paulo Freire, might place one foot. Once we see, with Foucault, how all-pervasive, how thorough, how insidious, and how resistant to reform is the power wielded by modern institutions, Freire's optimistic hope for liberatory education through organized culture circles comes to seem naive.

Discipline vs. Oppression

For Foucault, pedagogy is but one of a multitude of social mechanisms that control us through discipline. He argues in *Discipline and Punish* that discipline ought to be understood as a form of social power very different from oppression. Oppression appropriates a body, confines it, and restricts it under the weight of a master. Discipline insinuates itself into body and mind, makes a body docile *and* productive, and makes the person a participant in his own subjugation. Oppression constrains a body to be less than it could be. Discipline enables a body to become what it *can* be, to realize its potential. The unruliness of the body, with its Freudian polymorphous perversity, becomes "potential," not a threat. Disciplinary mechanisms channel "potential" into socially productive but humanly limited ends.

Disciplinary power overtook oppressive power at the end of the eighteenth century. It was based on the development of a "political anatomy of the body." The new disciplines of knowledge examined the body in minute detail, mapped its structures and functions in depth, and then deployed around the body sets of interventions and incentives to help the body become the best it could be, where "best" remained over decades and centuries an ambiguous term ready to be redefined again and again according to the requirements of historical circumstance. A body was no longer the site of character and virtuous action. It became something to be disciplined so it might become "fit," not for anything in particular, but for whatever happens to be "valued" in the circumstances. Under the reign of the disciplines, the power of the body no longer had to be restrained; instead, the body, through its powers, was made useful and productive.

Foucault warns:

> The "invention" of this new political anatomy must not be seen as a sudden discovery. It is rather a multiplicity of minor processes, of different origin and location, which overlap, repeat, or imitate one another, support one another, distinguish themselves from one another according to their domain of application, converge and gradually produce the blueprint of a general method. They were at work in secondary education at a very early

> date, later in the primary schools; they slowly invested the space of the hospital; and, in a few decades, they restructured the military organization. They sometimes circulated very rapidly from one point to another (between the army and the technical schools or secondary schools), sometimes slowly and discreetly (the insidious militarization of the large workshops).[20]

To try to distinguish between the disciplinary mechanisms of the military and the schools, between the training of doctors and the training of elementary pupils, or even between liberal and conservative pedagogy, is to fall under the sway of discipline itself. Such expertly drawn distinctions can only be made by those disciplined enough to see such distinctions. To spend one's time and rational effort organizing and ordering the social scene is to contribute further to "political anatomizing" and to miss the overarching, underlying fact of modern life that, for Foucault, is the inexorable spread of disciplinary action into every crevasse of life.

Foucault distinguished new forms of power from old ones in many ways, but his often-quoted admonition that modern power is not restrictive but "productive" points to what is most surprising and counter-intuitive about disciplinary power: "We must cease once and for all to describe the effects of power in negative terms: it 'excludes,' it 'represses,' it 'censors,' it 'abstracts,' it 'masks,' it 'conceals.' In fact, power produces; it produces reality; it produces domains of objects and rituals of truth. The individual and the knowledge that may be gained of him belong to this production."[21] Social power creates not only "truth," not only knowledge, but the individual himself. It effects this fruitful production through normalization.

Normalization

Foucault, more than anyone, has helped us appreciate the power of the norm and the disciplinary force of normalization. There is, for Foucault, nothing normal about normalization. The power of terms like "educated" or "healthy" comes from the disciplinary power of the norm. Disciplines formed around norms are what Illich has called a "source of axioms" for grounding all social discourse, the "mental frameworks in which [our social] institutions make sense."[22] The knowledge disciplines enable us to say what is normal, healthy or functional and thus to evaluate our social life.

Conceived in this way, disciplinary power cannot be spoken of as some thing certain groups of people wield at the expense of others. Since power is based in the assumptions and categories that underlie all social life—and the knowledge that justifies these assumptions and categories—it defines the normal for everyone. All members of society become subjects of power. Thus, Foucault speaks of power as an impersonal force affecting the weak and the "powerful" alike. "Power" replaces people, economic classes, or interest groups as the subject of his sentences; the people, classes, and groups become the direct objects of disciplinary power.

Normalization involves several component operations: (*a*) examination, (*b*) distribution, (*c*) creation of hierarchies, and (*d*) intervention. As a shorthand, we could say that the examination of people creates distributions of those people, which leads to their categorization in hierarchies. Properly categorized hierarchies of people enable interventions. The entire sequence of operations that underlie normalization requires (*e*) that the actions of individuals be made *visible* down to their smallest details.

Examination

The first component of disciplinary power, one that we certainly take for granted in the pedagogical encounter, is the examination. Examinations delimit a field of knowledge and help organize its structure. But once a field of knowledge is elaborated into a discipline, the examination is also used to discipline an apprentice to the body of created knowledge. The examination links these two meanings of "discipline": Examinations discipline people to a discipline.

It was during the nineteenth century that those exemplary disciplines, the professions, appeared. Along with them came licensing examinations. No longer were examinations conducted for the purpose of inquiring into the good character of an applicant; now they would assess the alignment of an applicant's knowledge of a subject matter with the known map of the discipline's object of study.

Examinations were designed not to discover if a person *was* of good character but to discern whether or not the person *had become,* through apprenticeship and close study or through training in a specialized disciplinary school, sufficiently informed to become a professional.

We are all familiar with the complaint that examinations objectify students. Foucault would say, "If they are well-functioning examinations, of course they will." In the same way that a discipline carefully articulates a body of knowledge by setting boundaries around it and by delineating its parts, the examination separates the relevant aspects of the student from the irrelevant, inquires only into the relevant parts (knowledge of the subject matter and skills) and by-passes all irrelevancies that fall under the confused and confusing rubric of subjectivity. Examinations are fair, we say, only when they are capable of by-passing the subjective. The examination ideally seeks to create a mirrorlike relationship between an object of knowledge and the would-be knower of that knowledge. To do that, the knower must be turned into an object as well. Because it must be objective, the good examination must objectify.

Foucault's acknowledgement of the objectifying quality of a good examination illustrates his critical strategy and differentiates him from other critics. Other critics would enter "objectification" as a complaint against examinations and would go on to develop a critical position that might point toward some better way to undertake the certification of knowledge or the selection of the knowledgeable. How often we hear of calls to make examinations more "sensitive" to individual differences, more accommodating to subjective aspects of the development of knowledge (e.g., learning styles, preferred cultural modes of expression). Foucault's strategy abandons such quick, facile criticism. He was more interested in attending to what social institutions do than in helping them to do their work better. In a discussion with a group of young students who were intrigued by the aborted but nearly revolutionary events in Paris in May 1968, Foucault indicated why he was reluctant to propose positive programs to replace that of which he was critical:

> Alain: This is a tiresome question, but it must be faced eventually: what replaces the system?

> Foucault: I think that to imagine another system is to extend our participation in the present system. . . .
>
> Philippe: If I understand you correctly, you think it's also useless or premature to create parallel circuits like the free universities in the United States that duplicate the institutions being attacked.
>
> Foucault: If you wish to replace an official institution by another institution that fulfills the same function—better and differently—then you are already being reabsorbed by the dominant structure.[23]

So Foucault is slow to offer "positive alternatives" to the operations of disciplinary power. Instead he takes seriously what serious people say and then puts all of their utterances together in provocative ways to help his reader see that we are confronting not just acts of power, which might conceivably be countered by oppositional acts, not just instances of oppressive behavior, which might conceivably be overturned or reversed, but a new form of power that is pervasive, resilient, rapidly responsive, and insidiously invasive into every aspect of personal and social life. So when Foucault "accepts" such unpleasant claims as "examinations objectify," we should appreciate that he is doing so to depict the place of this mechanism in an elaborate network of activities that together constitute disciplinary power.

Distributions and Hierarchies

The examination, as we know well, creates distributions of people. Some people do well on exams, some do poorly, and most fall in between. There is often a temptation to insert "naturally" at some place in a sentence like the preceding one. Foucault insists that rather than giving in to that temptation we try to understand its basis, for there is nothing "natural" about distributions of people along examination-based scales. Foucault carries the constructivist position[24] of critical social science to an extreme. For Foucault, examinations that create distributions are thereby creating nature as we know it. The "natural order" of things is a fiction that derives from social acts of ordering enabled by examinations. Examinations select criteria for assessment, provide an objective evaluation of cases on those criteria, contribute the data to be distributed along the continua of disciplinary knowledge, and then enable us to come to understand those distributions as natural, as reflective of an underlying "nature." The socially fit are as "naturally" distinguished from the unfit as are the short from the tall.

It is no accident that the discipline of statistics made its appearance precisely at the moment the other disciplines were rendering the natural world available for ordering. Statistics is, in part, the discipline of distributions and in the popular culture the Normal Distribution (or "bell curve") is an icon for this discipline. Francis Galton spoke of the normal distribution, which was known in his day as the Law of Error, with awe:

> I know scarcely anything so apt to impress the imagination as the wonderful form of cosmic order expressed by the "Law of Frequency of Error." The law would have been personified by the Greeks and deified, if they had known of it. It reigns with serenity and in complete self-effacement among the wildest confusion. . . . It is the supreme law of Unreason. Whenever a large sample of chaotic elements are taken in hand and marshalled in the order of their magnitude, an unsuspected and most beautiful form of regularity proves to have been latent all along.[25]

All one has to do to cut through confusion, to overcome unreason, to find the regularity that is there among the apparent chaos of everyday life is to distribute all the elements of a batch of data from the smallest to the largest. Order appears. The Greeks would perhaps have personified and deified this "law," but we moderns do not stoop to rituals. For us, Nature simply *is* as it is, and this "law" shows us that we can always find it to be orderly.

Distributions pave the way for the creation of hierarchies. By imposing a set of values on a distribution, we produce a hierarchy. Once a distribution has been hierarchically organized, each individual will have a certain distance from and a certain relationship to all the other positions in the pyramid, but especially to the apex—which will define the healthy, the fit, the functional, or the normal.

The beauty of this interlinking of distribution and hierarchy is that once it is effected, it is easy to claim that the hierarchical categories "emerged" from the distribution. In other words, neutral science in the pursuit of knowledge simply examined its subjects, and discovered that along certain dimensions people "naturally" distribute themselves in such a way. Any person can discover his own place in the hierarchy and the distance that separates him from the apex—from his "potential"—and this "knowledge" seems to have emerged uncoerced from the motiveless pursuit of pure disinterested science.

Intervention

Hierarchies overlaid on distributions enable interventions. Society can see to it that those who have to "work on" this or that "issue" will have the opportunity and the pedagogical possibilities to do so.

Statistics, a discipline closely linked to the eugenics movement in nineteenth century Britain,[26] could guide intervention even in instances where effects were individually uncertain. Francis Galton, his early protégé Florence Nightingale, Karl Pearson, and as late a statistical practitioner as R. A. Fisher all saw statistical procedures as leading to interventions that would "improve the stock," be that stock sweet peas, corn, cattle, the British army, or school children. For these researchers, problems were self-evident and the need for intervention clear. Corn should not be stunted in its growth; cattle should not be skinny; and the British army should not lose wars in southern Africa. The task of the newly emerging class of technical professions, of which the first statisticians were early members, was to design schemes of intervention to increase the frequency of cases at the "higher end" of a given distribution. Florence Nightingale applied to Galton for a university post and said that she would devote herself to the statistical study of social problems and collaborate with Galton on "how to use . . . statistics in order to legislate for and administer our national life with more precision and experience."[27] Karl Pearson was a Fabian before the society was formed.[28] Within his "socialism of professors" he was at ease proposing schemes for ensuring that only the fit be allowed to marry and for enabling the British people to improve itself by administratively overseeing family formation. The science of distributions led easily to all manner of schemes for the improvement of life.

The Visible Subject

The disciplines create "grids of observation"[29] in which *everyone* becomes completely visible. This visibility is the most compelling trap and the most essential operation of disciplinary power.

The operations that underlie normalization create the individual whose individuality is always on display, always visible. Unlike oppressive power, which crushes the individual and reduces him to some common denominator lower than the oppressor, disciplinary power raises the person to a visible position and makes his individuality manifest.

Visibility is effected by turning individuals into "cases." "The examination, surrounded by all its documentary techniques, makes each individual a 'case,'"[30] says Foucault, but he is quick to distinguish the disciplinary "case" from the juridical "case": "The case is no longer, as in casuistry or jurisprudence, a set of circumstances defining an act and capable of modifying the application of the rule; it is the individual as he may be described, judged, measured, compared with others, in his very individuality; and it is also the individual who has to be trained or corrected, classified, normalized, excluded, etc."[31] Statistics permits one to assess a case in terms of its deviations from other cases. Rather than rendering judgments on acts that break rules or contravene laws, statistics enables a non-judgmental description of the individual in terms of "variables." The individual gains an individuality by becoming known as a unique collection of deviations from a potentially infinite set of norms. The individual gains an individuality through the accumulation of a file, a unique, infinitely expandable, always amendable collection of facts that *become* (in both senses of that word) the individual.

In response to the person who protests that she is more than an aggregation of deviations around norms, the keepers of her file casually add another page, take out their pens, and encourage the individual to speak the terms by which the truth of her individuality can be better known. Teachers are often the first to protest the use of direct, blunt examinations; they are also the first to want to hyper-individualize a child's school file. Students are encouraged to "think critically" about social institutions, even about schools; when they do, a note is added to their file regarding their responsiveness to encouragement. The critical scream of "subjectivity" that presumably opposes the objectification of the individual in the "case notes" is a senseless act under a disciplinary regime because a case only becomes complete, accurate, and truthful by objectifying, among other things, one's subjectivity.[32] The scream will be duly noted.

Paradoxically, disciplinary power derives not so much from the way it makes the individual case visible to some centralized authority but from the way it makes the individual visible to himself! Unlike deviations from rules or laws, for which one is punished or for which one seeks absolution, deviations around norms become "issues" that one can "work on." It is the rare school child today who is marked as an unredeemable failure. Few are even kicked out of school anymore.[33] Most students on the lower end of some distribution acquire a term like "developmentally encumbered," along with an indeterminate sentence to a development-enabling program.

Foucault illustrates the power of visibility by recalling the structure and function of Bentham's Panopticon, a never-built prison whose principles of operation infuse our contemporary understanding of everything from corrections to medical care to national security to the pedagogical encounter. The Panopticon was, as the name suggests, a machine for creating visibility everywhere. It was to be a circular prison with each of the prisoners in an individual cell, each with an individual record perpetually recording all the facts of his case. The prison was to be light and airy, unlike the dungeons of old, which locked away in darkness the mass of indistinguishable members of "the criminal class." There were to be few bars in the Panopticon and its many windows would allow all the cells to be well illuminated. Each prisoner was to be free to do as he pleased inside the cell under the single constraint that all actions be always visible. Each prisoner looked out of his cell at a guard tower that might or might not, at any given moment, contain guards. The principle of visibility—the ever-present *possibility* of being seen—was to be more important than the fact of being watched. Foucault summarized the principle of visibility this way:

> Each individual, in his place, is securely confined to a cell from which he is seen from the front by the supervisor; but the side walls prevent him from

> coming into contact with his companions. He is seen, but he does not see; he is the object of information, never a subject of communication. The arrangement of his room, opposite the central tower, imposes on him an axial visibility; but the divisions of the ring, those separated cells, imply a lateral invisibility. And this invisibility is a guarantee of order. If the inmates are convicts, there is no danger of a plot, an attempt at collective escape, the planning of new crimes for the future, bad reciprocal influences; if they are patients, there is no danger of contagion; . . . if they are schoolchildren, there is no copying, no noise, no chatter, no waste of time. . . . The crowd, a compact mass, a locus of multiple exchanges, individualities merging together, a collective effect, is abolished and replaced by a collection of separated individualities.[34]

The Panopticon reveals an equivalence across the many sites of disciplinary power, which Foucault expressed in a rhetorical question: "Is it surprising that prisons resemble factories, schools, barracks, hospitals, which all resemble prisons?"[35]

Unforced Power

But who imposes disciplinary power? Who enforces the disciplinary effects achieved by the modern prison/hospital/schoolroom? Does it make sense anymore to talk about the people who are powerful and the people who are powerless? Foucault has a clear answer. Power is vested in structures that make all people both subjects of power and agents of its implementation:

> It is not necessary to constrain the convict to good behavior, the madman to calm, the worker to work, the school boy to application, the patient to the observation of the regulations. . . . The heaviness of the old "houses of security," with their fortress-like architecture, could be replaced by the simple, economic geometry of a "house of certainty." The efficiency of power, its constraining force have, in a sense, passed over to the other side. . . . *He who is subjected to a field of visibility, and who knows it, assumes responsibility for the constraints of power; he makes them play spontaneously upon himself;* he inscribes in himself the power relation in which he simultaneously plays both roles; he becomes the principle of his own subjection.[36]

It no longer makes sense to think power can be owned, seized, or wielded by some people at the expense of other people. Power operates on all people through its own structures and according to its own rules.

The radical notion that the person who is the object of disciplinary power is simultaneously the active agent of that power makes even clearer the importance of the file in the process of achieving individuality. A well-disciplined person comes to experience life through the facts inscribed in his file. Social norms define what is important in life, and his file documents how much he deviates from each norm. The aware person disciplines himself; the institution's job is to make him aware. Whether a student does well or poorly in arithmetic is not of principal concern to schools today; what matters is that all students judge themselves by means of the established developmental norms for arithmetic. What matters is that all students take responsibility for their own arithmetic development. Educators might chastise a particular school by pointing to relatively low test scores and they might propose schemes for "improving student performance." But these common activities mask the terms of success by which modern schools measure themselves: First, has a school created an efficient record-keeping mechanism that permits the moment-to-moment assessment of all students individually? Second, does the system make the students aware of the various measurements that "must" be made. And third, does the school get the students to muster some initiative, show some interest, take some responsibility, as we say, for their own educations? Put somewhat differently, do schools, through centralized record-keeping systems, make students visible to themselves?

Well-functioning disciplinary institutions will always produce individual "failures." But schools themselves fail only when their record-keeping systems fail to alert them to the "failures" of the system. Debates about ways to improve student performance will be endemic to the successful school system. Standards may change, expectations may change, and teaching schemes may change. What must not change is the constancy of the field of visibility and the awareness of those subject to disciplinary power that they are always visible. As Foucault puts it, when visibility is the rule, "external power may throw off its physical weight; it tends to be non-corporal; and, the more it approaches this limit, the more constant, profound and permanent its effects: it is a perpetual victory that avoids any confrontation and which is always decided in advance."[37]

Foucault's view leads to the paradoxical notion that the more freedom an institution accords its subjects, the more power it exercises upon them. Institutions that must rely on force are failures from the start. In a good disciplinary institution, the need to exact a punishment is a sure sign that it is time to rethink the institution's strategies. In good disciplinary institutions no one is a criminal—for there are no laws to transgress—but everyone is a potential delinquent. In a good disciplinary institution, everyone has the freedom to change, the liberty to comply with what counts (for now) as expected behavior. "The 'Enlightenment,'" says Foucault, "which discovered the liberties, also invented the disciplines."[38] Foucault would understand well B. F. Skinner's paradoxical-sounding view of freedom expressed succinctly in his *Walden Two* when Frazier, the founder of the community, says, "All that happens is contained in an original plan, yet at every stage the individual seems to be making choices and determining the outcome. . . . Our members are practically always doing what they want to do—what they 'choose' to do—but we see to it that they will want to do precisely the things which are best for themselves and the community. Their behavior is determined, yet they're free."[39] To disciplinary institutions there is no contradiction between being free and being determined.

Good disciplinary institutions force nothing. They provoke everything. Through their silence, institutions incite speech. Through the calm of the ever-open record-keeping notebook, through the blank projective screen of the therapist/teacher, through the creation of a Rogerian nonjudgmental environment, through a Piagetian curiosity about "errors," the disciplinary subject is incited to speak about that which would otherwise remain invisible to the record. Disciplinary subjects are encouraged to keep speaking because they can never say anything that is incorrect since there is no firm rule for delimiting the correct from the incorrect. The speaking subject can fill pages with his speech while the panoptic institution files each page in his file. "Free speech" has become not only his right but his duty.

Foucault's project was to appreciate the dark side of this form of "freedom." Perhaps it is better to say that Foucault's project was to help us appreciate this "liberty" and this "freedom" *as* the dark side of the social. Life in disciplinary institutions is not a life lived in the chains of oppression. It is a life in which we are free to speak our subjectivity. It is a life in which we are free to be the best we can be. It is also a life in which there is no darkness in which to hide. It is a life where, ideally, norms rule everyone and everyone polices himself in every respect. It is a life where life-long education is no longer a luxury, but has become an indeterminate sentence.

Foucault and Illich both think modern pedagogy is one of the major disciplinary agencies that construct human needs for nonhuman purposes. What do they think about the possibility of liberating students through educational reform or even through the radical restructuring of schools? Is a revolutionary, Freirean, liberatory educator possible in modern society?

The Unprivileged Critic

For Rousseau, the tutor was the privileged agent of his pupil's education. Freud's transference removed the privilege and forced us to see a kind of equivalence between tutor and pupil within the dynamics of the transference and the counter-transference. Freire's liberatory educator trades on her position of institutional privilege so that, as true educator, she can commit that last act of "class suicide." Only through the efforts of the educator can the problem of constructed inequality be solved. For Foucault and Illich, such an optimistic understanding of the social situation of pedagogy is too simple. The social constructions that social institutions effect are more resilient than Freire allows. With respect to the institutional order of schooling, no one is a privileged party. The critic merely doubles the expert. There is no outside.

Illich's Well-Schooled Critics

Schooling so invades the fabric of everyday life that even when one thinks about protesting against it, says Illich, one almost always does so in well-schooled terms. "Many self-styled revolutionaries are victims of the school," Illich says. "They see even 'liberation' as the product of an institutional process."[40] Indeed, the school system breeds its own reformers! A good disciplinary institution will foster dissent and nurture "good and thoughtful criticism" because good criticism is the fuel that sustains disciplinary institutions and, in Foucault's terms, reabsorbs the reformers into the dominant system. Modern educational reformers of whatever stripe "feel impelled to condemn almost everything which characterizes modern schools—and at the same time propose new schools."[41] Liberatory pedagogies of all sorts—ungraded courses, student-centered learning, issue-centered relevance, portfolio-based assessment, hyper-mediated instruction—are seen, from this perspective, as but a gloss on the underlying function of the school, which is to discipline students to need more schooling.

Different approaches to school reform, even when they appear contradictory, are for Illich "irrational consistencies." For example,

> The criticism directed at the American school system by the behaviorists and that coming from the new breed of radical educators seem radically opposed. . . . [The behaviorists'] style clashes with the nondirective cooption of youth into liberated communes established under the supervision of adults [by the radicals]. Yet, in historical perspective, these two are just contemporary manifestations of the seemingly contradictory yet really complementary goals of the public school system. From the beginning of this century, the schools have been protagonists of social control on the one hand and free cooperation on the other, both placed at the service of the "good society" conceived of as a highly organized and smoothly working corporate structure.[42]

Protest and calls for reform are merely a mask for what Illich calls the "escalation of the schools," which, "is as destructive as the escalation of weapons but less visibly so."[43] Thus, the perpetuation and escalation of school is abetted by its most able critics who conduct the critical research and develop the keenest insights about the social and psychological effects of schooling only to propose "viable alternative programs" or some similar sounding euphemism for "more schooling":

> The established teachers unions, the technological wizards, and the educational liberation movement reinforce the commitment of the entire society to the fundamental axioms of a schooled world, somewhat in the

> manner in which many peace and protest movements reinforce the commitments of their members—be they black, female, young, or poor—to seek justice through the growth of the gross national income.[44]

Everyone—students, teachers, critics—becomes trapped by the logic of the schools. "Surrounded by all-powerful tools, man is reduced to a tool of his tools. Each of the institutions meant to exorcise one of the primeval evils has become a fail-safe, self-sealing coffin for man," says Illich.[45]

Foucault's Disciplined Intellectual

But isn't there a way out? Is there no way to criticize the system of schooling other than in its own terms? Freire certainly thought so: The politically committed teacher whose consciousness is fully developed can be the agent of liberation for her pupils. But Foucault's analysis of disciplinary institutions is more relentless than Freire's. For him, *there is no privileged agent* of reform. Although there *may* be a way out,[46] it was not Foucault's way to point toward it. His analysis of modern structures of power shows, as Illich's view implies, that would-be agents of reform are as trapped by these new forms of power as are those subjected to (and longing for) programs of reform. The new panoptic structures of power exercise their discipline on the guard as well as on the guarded. This analysis distinguishes Foucault from other critics because he provides his reader with no positive, firm ground from which to launch a program of change.

The cover of the Allen Lane, London, edition of *Discipline and Punish* shows a reproduction of a nineteenth century engraving of men on a treadmill. It features six men each visually separated from one another even though they are all involved in the task of keeping the machine running. Each has an identifying number. At the moment depicted, three are on the treadmill, three are not. One man is distinguishable from the other five because he has a set of keys on his belt. He is the guard. The engraving illustrates one of the most potent features of the panoptic machines of power Foucault describes: Although guards may be distinguishable from the guarded, the machine makes them equivalent in crucial respects. The machine removes any privilege that might fall to those who are in the seemingly privileged position of "keeper of the keys":

> The Panopticon may even provide an apparatus for supervising its own mechanisms. In the central tower, the director may spy on all the employees that he has under his orders . . . ; he will be able to judge them continuously, alter their behavior, impose upon them the methods he thinks best; and it will even be possible to observe the director himself. An inspector arriving unexpectedly at the center of the Panopticon will be able to judge at a glance, without anything being concealed from him, how the entire establishment is functioning. And, in any case, enclosed as he is in the middle of this architectural mechanism, is not the director's own fate entirely bound up with it? . . . "'By every tie I could devise,' said the master of the Panopticon, 'my own fate had been bound up by me with theirs.'" (Bentham, *Works*, 1848, 4:177)[47]

The Panopticon accumulates records on its prisoner-clients, but it also creates records on its guard-employees. And it accumulates records on the guards according to the same principles by which it assembles all other files: everything must be noted, distributions must be created, hierarchies according to which better guards can be differentiated from worse guards must be invented and imposed on the distributions, and the effects of experiments to "improve" the guards must be diligently recorded so that the criteria by which "improvement" is evaluated can be constantly improved. Examinations may grade students, but aggregated scores also assess teachers, schools, districts, and the "educational performance" of whole nations.

Foucault is so relentless in his insistence that no one is exempt from panopticism that he includes even himself and his own work in the category of the unprivileged. The following passage from *The Archeology of Knowledge* points to the dispersion of his work that Foucault is at pains to effect:

> My discourse, far from determining the locus in which it speaks, is avoiding the ground on which it could find support. It is a discourse about discourses: but it is not trying to find in them a hidden law, a concealed origin that it only remains to free; nor is it trying to establish by itself, taking itself as a starting point, the general theory of which they would be

> the concrete models. It is trying to deploy a dispersion that can never be reduced to a single system of differences, a scattering that is not related to absolute axes of reference; it is trying to operate a decentering that leaves no privilege to any center.[48]

The passage is stylistically dispersive. All of those commas and semicolons usually cause one to think that the author is having trouble making his point and that he is trying to spiral in on it. Foucault uses those devices to achieve the opposite effect: he is pointedly trying to avoid making his point. He even undermines the importance of his elegant and compelling case studies as he argues that they are likely as not to become part and parcel of the structures of power of which his work is so critical: "After all, is it not perhaps the case that these fragments of genealogies are no sooner brought to light, that the particular elements of the knowledge that one seeks to disinter are no sooner accredited and put into circulation, than they run the risk of re-codification, re-colonization?"[49] Foucault seems to take a perverse pleasure in building up in order to destroy, and his first target is usually the importance of his own work.

Foucault's work is fundamentally a caution about the role of the intellectual. If his analysis is right, he seems to suggest, then there is no escape from structures of power that can last longer than a laugh. Laughs are, following Freud, events that escape through the weaknesses of the defensive structures. After a good laugh, you are ready to get back to work. Foucault knows his work will probably be put into the service of the system, as any good critic's work must be. With echoes of Freud's admonitions to therapists regarding the transference, Foucault says:

> There exists . . . a power not only found in the manifest authority of censorship, but one that profoundly and subtly penetrates an entire social network. Intellectuals are themselves part of this system of power—the idea of their responsibility for "consciousness" and discourse forms part of the system. The intellectual's role is no longer to place himself "somewhat ahead and to the side" in order to express the stifled truth of the collectivity; rather, it is to struggle against the forms of power that would transform him into its object and instrument in the sphere of "knowledge," "truth," "consciousness," and "discourse."[50]

Even a critic who tries to construct discourses with no ground under them is in danger of being made to occupy neatly the niche the system has carved out for him.

After the Catchphrase, What?

Illich's view of the unprivileged position of the intellectual can be inferred from his commentary on his own personal experience as a critic. After proposing that societies be deschooled, Illich underwent the experience of the would-be critic/intellectual precisely as Foucault describes it. Instead of being taken as a radical critic, he was instantly elevated to the position of new guru. His work appeared at a critical educational moment, just at the time when the idea that schools are in crisis was becoming popular, and his book became for many a godsend. Shortly after his book appeared, he wrote, "Phrases such as the 'deschooling of society' and the 'disestablishment of schools' become instant slogans. I do not think that these phrases were used before [1970]. This year they have become, in some circles, the badge and criterion of the new orthodoxy."[51]

Illich's proposal to deschool society is radical and difficult if one removes the quotations marks from what the editors of *After Deschooling, What?* called "the catch-phrase 'deschooling.'"[52] Illich's writing is easier to take if one tames his urgent proposal by the deft use of those quotation marks, making "deschooling" into a catchphrase. Illich the critic is easier to take if one "elevates" him from the dirty, root-bound level of radical critic to the lofty level of serious, rabble-rousing intellectual.

Recently Illich has said that he felt *Deschooling Society* had been an effort of "climbing up the wrong tree." His research emphasis shifted, and so did his popularity:

> And then during the '70s, most of my thinking and reflection, to put it very simply, was on the question how should I distinguish the acquisition of education from the fact that people always have known some things, many things, have had many competences, evidently therefore have learned something. And I came to define education as learning under the assumption of scarcity. . . . At this point, my reflection wasn't rabble rousing any more. Nobody on the campus discussed it. I tried to bring it into

> the educational research associations, completely failed, and even five years later, I barely see a little response here and there.[53]

Illich's realization that even a radical proposal can become a reformist cliché and Foucault's insistent refusal even to offer suggestions for social change point to what is paradoxical in each of their writings.

The Paradox of Producing Social Critique

The principal paradox of Foucault's work is that it is not clear what is to be done, or, indeed, whether there is any basis for even beginning to think about doing anything. He has formulated for himself and all those who read him the ultimate trap. No matter what his utterance, no matter how well aimed and acute his critical commentaries may be, good disciplinary institutions will absorb his utterances and his commentaries and turn them to the uses of those institutions, to the uses of power. Illich expresses his experience of the paradox of his position directly. He says he "feels very badly about this whole thing frequently," and adds, "I know that our criticism is destructive of one of the great creations of the last two generations. It pulls the rug out from under the only ritual which at this moment keeps stability. It calls for a radical alternative which we cannot imagine, because I do not know how one imagines the sense of the future."[54]

Foucault seems to say that the very best one can hope for is the fate suffered by Illich at the hands of his good and faithful editors, colleagues, and disciples, to have the most seriously critical commentary turned into a catchphrase, to have one's proposal for the absolute disestablishment of social institutions become a point of debate within circles of power, and to be left to write paper after paper and study after study saying, "But I was serious," against the tide of politely receptive academic and institutional opinion. Illich persisted in his work but turned away from all invitations to become a leader of the reformers. He said, "I have chosen the politics of impotence, bearing witness to my impotence because I not only think that for this one guy, there is nothing else left, but also because I could argue that at this moment, it's the right thing to do."[55]

In like manner, Foucault turned away from any suggestion that he was doing "useful" work. Instead of doing work "which you judge *useful* to do right now," as an interviewer put it to him, Foucault responded by saying he was doing work "which I find *important* to do now."[56] What Foucault found it important to do was question. Keith Gandal, an astute commentator on Foucault, says that Foucault had values but he was reluctant to let them structure any discussion. Gandal writes, Foucault's "radicalism consisted in his dedication to questioning just what seemed most obvious and least open to question, to giving 'some assistance in the wearing away of certain self-evidences and commonplaces.'"[57] He strove only to question, not to find answers. Illich is interested only in doing "archeologies of modern certainties," not in building new structures on sands that he knows shift throughout history.

What are we to make of the paradoxical positions of these two social critics? What is the point of writing criticism if one offers no program for improvement through that writing? For us, the positions Foucault and Illich have taken as writers point to a fundamental paradox, namely, that anything directive they might be saying is said more through silences than words.

Foucault enjoyed his role as a teacher,[58] but in his teaching everything that needs to be said, everything worth saying, is never said. A particularly insightful interviewer once asked Foucault, "One of the many things that a reader can unexpectedly learn from your work is to appreciate silence. . . . Would it be correct to infer that there is a strongly autobiographical element in this?" Foucault responded,

> I think that any child who has been educated in a Catholic milieu just before or during the Second World War had the experience that there were many different ways of speaking as well as many different forms of silence. There were some kinds of silence which implied very sharp hostility and others which meant deep friendship, emotional admiration, even love. . . .
>
> Maybe another feature of this appreciation of silence is related to the obligation of speaking. I lived as a child in a petit bourgeois, provincial milieu in France and the obligation of speaking, of making conversation with visitors, was for me something both very strange and very boring. I often wondered why people had to speak. Silence may be a much more interesting way of having a relationship with people.[59]

Illich, also a teacher, is also compelled to silence in some instances. In his effort to question and understand the "certainties" of the modern world, those goes-without-sayings that let us say all that can be said, he necessarily encounters "constructs of an epistemologically explosive nature," "deeply corrupting images" of life that he "will not allow to enter conversation except to exorcise them." Facing the new concept of "Life" that structures public discussion in so many arenas (abortion, capital punishment, euthanasia, genetic engineering) or facing the horrors of nuclear armaments, Illich "claim[s] the privilege to horrified silence . . . if I can make my horror visible." Of an invitation to speak about horrible things that might come from a well-meaning critic, Illich says that as soon as you begin to speak you implicitly condone violence and participate in an "apocalyptic randiness." By speaking about horrible things you make them into "issues" and accord them a status they should not have. Illich, like Foucault, falls silent.

Beyond their silences, both simply continued to offer analysis after analysis of institutions that would trap us all. We know Foucault principally for his case studies of the prison, the medical clinic, psychiatry, and so on. We know Illich for his "little pamphlets" on the school, medicine, transportation systems, and the mechanisms of literacy. Neither man offers a magnum opus, a grand synthesis. Foucault thinks of himself as a map maker, and he describes the work of intellectuals in terms that would apply well to Illich:

> The intellectual no longer has to play the role of advisor. The project, tactics and goals to be adopted are a matter for those who do the fighting. What the intellectual can do is to provide instruments of analysis, and at present this is the historian's essential role. What's effectively needed is a ramified, penetrative perception of the present, one that makes it possible to locate the lines of weakness, strong points, positions where the instances of power have secured and implanted themselves by a system of organization dating back over 150 years. In other words, a topological and geological survey of the battlefield—that is the intellectual's role.[60]

Illich might reach back a few more centuries, but he is, like Foucault, an "archeologist of modern certainties" eager to map the present in terms of its past.

Neither Foucault nor Illich is ultimately concerned about the paradox of being so productive of books that are ultimately not concerned with producing anything. To the extent that they have been successful teachers through their work, they have been so through the most vigorous indirection and through the creation of the most fecund silence.

A Way Out?

Foucault and Illich both participate in the paradox of pedagogy first enunciated by Rousseau's *Emile.* They differ from Rousseau in the extreme severity of their understanding of the corrupting power of the social. For Foucault and Illich, there is simply no route of appeal by which one might get out of the trap of the paradox their works reveal. There is no reason to do anything, *and yet* they continue to work. We think it best to attend to the *nature* of that work to appreciate what enables them to carry on in the face of the bleak, relentless understandings they develop. Both men are, after all, writers, and even though there are great differences in their approaches to writing, at the root, we think, lies a common concern.

The difference between Illich and Foucault is manifest most clearly in the very ways they conceive of their books. Foucault worked alone and thought of his books as "bombs directed against extant reality, [he wanted] them to self-destruct after use, like fireworks."[61] He fashioned himself as the lonely guerilla fighter taking pot-shots as "what threatens us, as well as what serves us, . . . less reason than the various forms of rationality."[62] His ending for *Discipline and Punish,*

> . . . we must hear the distant roar of battle.
>
> At this point I end a book that must serve as a historical background to various studies of the power of normalization and the formation of knowledge in modern society,[63]

is neither a call to arms, a request for grant money "for further research," nor even a request that the author be somehow remembered for what has gone before. It is more like the refuse left behind by a single-combat warrior, his job finished, slinking back to his anonymity among the troops.

Illich, in contrast, thinks of his books as reports on conversations among friends. He uses his prefaces to let us know the collegial circumstances of each book's genesis, whose homes the conversations occurred in, the continents spanned by the network of people who have helped him think through his ideas.

Illich's books are invitations to his reader to carry on the conversation with him, to join the circle of colleagues engaged in this work. His collaboration with Barry Sanders on *ABC* is, in some ways, forced, and the friendship, out of which the book grew, seems more important than the substance of the book itself. In fact, the book ends with,

> As the two of us wrote this book, the literary *we* constantly silenced us, a deafening silence that makes it impossible for the reader to know anything about the writer. Using this contemporary *we*, the speaker engages in semantic violence, incorporating groups, whose way of formulating the *we* is heterogeneous to that of the observer, and thus driving them into silence.
>
> We are not fools enough to propose, even as a joke, to return to ethnic silence, the silent co-presence before words, language, and text came into being. We are children of the book. But in our sadness we are silly enough to long for the one silent space that remains open in our examined lives, and that is the silence of friendship.[64]

Foucault, in contrast, displays few marks of collegial engagement. His footnotes are garish and often destabilize the authority of the person honored with a citation.

And yet—*and* (paradoxically) *yet*—Foucault has a keen interest in friendship, just as Illich does. Recall his remark about silence being the breeding ground of fine relationships. He spoke several times about friendship as a "way of life" or as a "mode of life" and discussed his own "sexuality" in these terms: "We have to work at becoming homosexuals and not be obstinate that we are. The development towards which the problem of homosexuality tends is the one of friendship."[65] His final studies were motivated, in part, by an interest in the possibility of "becoming 'gay,'" a concept that "contributes to a positive . . . appreciation of the type of consciousness in which affection, love, desire, sexual rapport with people has a positive significance,"[66] as opposed to "being homo- [or any other categorical prefix] sexual." There is a subversiveness to sexual pleasure, especially that ungoverned by a code of conduct:

> But two men of noticeably different ages—what code would allow them to communicate? They face each other without terms or convenient words, with nothing to assure them about the meaning of the movement that carries them towards each other. They have to invent, from A to Z, a relationship that is still formless, which is friendship; that is to say, the sum of everything through which they can give each other pleasure.[67]

Foucault's silence on future institutional forms has a few cracks in it through which we can see something of his interest in the surprise that can occur when unsupervised personal relationships become the ground of social interaction.

This kind of talk by Foucault is suspiciously close to Illich's concern for the development of "institutions of conviviality." He speaks of convivial institutions promoting an openness to the "surprise" of other people encountered outside of the usual rules of conduct, enabling an appreciation of "unmeasured experience,"[68] and he approvingly invokes Aristotle's view of the "true master-disciple relationship" as "priceless [in] character":

> Aristotle speaks of it as a "moral type of friendship, which is not on fixed terms: it makes a gift, or does whatever it does, as to a friend." Thomas Aquinas says of this kind of teaching that inevitably it is an act of love and mercy. This kind of teaching is always a luxury for the teacher and a form of leisure (in Greek, *schole*) for him and his pupil: an activity meaningful for both, having no ulterior purpose.[69]

Illich prizes "autonomous and creative intercourse among persons, and the intercourse with their environment."[70]

Both of these authors write themselves into the darkest corners through their unrelenting analyses of the social situation in which the pedagogical encounter takes place. They both reveal for us the unbreakable traps of all the conventional aspects of modern schooling; they give voice to all the goes-without-saying aspects of schooling that our silences on schooling illuminate. But then, out of *their* near silence comes the suggestion that in that well-regulated, brightly illuminated pedagogical encounter, there is the dark possibility of vitalizing connections of mixture, of the possibility of inventing "a manner of being that is still improbable" in which we "escape . . . the ready-made formulas" and "make ourselves infinitely more susceptible to pleasure," including the pleasure of learning, and of learning together. But even to suggest this possibility is to invite a silence of a very profound sort.

FREUD CAST A CLOUD of suspicion over Rousseau's pedagogy that occurred in the intimate, loving, master-pupil relationship. Freire's reformulation of the pedagogical encounter as a study circle of equals born out of a common confrontation with their common social lot suggested a way to save the promise of pedagogy that prepares a path toward freedom. Freire thought there was an "outside" to the institutional locus of the pedagogical encounter where he could keep one foot firmly planted. Illich and Foucault say no, there is no outside. They cast a cloud of suspicion over the project of liberatory pedagogy. The scene of the pedagogical encounter darkens once again.

It is time to move on, even if we cannot get out. Perhaps we should stop talking, finally, about revising the pedagogical relationship between students and teachers. Perhaps we should begin to ask whether there might not be other ways of educating. "The way out is via the door." Maybe we should try to walk through it.

PART 2

COLLEAGUES

Have recourse to older men who make themselves difficult of access and in no way harm the young by the charm of their countenance.

—Basil, "On Renunciation of the World"

5

TURNING AWAY FROM THE STUDENT-TEACHER RELATIONSHIP / TURNING TOWARD COLLEAGUES

> [For Rousseau,] professors . . . represented an unsatisfactory halfway house between the two harsh disciplines that make a man serious—community and solitude.
>
> —Allan Bloom, *The Closing of the American Mind*

WE STARTED WITH ROUSSEAU'S innovative, developmental vision of a progressive and humane pedagogy that appeals to nature and aims toward freedom. We discovered, even before we left our analysis of Rousseau, a paradox inherent in his pedagogy: a liberatory education is inherently social and its social dimension has an almost unlimited power to corrupt, distort, and thwart the aims this pedagogy sets for itself.

Freud made the prospect of living with the paradox more daunting. His concept of transference with its Siamese twin, countertransference, showed us how deeply rooted and firmly entrenched "the social" is in all human affairs. Worse, the psychoanalytic framework revealed the social to have an infantile, and hence all the more corrupting, dimension. We left Freud more pessimistic than we left Rousseau.

Freire restored some hope. He restructured the network of personal relationships in which teacher and pupil find themselves joined. They will manifest their essential equality by undertaking a common task, an analysis of culture. The one-to-one student-teacher relationship gives way to the group, the study circle or "culture circle."

Freire restored our hope for a liberating pedagogy. By shattering the unequal two-person relationship at the center of education, he seemed to find a way to unburden himself of the dark dangers this relationship brings to education. "The social," in its transformation from "relationship" to "group," seems to have been transformed from a limitation on development into its very engine. By making the social the *object* of study and by making the group the *agent* of study, Freire appears to have found a way to "finesse the transference"[1] and to reopen the door to a pedagogy that is progressive, democratic, humane, and liberating.

Our sunny moment was short-lived as Illich and Foucault entered the discussion and showed us that the social has far more profound, minute, complex, and ineradicable ways of corrupting any pedagogy than Rousseau or Freud could ever have imagined. Freire's ingenious recasting of the personal relationships within the educational box[2] does nothing to change the walls of that box. The paradox of pedagogy we encountered in latent and undeveloped form in Rousseau returns to haunt us. But after Illich and Foucault, it is neither latent nor undeveloped.

We can now state the paradox in one sentence: *the primary vehicle necessary to a liberating education, the personal relationship, is also the fundamental obstacle to the achievement of genuine liberation.* Our analyses showed that the paradox holds whether the personal relationship at the center of education takes the shape of the intensely focused two-person Rousseauian dyad or whether it takes the shape of the more extended social grouping of the Freirean cultural circle. In both cases, impersonal institutional power from the outside collaborates with psychological transference from the inside to turn potentially liberating personal relationships into shackles. In the face of this paradox, self-reflective teachers surely must stop to ponder what or whom they are serving in their work.

Turning Away from the Student-Teacher Relationship

If we want to move on from the stall in which we find ourselves after appreciating the severity of Illich's and Foucault's critiques, perhaps we will have to tack. Perhaps we should turn away from a pedagogy based in the student-teacher relationship. In part 2 we consider a pedagogy that begins with a turn toward colleagues, a turn that becomes possible only in conjunction with a turning away from the student-teacher relationship itself. The turn toward one's colleagues results in something we mildly call "collegial teaching."

Collegial teaching is teaching that is informed by *equality* and *difference*. The student-teacher relationship takes its life from a set of differences that amounts to an inequality. A relationship between colleagues, the kind of relationship that animates collegial teaching, takes its life from a set of differences that presupposes equality.

We discovered our own differences as teachers in many details of teaching and reacting to students. Most dramatically, however, we discovered the divide between us in our responses to the figure who started the conversation on pedagogy in the West, Socrates. By chance, we were two members of a five-person team in a year-long freshman program that was using Plato's *Meno* for one of its first texts. One of us (we shall call him B) offered to deliver a lecture on this text and did so. Upon hearing the lecture, the other (we call him A[3]) was moved to give his own lecture, a strikingly different interpretation of Socrates and the Socratic project. These two lectures, included below, pushed us to articulate our own differences as teachers precisely because they were about Socrates. The Socratic dialogues of Plato raise almost all of the interesting questions about education in one form or another, and the *Meno* is particularly rich in educational material. Because Socrates is so enigmatic, paradoxical,[4] and devious, and because so little is actually known about him, he is a perfect target for pedagogical projection. W. K. C. Guthrie has said, "In spite of the application of the most scientific methods, in the end we must all have to some extent our own Socrates, who will not be precisely like anyone else's."[5] It was in finding his "own Socrates" that each of us came to see how he differed from the other as a teacher. This difference, within the equality of a collegial teaching relationship, animated our work together.

"Tragic" vs. "Progressive" Educators

"The two harsh disciplines that make a man serious," according to Allan Bloom, are "community and solitude."[6] Education can take either of these disciplines seriously. It can try to create people equipped to live truly with their fellows, or it can try to create people equipped to live truly knowing that each is alone. Does the educational path to which Socrates summons his students and friends lead to solitude or to community?

How one answers this question will depend on who one is; it will depend on one's own Socrates. B's Socrates is an ironic figure. His Socrates is, as Kierkegaard put it, "hovering."[7] His irony and his hovering posture lead to a pedagogy that requires an audience, a community of some sort. This Socrates is always talking indirectly to someone besides the person he is talking to; his dialogue, his laconic questions, his barbs, are always pitched with a community of listeners in mind. This three-part dialogic structure (Socrates, an interlocutor like Meno, and the larger audience) implies a developmental sequence. With the right kind of effort and work and thought, Meno can hope to attain the status of the other audience members. As he moves from poor student to privileged auditor, he will come to be in on the jokes and he will be open to learn from the moves of the dialogues. In the same way, the audience members, with the right kind of effort, work and thought, may someday develop the capacity to occupy Socrates' position. The ironic Socrates is one who knows that there may be someone wiser than he; he is one who takes his own development seriously. Our B uncovers the link between irony and a developmental perspective, a link that undergirds his progressive faith.

Plato's parable of the Cave, in B's view, makes it clear that even though education requires a temporary alienation and removal of the learner from society, the final aim is to return to the human group and make it better by means of the knowledge one has acquired. Knowledge of the Good requires one finally to leave the light and return to the darkness of the Cave to help one's brothers and sisters. Socratic education appears to begin socially and to have as its end a social good.

But only for B.

A's Socrates is a more solitary figure. He is "humorous" rather than ironic. His aim is to disrupt, to deflate, to make one laugh at all treasured truth. He attacks not ignorance or self-delusion, but truths "lewdly" held.[8] Kierkegaard characterizes A's Socrates as "vanishing."[9] Instead of hovering around as his students develop, he departs and leaves his students to do their best on their own. This Socrates acknowledges that education begins in conversation and in society, but he sees, even if he does not say it, that the path leads out of social conversing and into solitude, a potentially lonely solitude. This is a Socrates who rigorously pursues his vocation of seeking someone wiser than he, but who never succeeds. The essential educational moment is when Socrates has vanished and the student is left alone to face his ignorance, his answers, his responses, or whatever it is he has discovered about himself from talking with Socrates. In fact, he is unlikely to have discovered anything at all from talking per se; it is only afterwards, alone, that he has a chance to discover something important. The faith of A's Socrates, if you can call it that, is that a person who sits quietly will have thoughts of his own. In some sense, then, for this Socrates, conversation, social life, and the common search for truth, are all important activities, inescapable, essential, and necessary activities, but it is the limits of these activities that are most important and that merit attention. A's Socrates takes it as his pedagogical mission to direct attention to those limits.

The humorous, vanishing Socrates is a "tragic" pedagogue. He is a Freud or a Foucault who speaks and writes to his fellow humans with energy and commitment and yet who always seems to know that he is destined to be misunderstood and alone. This pedagogue, too, will return to the Cave, for he knows there is nowhere else to go, but he despairs of helping his fellows with his knowledge. He would love to see the creation of the Good Society, but he is more pledged to clear vision and plain speaking than to utopian dreams. This pedagogue understands why Socrates had to be condemned and cannot understand why the vote was close. His humor, his clever definitions, his artful moves are all designed to stop the student in his tracks and to make him give up ideas, thoughts, opinions, and conceptions. Are there other thoughts (knowledge) with which the student can replace his abandoned ones? To this question, A responds with silence. We can well imagine him posing the same question to himself and, in response, once again, remaining silent.

Differing Approaches to Paradox

The tragic and progressive pedagogical stances represent different responses to paradox itself. A reconsideration of Foucault and Illich shows how "tragic" and "progressive" educators respond differently to the paradox of pedagogy.

Illich permits his reader to feel a part of a community of inquiry. Illich, the writer, is inviting and encouraging. He stimulates a certain kind of hopeful energy. His voice and the formats he uses suggest there is a substantial and ongoing community (a research group) available to him. Though his analyses may make us feel helpless and alone in a brutal social world, his mode of writing counters this effect. He has a three-pronged faith in people that transcends his analysis: faith in what people might do if only they were given more latitude in their lives, faith in what a community of intelligent scholars and political actors might do to help create that latitude, and faith in the reader—that he or she might join this community of intelligent scholars and actors.

Foucault offers no social solace. In content, mood, and form, his writing says there is no way out. Social institutions, not people, always have the last word. Foucault writes as someone solitary and alone. He issues no invitations to the reader. His writing suggests faith in nothing but the irrevocable historical restructuring of power relations, relations that control everyone and can be controlled by no one. His writing is bleak. He pushes us away, leaving us alone to figure out how to regain the equilibrium we have lost from reading his books or essays.[10]

Neither Illich nor Foucault is one of those "professors" Rousseau or Allan Bloom find so lamentable. Neither represents an "unsatisfactory halfway house" between "community" and "solitude." Each has staked out his territory at an opposite pole: Illich, with his communitarian orientation, responds to paradox from a progressive posture; Foucault, the loner, is a more tragic writer.

By calling Illich "progressive," we do not suggest he is optimistic. We do not even mean that he is fundamentally concerned with doing something about the future; after all, it was he who said he refuses to let the future cast its shadow on the present.[11] But at root, he seems to believe in the *possibility* of progress in human endeavors. No matter how constraining he finds social institutions, he writes as one who believes humans can have the upper hand, and that regardless of the odds, it is better to speak and act *as if* humans can and will shape their own destiny. By using the term "progressive," we also do not suggest that Illich believes that the course of history so far as been one of improvement. Much of his writing suggests (though it refuses to assert) the opposite. His work conjures up an earlier era when humans *seemed* to have had it better. He does not think we are embarked upon some one-way path of development, each stage an improvement over the last. But he has a fundamental faith in human nature and in human intellect. Illich is a man of faith and a man of hope.

By calling Foucault tragic, we do not suggest that reading his works will produce any kind of Aristotelian purging of emotions in the reader. We do not suggest his works evoke grand passions or strong identifications with fallen human figures. To the contrary, the human figure has no height from which to fall in Foucault's work. All traces of heroism or tragic grandiosity have been expunged. The human appears in Foucault's works more as a Kafkan beetle than as any kind of Antigone or Oedipus. The best one can hope for, according to this view, is to gain some leverage in order to "sap power," much as a judo fighter draws on the power of his opponent to make a throw. Foucault suggests that countermoves against power are possible and welcome, but his analysis offers no hope that such countermoves are likely to succeed. Even if the odd one or two resistances do succeed, it seems clear that they could never add up to yield any substantial, cumulative effect. Thus, as readers, we are thrown back on our own devices, left with no encouragement to hope or to faith, yet disturbed by the strong sense of pervasive injustice that Foucault's analyses inevitably provoke. We are left to do our best in a hopeless and bleak world. Thus, we term Foucault's orientation "tragic."

A paradox, according to one scholar, is "a dilemma inherent in the thing itself, the kind of inner breach not improperly called tragic, a grave difficulty that enhances rather than degrades its matter."[12] The tragic teacher, like Foucault or our A, will find the paradox of pedagogy puzzling, invigorating, humbling, but finally, it will be taken to set fixed limits around his work. The "progressive" teacher, like B or like Illich, tends to view a paradox as an inner breach *not yet* resolved. The "not yet" is the premise of his developmental/progressive orientation. Paradoxes, to a progressive, are potentially unlimited sources of challenges that arise *within* work, challenges that spur the teacher on rather than limit his ambitions.

Our A and B are different. They think differently and they teach differently. But they share certain goals and assumptions. They are both pedagogical liberals. That is, they hope that education will affect people so they might think about making life together better. They both accept the two basic Rousseauian assumptions: (*a*) that there is something fundamentally wrong with the social structuring of human relations in the modern world and (*b*) that education just might be one place to begin thinking about doing something about this "something wrong."

A and B also accept as a starting point that the personal relationship between student and teacher is crucially important. Both see it as providing the matrix within which virtually all that is important in the educational encounter will occur. Both see it as a relationship that must change with time. And both agree that in the long run their students might become their colleagues, perhaps their friends. Both look toward a renunciation of the roles of both "student" and "teacher."

Beyond these similarities, A and B differ. By means of the contrast between A's and B's understanding of Socrates, we will be able to see much more clearly how those with a "tragic" and those with a "progressive" orientation articulate their responses to the paradox of pedagogy.

B's Lecture: The Poor Student and the Privileged Auditor in the *Meno*

> It is suggestive that European philosophy originated (among the Athenians) under the direct pressure of educational questions.
>
> —John Dewey, *Democracy and Education*

> And, for those who wish to see, contemplation of Socrates is our most urgent task.
>
> —Allan Bloom, *The Closing of the American Mind*

I wish to begin my contemplation of Socrates with the *Meno* for it is there that the connection between education and philosophy is most immediate. The dialogue begins with an educational question, Can virtue be taught? Immediately, Socrates poses the philosophical question: What is virtue? Without knowing what it is, how could one ever know if virtue is teachable? The dialogue never disentangles these two questions. We should never expect our contemplation of Socrates to help us with an educational question without involving us in basic philosophical problems. And we should not expect to be able to approach philosophical questions without having to confront problems in education.

Without doubt, Socrates is a philosopher-educator. The *Meno* does raise the question, however, of who might be the proper students for this philosopher-teacher. In my view, whoever the proper students are, Meno himself is not one of them. The best students for Socrates are rather those who are the *auditors to the dialogue.* We can imagine these to include first, the young Plato, who was a great admirer of Socrates, and then, much later, you and me. We, the audience to dialogue, are in an educationally privileged position. You and I can learn from Socrates, if we can find a way to watch and to listen to what is actually going on in the conversation between Socrates and Meno.

To begin, I must point out the irony of my lecturing on the *Meno.* The *Meno,* remember, begins with a request for a lecture. Meno has just arrived in town from Thessaly, entourage following him, and no doubt making himself quite a spectacle for the democratically inclined Athenians. He is staying in the house of Anytus, a man who is known from the *Apology* as a later prosecutor of Socrates and who eventually enters this dialogue. In Thessaly Meno has associated himself with the sophist Gorgias and has heard many fine speeches on many fine topics. Now in Athens he meets Socrates and invites him to give yet another fine speech so that he, Meno, can compare Socrates to Gorgias, much as a traveler might compare the landscape or the fine buildings of one city to those of another.

"Can you tell me, Socrates—is virtue something that can be taught? Or does it come by practice? Or is it neither teaching nor practice that gives it to a man but natural aptitude or something else?" (*Meno*, 70a). Come, give us a lecture, Meno seems to say. Socrates refuses. This is Socrates' first educational act. It is his first step in making a certain kind of learning possible. The learning that Socrates would have Meno undertake may never occur for him, but this refusal to lecture is what makes anything educational *possible*. This refusal is no small feat.

So, the irony of our situation is that here I am, lecturing about a refusal to lecture. I did not refuse the seductiveness of the offer to fill this time with some fine and pretty words. Have I made education *impossible* by making this decision? To answer that question, we must think for a moment about the dialogue form.

At first glance, the dialogue form seems simple. Two people meet. They talk. They pursue a mutual inquiry. They continue to talk until they reach an end or until one of them leaves. They do this with the intention, implicit or explicit, of discovering something that neither of them knew before.

But, if the dialogue form is that simple and this is the goal of dialogue, we are forced by the evidence from this earliest set of dialogues to doubt the educational efficacy of the dialogue form. Why? Because over and over again, the dialogues seem to go nowhere. They tend to end in *aporia*, in complete bafflement. Over and over again, Socrates befuddles and numbs his interlocutors, occasionally drives them to anger, always seems to destroy their best arguments or, more subtly, drives them to contradict themselves. They come out seeming to know little more than when they started.

All of this takes place in the context of Socrates' claiming that he himself has no knowledge of the topic under discussion. Socrates' refusal to lecture on the question of the teachability of virtue is premised on the fact that "far from knowing whether [virtue] can be taught, I have no idea what virtue itself is" (71a). So the Socratic dialogues begin and end in an absence of knowledge. No one seems to get anywhere. What is so great about dialogue as an educational method, what is so great about Socratic inquiry, if no one learns anything from it except how ignorant he is?

I hope to convince you that the dialogue form is more complicated than it seems at first.

We need to think carefully about how these dialogues might have taken place. Here is how I picture them: First, there is Socrates encountering a person of authority in education, the arts, or politics. (To try to find someone wiser than he, after all, is Socrates' vocation.) In addition to Socrates and the interlocutor, I also see a small gathering of young men nearby. They are listening, whispering to one another, and reacting to what they hear. More important, I imagine this group of young men having what we would call seminars on these conversations after they had ended.

So, instead of there being only two parties to each dialogue, there are three: Socrates, the interlocutor, *and* a new element, an audience.[13] I will try to convince you that in a Socratic conversation, *the audience is in a position to learn more and to learn better than the interlocutor.* Socrates may be right when he tells Meno that neither of them is much good (96b), that both are poor specimens. But those audience members would not necessarily fall into that category. And you can see why. A member of the audience has some distance on the conversation. He is removed from the emotional dynamics. He can experience the dynamics vicariously, but he won't actually be stung and numbed by the torpedo fish, the sting ray, which Meno says Socrates is. He will be in a position to reflect on what Socrates said *and* on what Socrates did in response to his interlocutor. And he will have other members of the audience to talk with, who will, like good seminar participants, help him sort out what has occurred.

By writing dialogues Plato constituted his readers as an audience. He recapitulates for *us* the situation *he* fell into by accident. Plato allows us to assume the educationally favorable position that he himself occupied during Socrates' lifetime. We have a chance—roughly the same chance that Plato had—to learn more from the dialogue than Meno did. We certainly have more of a chance to learn something than if Plato had chosen to lecture us about virtue and its teachability. Had he done that, we would have been cast, at best, as his distant interlocutor and we would have lost the educationally favored position of auditor.

That takes me back to the question of whether, by choosing to lecture about the *Meno,* I have made it impossible for education to occur here. I am, it seems, violating the educational principle Plato discovered, a principle I think is truly insightful. When you read the *Meno* and when you discuss it with your friends and have a seminar about it, you approach the dialogue from the position of the third party. When I lecture to you, I put you in the position of the second party to the dialogue. That decreases your chances of learning anything. I run the risk of making you into a Meno, a "poor specimen." Is there a justification for my decision to lecture?

My justification may shock you, but I will risk telling you the truth. I am doing this mostly for myself. Preparing this lecture gave me the chance to talk to myself for a while about what I saw as I reread the *Meno.* This is the culmination of my activities as an auditor. I am also doing this to impress my colleagues a little. I am not interested in teaching them; I would just like to dazzle them a bit. So, unflattering though it is to admit, I am here talking mostly for me, a little for them, and if you learn anything . . . well, so much the better.

But that may give you a hint as to how to treat this performance. Think of me as a little mad up here, just talking to myself. Make me both the party of the first part and the party of the second part. Don't try to take part in my madness. Make yourselves into auditors. Listen to this conversation. Watch it. Don't think I am talking to you. Don't let me turn you into a Meno.

With that introduction I can turn to the main topic of my lecture, the relationship between education and character. In order to be a good auditor and to learn something from listening to a dialogue, you must be of a certain character. We might say that you must be of virtuous character. But along with that philosophical claim of which I hope to convince you, there comes, naturally enough, the educational question of whether one can acquire that kind of character in a relationship with a teacher. I will take up this question also.

Now, there are two standard interpretations of this dialogue. The first is that Socrates uses his method of inquiry to draw the truth out of his interlocutor or to have him follow a path of his own making toward the truth. Gulley, for example, argues that Socrates' method is "an expedient to encourage his interlocutor to seek out the truth, to make him think that he is joining with Socrates in a voyage of discovery."[14] By this account, Socrates may or may not have knowledge or at least answers to pointed questions like Meno's, but his method, including his profession of ignorance, is a device for getting the second party to the dialogue to develop on his own. This interpretation strikes me as having some difficulty with the evidence. The evidence overwhelmingly indicates that the dialogues are, for the interlocutors, educational failures. There must be something more subtle at work.

The second standard and reasonable interpretation of the dialogues is more in accord with the evidence. This interpretation allows that the dialogues do end in failure, but the fundamental point of them was to illustrate a method of inquiry. I. F. Stone is a proponent of this view. He writes, "The only definition of virtue Socrates ever ventured in his many fruitless attempts to define it was to equate virtue with knowledge."[15] But, of course, to say that virtue is knowledge is not to venture a definition at all. And notice Stone's phrase, "his *many fruitless attempts* to define virtue." In the *Meno* and elsewhere we see Socrates using his method of inquiry and we see it fail again and again. This failure, according to this interpretation, points to the fact that it is the method itself that is the point of the dialogues and that the topic of the dialogues are but means to *this* educational end.

Socratic method is important and we should not slight it. It is a commonplace for us to ask someone, "What do you mean by that? Define your terms." We should not forget that Socrates was the first to ask this question. He was the first to insist that his interlocutors put forward general definitions of essential ideas, develop logically the consequences and implications of those general definitions, and then ask whether those consequences and implications made sense, whether they were in accord with experience, or whether perhaps they produced contradictions. He proceeded iteratively. If a general definition failed, he asked his interlocutor to go back to the beginning and be so kind as to start over, revise the definition, trace out the consequences yet again, and try to do better this time. Eric Havelock suggests, in his *Preface to Plato*, that Socrates was the first to use a method of inquiry that relied on the alphabetical technology of freezing the flow of words, fixing words in place so that they might be subjected to a radical scrutiny. Socrates is always reminding his conversants of their original definitions, as if they were written on a blackboard, and is always pointing out subsequent problems with that original definition. An oral culture, in which Socrates moved, would never proceed in a conversation this way. An oral culture would never think of circling back to the starting point with an eye to revision and to retracing one's steps. So let us give this method its due. It was a wonderful discovery, the basis of a form of critical reasoning that enables one to get beyond the grip of one's culture and traditions. It is indeed useful to know this method, but it is a little strange that we never see anyone making much progress with it. All we ever hear is Socrates saying, "Let us begin again at the beginning," his eternal refrain. Stone calls Socrates' search for absolute definitions "a wild goose chase," and we should wonder why Plato would spend so much effort illustrating a wild goose chase time after time.

This second interpretation of the dialogues is sensible, but it is superficial. A careful reading of a dialogue like the *Meno* suggests that Plato is doing something much more than showing Socrates' cleverness with a recalcitrant student and that something much greater is at stake than an illustration of a useful method of inquiry. I believe, in fact, that Plato does have Socrates answer Meno's question of whether virtue can be taught and that Plato also suggests an answer to Socrates' philosophical question, "What is virtue in the first place?" But Plato provides answers to both questions in a way that is accessible only to an audience, not to Meno. If we simply *listen* to Socrates with Meno's ears, as if the philosopher-teacher were going to simply teach us something, we will miss everything. If, following Bloom, we use our eyes and *watch* Socrates and Meno together, if we reflect on what we see, we have a chance of appreciating the answers Plato provides.

The dialogue is more than two people talking; it is a performance. We must focus our attention on what Socrates and Meno *do*, not on what they say. We must focus on their motives, not on their ideas. The dialogue is really a drama.

How does this play begin? Meno poses a debater's question. He invites a fancy speech that he could then compare to the speeches of Gorgias, whom Meno admires. He might even be able to take a little gossip about this renowned Socrates back to Thessaly. But Meno does not pose just any question. He poses a question about virtue, a question a man might take seriously, a question the answer to which might have consequences for the state of one's soul or the state of one's state. We should not forget that Thessaly was a city known principally for the breeding of horses and for the strict control of its citizenry through the state's honing of the will-to-power of its citizens. Thus, the question is something like a set-up for Socrates. It was an invitation for Socrates to defend the democratically oriented city of wisdom, the city of Athena, against a city with a completely different ethos.

Now, people like Meno ask debaters' questions not because they seriously want to consider possible answers. They pose such questions with an eye to winning the ensuing debate. But Socrates does not respond in these terms. He chooses to take Meno seriously even though Meno is not taking himself seriously. Socrates acts as if Meno really cared about this question. Socrates' refusal to deliver the invited speech is, first, an act of respect for the seriousness of the question.

It is instructive that instead of telling Meno anything about virtue, Socrates tells Meno that he knows something about Meno's biography. He knows, for example, Meno's background, who his lover is, which sophist he admires. Socrates makes Meno's biography relevant to the conversation because he wishes not to discuss the question of Virtue in the abstract, but the question of virtue in the concrete embodied presence that these two men are enacting before one another. After only a few lines of this dialogue, the question is no longer: Can virtue be taught? Instead, it is shifting toward the concrete question: Can Meno be taught virtue? In a line that is easily mistaken for an illustration of his general method of inquiry into the problem of virtue, Socrates summarizes what he has done in 70a—c by saying that in order to know anything in particular *about Meno* we first have to know Meno: "How, if I know nothing at all of Meno, could I tell if he was handsome, or the opposite; rich and noble, or the reverse of rich and noble?" (71b). Socrates is not just suggesting an approach to all questions. He is telling Meno that it is time now to consider himself seriously, if he is going to ask such serious questions.

Socrates makes it clear to Meno that they are about to undertake a moral inquiry. "I confess with shame," Socrates says, "that I know literally nothing about virtue." Be careful, Socrates is saying. In Athens, people can be *shamed* as a result of their inquiries. This Socrates, says one scholar, "is a moralist pure and simple who practices moral inquiry but never inquires into the theory of moral inquiry."[16] Socrates' first effort is to lure Meno into a conversation and to get him to take himself seriously, because the conversation might eventually turn out to have personal consequences for him. You are not in Thessaly anymore, Meno, Socrates says. You are in Athens, new territory, and we do things differently here. All wisdom appears to have migrated from Athens to Thessaly and we Athenians are a bankrupt lot. We have only ourselves to rely on now. If you want to give up the wealth of wisdom that the sophists have imparted to you and come to rely on yourself now, come along; do so. I am always ready to pursue philosophical questions seriously, if I can find anyone else to do so with me.

Meno is not quite ready to leave Thessaly and arrive, finally, in Athens where the rules of the game of moral inquiry are different. He appeals to Socrates to remember that Gorgias himself had come to Athens, had no doubt delivered many fine speeches, and, Meno asks, could not Socrates possibly remember what Gorgias had to say about virtue and could he not perhaps use that as a starting point? Socrates allows that Gorgias probably does know what virtue is, but he gets Meno to "leave Gorgias out of it, since he is not here" (70c). This is crucial to everything that will come. If Meno wants to learn something important, he cannot rely on some authority to do the work for him. He must do the work himself. If virtue is teachable, it is not teachable by an expert's using the appropriate tuition to tell a novice what virtue is. If there is a way, it involves entering into the conversation yourself. Moral inquiry is mutual inquiry. "Tell me your own view," Socrates says at the conclusion of his first effort to get Meno to take the question seriously.

Meno tries. But he is is a poor student. He is not of good enough character for mutual inquiry.

Meno tries all the studentlike ploys to get out of doing the hard work of mutual inquiry. He gets Socrates to do the work for him in a discussion of shape and color (with the promise that he, Meno, will do the work with regard to virtue later). But then he tries to quit. He complains of being numbed. Then he presents the paradox that one cannot learn anything that one does not know already. Then he says, no, his original question was the right one anyway and, if he is going to continue, Socrates must agree to go back to the pedagogical question without linking it to the philosophical problem of what virtue is.

Socrates responds to Meno's ploys with a double tactic.

First, he does whatever is necessary to keep Meno in the conversation. He agrees to take the lead on the inquiry into color and shape. He paries Meno's accusation of being numbed by saying that he, Socrates, is numbed too. He puts on the little show with the slave boy to show that the process of moral inquiry is one of recalling that which one knows already, so one need not worry about learning something that one does not know.

At the same time, Socrates tries to draw attention to Meno's own weak character. He suggests that Meno needs to develop some self-control, some determination, a willingness to examine himself and his life, before he will ever be able to make progress in this kind of moral inquiry. Socrates comforts Meno with the myth of the soul's recollecting knowledge, shames him by showing that even a slave boy can reason through geometry problems, and finally appeals to Meno's Thessalonian nature by saying that there is one thing worth fighting for and that is the belief that "we shall be better and brave and less hapless if we think that we ought to inquire, than we should have been if we thought there was no way of knowing and no duty to seek to know what we do not know" (86b).

Meno agrees to continue. Socrates agrees to go back to the pedagogical question without taking up the question of what virtue in itself is because, now, he senses that Meno will just quit completely if he does not compromise. And Socrates does not want Meno to quit, for then all would be lost. And perhaps—Socrates never knows—they are on the verge of finding an answer to their common question(s).

Indeed, I would suggest that it is precisely at this point in the dialogue that we, the audience, are able to discern the definition of virtue that motivated this whole play. Look at what happens. Socrates chides Meno, "Had I command of you as well as of myself, Meno, we should not have inquired whether virtue is given by instruction or not, until we had first ascertained 'what it is.' But since you never think of self-control—such being your notion of freedom—but think only of controlling me and do control me, I must yield, for you are irresistible" (86d). Wisdom has indeed migrated from Athens to Thessaly, and the rule of the other has taken over the dialogue. But in this there is that grand Socratic irony that points toward what we seek (even if Meno is unable to stay the course). Virtue is, the dialogue suggests, the ability and the willingness to rule oneself (and to renounce the will always to rule others) so that one might have the right kind of conversations with the right people about the right subjects.

We members of the audience can recall, at this point in the dialogue, intimations of this definition of virtue that we have already seen. Socrates accused Meno of flirting with him and of trying to manipulate him by employing imagery (the image of the torpedo fish). He accused Meno, that is, of trying to rule over him in subtle ways. Socrates had also asked if he could not add to Meno's definition of virtue (viz., virtue is the capacity to rule over one's domain, men over the state and women over the household) the fact that rulers must always be temperate and just. Again, we can recall that we have heard this theme of ruling over oneself instead of always ruling others sounded before. We can recall it even better than Meno can because he is caught up in the heat of the dialogue. We have the space in which to reflect on what we have seen and heard. We have seen an enactment of virtue as we watched and contemplated Socrates.

So, can virtue be taught? We see Socrates trying to teach it to Meno. But here is the paradox of this act: To figure out if virtue can be taught, you have to know what virtue is in the first place, as Socrates said. To define virtue you must engage in a mutual, moral inquiry that leads to a suitable definition. You have to have a conversation with Socrates that leads somewhere. To do that, you have to be of a certain kind of character. You have to be able to stick with the conversation when it gets tough. You have to avoid the temptation of being insulted when the conversation implicates you and your own behavior. You have to be willing always to go back to the beginning, no matter how many times it takes. You have to be willing to rule yourself and you have to renounce trying to rule Socrates. In short, *you have to possess virtue already.* It's a paradox.

But what if you don't already possess virtue and you want to? In my view, the dialogues do not *give* an answer to this question; they *are* the answer to this question. If you want to possess virtue, you must engage in mutual inquiry. But things are not as bleak as the paradox of Socratic inquiry may make them seem. You will find help in the dialogue. Socrates will be there not only as an opponent in philosophic exchange. He will be there as your teacher and guide. Every time your weak character begins to show itself and tries to take over the conversation, Socrates will point it out to you so that you can have the chance—an opportunity offered to Meno but never accepted by him—to examine your own character. Exactly what Socrates will do will depend on his assessment of your character in the instance. He will chide, he will shame, he will be lenient, he will give in, he will press his case. But it will always come back to you, as mutuality demands. It may seem like a circle, but the circle is not a vicious one. Every small gain you make in ruling yourself will feed back into the process. You will come to participate better in the conversation. The conversation will strengthen your character. You will participate better. And so on. By the time you are ready to inquire into the nature of virtue using the Socratic method, you will already have acquired virtue.

We can turn briefly to another of the great dialogues to deepen our appreciation for the importance of the interlocutor's character to the success of the inquiry. The first book of the *Republic* ends with one of those famous Socratic disavowals of knowledge: "So that for me the present outcome of the discussion is that I know nothing. For if I don't know what the just is, I shall hardly know whether it is a virtue or not, and whether its possessor is or is not happy" (354b). Another Socratic failure. But why? The inquiry into justice proceeds with first Cephalus and then his son, Polemarchus, occupying the role of interlocutor. At a certain point, Thrasymachus enters the conversation, a man Plato describes as a "wild beast," a man who hurls himself into the conversation because he is unable any longer "to hold his peace" (336b). Thrasymachus is an angry man, hardly one capable of ruling himself. He, like Meno, is more interested in defeating Socrates than in pursuing the question at hand. He, like Meno, is dominated by a concern with *appearance*. He is unable to penetrate surfaces and engage in a mutual inquiry that might plumb the depths of a truth. He may be a worthy opponent for Socrates, but he is not a worthy inquirer for exactly the same reasons Meno is unable to learn. The dialogue between Socrates and Thrasymachus must, again, end in failure because it is incapable of ever beginning.

But that is so only for Socrates' encounter with Thrasymachus. At the beginning of the second book of the *Republic*, Thrasymachus's argument is restated, this time by Glaucon and his brother Adeimantus. They too are dominated by a concern for appearances, but Socrates does not rebuff them with his plea of ignorance. He takes up their concern directly: "Then since it is 'the seeming,' as the wise men show me, that 'masters the reality' and is lord of happiness, to this I must devote myself without reserve" (365c). Socrates himself is willing to involve himself, *for the sake of argument*, in the world of appearances, an act that looms large in the dialogue and, from Book 7's parable of the cave, in Western philosophy generally.

Why does Socrates rise to the bait when it is dangled by Glaucon and Adeimantus, but not by Thrasymachus? Why the profession of ignorance in response to the latter and the lengthy inquiry into "What is justice?" in response to the former? In light of our discussion of the *Meno*, the answer should be clear. Glaucon and Adeimantus are not interested in defeating Socrates. They have made the most powerful case of which they are capable in order to bring out the best in Socrates. The have shown themselves interested in the question they hold in common with Socrates; they are not interested in combat. Their interest is intellectual, yes, but also moral. They are people *committed* to leading a just life, and their interest in knowing what justice is is grounded in this personal commitment. Book 1 sees the climate change from one of hospitality and conviviality to one of angry confrontation. The climate of Book 2 is one of friendship. In that new air, Socrates allows himself to think aloud in order to honor the inquiries of his interlocutors. In the *Republic*, after Book 1, Socrates conducts, essentially, a dialogue with himself, but he abides by the form of the dialogue in that he keeps checking his conclusions at each step to see if he is still making sense.

In the transition from Book 1 to Book 2 of the *Republic*, there is a movement from strife to harmony. This is a critical axis for Plato. This strife-harmony axis parallels two other crucial Platonic axes, one that leads from appearances to reality along the Platonic "divided line" and another that leads from multiplicity to unity. The dialogue moves from strife to harmony so that, we might say, it can move from appearances to the truth. One must begin with appearances, with culturally accepted beliefs; one then submits them to scrutiny via the dialogue; then one stands a chance of moving beyond appearance. One begins with multiplicity—the many forms of virtue that Meno mentions and that Socrates compares to a swarm of bees, or the many forms of justice mentioned in *Republic*, Book 1—and moves toward a unity—virtue itself, justice itself. Society presents us with a swarm of opinions, nature a swarm of appearances, both cause anger, conflict, and strife. It is the method of philosophy to take these starting points seriously and to move beyond them toward unity, reality, and harmony. For Plato, these are the attributes of truth.

But the transition from appearance to reality, from confusion to truth, can only be made in a special context, a context that admits opposition but that aims toward harmony. In a dialogue, ideas may clash, but the people who hold these ideas must converse as friends in a manner that is fundamentally harmonious. The harmony that is this prerequisite to successful mutual inquiry has as *its* prerequisite the virtuous, self-disciplined character of the participants. The person who would inquire into moral questions of justice and virtue must already be just and virtuous.

For a person of virtue, the question of whether virtue is teachable—the question with which the *Meno* begins—is an academic question, for he does not need that instruction. Here is the irony: Meno begins with a question that, for him, is an "academic question" in the worst sense of that term. He wants to treat the question glibly and does not want to have to take it seriously. Socrates turns the tables and lets Meno know that this question is of vital personal importance. It should be treated as a life or death question. Meno doesn't get it. But you—the auditor to dialogue—you have a chance to get it. You have a chance of pursuing the conversation to its end, where Meno could not go. And it is only at the end of the inquiry that the question of whether virtue can be taught becomes an academic question, in the first sense.

Recall the end of the dialogue. Socrates says, "I fear that I must go away, but do you . . . persuade our friend Anytus [of the conclusion which we agree we have reached together]." This line forcefully encapsulates the life-or-death nature of the inquiry that has just ended. Socrates tells Meno that if he can "conciliate [Anytus], you will have done good service to the Athenian people." We know the rest of the story. Anytus prosecutes Socrates and Socrates is put to death. Meno failed. The question is whether you, the audience member, will be able to succeed with Anytus where Meno was doomed, by his own character, to fail.

We can frame the question of the teachability of virtue in a testable way. We know Plato was a member of Socrates' audience and we can hope that he became virtuous as a result of watching Socrates. Can Plato then go on to help other people acquire virtue? He undertakes to put Socrates in dialogue before a much larger audience than Socrates ever had. He allows you, here in this room some twenty-five hundred years later, to occupy the favored position of the third party to this dialogue. He allows you the chance to contemplate Socrates. Will he help you acquire virtue? Here's the rub: It will depend on you. It will depend on your willingness to examine your character. Just as the question of whether virtue is teachable remains open at the end of the dialogue, the question of whether those of us who read Plato can acquire virtue is an open question in the present moment. Perhaps we can.

I will not take any questions as is customary at the close of a lecture. I have, I hope you understand, just explained my reason for this refusal. Thank you for listening to me talk to myself and for being so attentive.

A's Lecture: Socrates as a Comic Figure

> Socrates was the buffoon who *got himself taken seriously;* what really happened there?
>
> —Friedrich Nietzsche, *Twilight of the Idols*

My friend and colleague, B, may please himself by thinking that he was talking to himself and that he was only dazzling his peers in his audience while providing the rest of you with something that was *perhaps*, as he puts it, educational. I admit to having been dazzled. I was not starstruck, however. I was listening closely and now wish to try to elbow my way into his private conversation. Perhaps he will let me in.

I begin by telling you a truth. I, like every other person who must earn a meager living by lecturing, am writing The Great Academic Novel. It opens this way:

> Jean-Louis neared the end of his first lecture since assuming the new chair in grammatology.
>
> "The task, then, is to keep the conservation . . . I mean, the *conversation* going."
>
> Jean-Louis smiled since he hadn't known you could make such grand slips in what was still for him a foreign language. He used that smile instead of the one he had practiced to set up his final line.
>
> "For the end of the conversation"—the practiced pause was still necessary—"is death."

"You have to rule yourself so that you may be free to participate in the important conversations." How could I disagree with this? What I disagree with is B's presumption—how can I convey to you the depth of my concern about this?—his *megalomaniacal* presumption—that these conversations will get you anywhere, except to their own end. Keep the conversation going, yes, absolutely, but not for any good reason. Do so only because it's better than the alternative.

Before I join in B's conversation directly, I want to tell you something about why I choose to lecture on this material. There is no irony, for me, in this decision. Lecturing, for me, requires two complementary acts by the lecturer that together signal a certain respect for his audience: (1) that he allow the audience to confront embodied ideas (and that the lecturer embody his ideas) and (2) that the lecturer leave.

The embodiment of ideas is very important to me. It is, for me, the crux of those passages in the *Meno* that follow on Socrates' telling Meno to leave Gorgias out of it. "Come, tell us what *you* think. Stand there, Meno; stand for something," Socrates seems to be saying. I have been quite influenced by some feminist thought that suggests that something beyond "voice" is important in writing and speaking. Putting ideas on the line effectively involves putting yourself on the line; ideas need a body; otherwise they float free, ungrounded, and are without meaning. Socrates is always bodily present to his interlocutors. (Didn't he, at one point, concede a tactical matter to Meno because, he said, he found Meno attractive? Isn't the direction of the dialogue as much influenced by the pull of Socrates' body as it is by the flow of logic?) He is always *there,* and even when people like Meno would rather invoke a surrogate, like Gorgias, to stand in their places, Socrates invites them back to be *there* as well. I will, for a time, try my best to be *here* for you.

The importance of the second act—the lecturer's leaving—should become clear once I start the body of the lecture. Socrates was not in a school. He could get away with asking, over and over again, that disrespectful question, "What do you mean by that?" because he was in an arena where this question could be destabilizing without necessarily being threatening. (We can note the obvious: the question *was* a threatening one for many interlocutors, like Meno, like Thrasymachus, but it wasn't *necessarily* threatening.) I choose to lecture, in part, because were I to engage you in a dialogue in this schooled setting, my "eternal refrain" of demanding that you go back to the beginning, of demanding that you say what you mean by that, would necessarily be threatening. So I think that it is partly out of respect that I wish to leave, and to leave you alone. But more important, I don't think that what I have to say is of crucial importance; certainly, it is not so important that I should do anything to force those ideas on you and insist that you deal with them as would be the implication of my hanging around and insisting, in some way or another, that you or we come back to these ideas. I respect the fact that you may conclude that there is nothing worth pursuing in my talk, and so I leave. I am with Socrates—*my* Socrates—a person who is "never anyone's teacher" (*Apology,* 33a). Consequently, my preferred mode of teaching is to lecture and leave. (But also following my Socrates, I will be there waiting if you want to talk. I try, as my Socrates tried, not to withhold myself from anyone who wishes to keep a conversation going.)

I am almost ready to begin my conversation with B, but there's a word of caution that I must utter first. There are differences between us that will become clearer as we progress. Those differences are a part of what makes the conversation between us interesting enough to continue. As you listen to us, you will hear us taking different sides in an argument. We will look at things from different perspectives. We will confront one another. We are *not*—and this *is* crucial—inviting you to choose a side and, for example, stand with one of us. You are not asked to use one of us as your surrogate. When you hear us carrying on an implicit or explicit argument, when you hear and see profound differences between us, try to hear also the respect that we have for each other. We are not interested in *defending* our ideas in the face of another's different ideas. We have no interest in combat. We are simply engaging in a conversation, and I think we both understand our task to be one of keeping the conversation going.

Now, with that rather solemn introduction, I can turn to my topic, "Socrates as a Comic Figure." My Socrates is, following Nietzsche, a buffoon who got himself taken seriously. But he *is* a buffoon. He is a clown, a comedian.

You know Socrates. Inquirer into virtue, justice, piety, and other big ideas. Gadfly on the horse of state. The world's greatest lover.

Consider now the image of Socrates in Aristophanes' play, *The Clouds*. The play opens on a promising Socratic note. Strepsiades is in search of the great Socrates because he knows that Socrates argues well. Socrates can, or so says his reputation as he tells us in the *Apology*, make the weaker argument overcome the stronger. Strepsiades is in a bit of a financial bind. He has suffered a "business reversal." He's broke and he's got his creditors on his tail. He knows Socrates can show him how to argue his way out of his creditors' clutches. So he makes his way to the Thinkery, Socrates' academy.

Upon entering the Thinkery, he sees some people looking at the ground. A student of Socrates tells him that these are students and they are studying geology. Nearby is another group of people looking at the ground, but these are bent over double and have their rears in the air. "Graduate students," Strepsiades is told, "and they are studying Hades." And the reason they have their rears in the air? "They are taking a minor in astronomy." Socrates has just finished an experiment designed to answer a studentlike question. How many flea-feet, a student has asked, can a flea broad jump? It's a reasonable question in the context of the play since a flea has just bitten this student on the eyebrow and jumped from the head of the student to the head of the teacher. Socrates, always the clever man, caught the flea, dipped its feet in melted wax, waited for the wax to harden, and measured the length of a flea foot. A little measuring, a little division, and presto, you have the answer to a pressing question.

After this introduction to the works of the great man, Strepsiades is introduced to Socrates himself. Inside the Thinkery, Socrates carries out his researches while suspended in a basket. Strepsiades calls to Socrates saying, "What in the world are you doing up there?" Socrates responds, "Ah, sir, I walk upon the air and look down upon the sun from a superior standpoint." Strepsiades says, "Well, I suppose it's better that you sneer at the gods from a basket up in the air than to do it down here on the ground."

> Socrates: Precisely. You see, only by being suspended aloft, by dangling my mind in the heavens and mingling my rare thought with the ethereal air, could I ever achieve strict scientific accuracy in my survey of the vast empyrean. Had I pursued my inquiries from down there on the ground, my data would be worthless. The earth, you see, pulls down the delicate essence of thought to its own gross level. [And then as an afterthought, he adds] Much the same thing happens with watercress.

From this first encounter with Socrates suspended in a basket, his feet not on the ground, his head not quite in the heavens, the play is rollicking good fun as it presents Socrates expounding his theory that the clouds are the gods, that thunder is simply the clouds passing gas (he uses a less delicate term), and lightning is not the work of Zeus, but is instead, the gas catching on fire as it escapes at very high speed from colliding, bursting clouds. The Socrates of Aristophanes is quite a comic figure.

But I have something more than caricature in mind. I want to argue that the Socrates we have come to know from the *Apology,* from the *Meno,* and perhaps less so from the *Republic, that* Socrates is a comic figure. But in order to make this argument, I have to spend a little time talking about comedy, about the humorous.

The best way to develop an understanding of the comic in this context is to contrast the comic with another form of expression. I am going to contrast the comic not with tragedy, as you might expect, but with irony. This is apt because B has set the stage for us so well. He urged us to read the Socratic dialogues as ironic.

What does this term, "irony," mean? *Webster's* says irony is "a method of expression in which the intended meaning of the words used is the direct opposite of their usual sense." Also, irony can mean, the dictionary says, "the feigning of ignorance in argument; more frequently, *Socratic irony.*" The author who writes ironically has an intended meaning; it is just that he chooses not to express the meaning directly. Allan Bloom, who urges the contemplation of Socrates as our most urgent task, does not think that our American openness of mind is a virtue in the usual sense of the term "virtue." He is ironic in saying that openness is our virtue; we eventually learn from reading his book that he believes our openness, in truth, is our vice. Why would he choose not to write directly and sincerely what he truly believes to be the case? Because truth, for a Platonist, must always be approached indirectly. Hence people like B usually argue that teachers must always teach by indirection. As he says, one must begin with the world of appearances because the real world cannot be apprehended directly. Socrates will agree, finally, to re-enter the Cave and begin in the world of "seeming." Language, the medium of dialogue, is part of *this* world, the world in which we live, the world that is for Plato the unreal world, the world of images and appearances. Language could never hope to present the Truth directly. As Candace Lang puts it in her book, *Irony/Humor,* a text on which I rely here, "meaning, or truth, is equated [in Plato and since] with gold (an absolute standard), whereas language functions as a kind of paper currency or other medium of exchange, false or insincere language naturally being regarded as bogus or counterfeit money."[17] The task of the reader in relation to an ironic writer is to penetrate the facade that the words make in order to apprehend the gems of truth that lie buried beneath the words.

According to most scholars, Socrates is an ironic figure. B taught us how to appreciate the irony and, perhaps, to cut through it. Read the *Meno,* he said, as a drama. Pay attention to the action of the drama, not to the words. Don't be suckered by the words of the text into the "educationally unfavorable" position of Meno, who thought that one learned by learning the right and true and pretty words with which to answer fancy questions. If you do this, you will become trapped by appearance and forsake any possibility of discovering truth. The words, B told us, don't contain the answer to Meno's question. But if you know how to get behind the words, the drama of the dialogue as a whole might contain an answer to the question of what virtue is. Your job, as an auditor or reader, is to attend to yourself and to develop the character necessary to remain in the educationally favorable position of a good interpreter of the irony, the educationally favorable position of the discoverer of the intended (not the expressed) meaning of the author. For most people, Socrates is an essentially ironic figure and even though he did not say directly what he meant, there is in the dialogues a message for those who are of the character to hear it.

I do not want to do an injustice to the subtlety of B's view. He does not think that Socrates was feigning ignorance in order to have a chance of teaching something to Meno or, elsewhere, to Thrasymachus. In B's view, these two and others like them have no chance of learning anything true. They will remain forever mired in the world of appearances. The subtlety of his view is contained in his notion that Socrates understands this from the outset. Socrates assesses these two characters and finds them wanting. Socrates persists in the drama, however, for the benefit of the audience. So B does not develop a naive understanding of Socratic irony that would conceive of Socrates being ironic for the purpose of teaching those directly in front of him. B's Socratic irony is, if we may use the term without being redundant, an indirect irony. Only those outside the immediate action have the chance of penetrating the words to get to the meaning, of getting behind the appearances to get to the truth.

But regardless of the form of irony in ironic discourse, there is always a meaning to be apprehended. There is an authorial intention that drives a particular ironic work, and with correct training the good reader can discover that intention. This is possible because all Being participates in an original Intention. We may not be able to apprehend the full meaning of life as Rousseau's "First Author" intended, but it is our obligation to ferret out, through language, exploration, and dialogue those fragments of the truth that are available to us.

Lang points out the "irony of the ironist's situation" as he goes around looking for little fragments of truth by trying always to penetrate appearance. Even though the dialogue might be the best or even the only way to get beyond appearance, the second party to the dialogue is never terribly important. It could be Meno now, Thrasymachus later, a slave boy in between; the particularity of the ironist's interlocutor is not of consequence. Glossing on Kierkegaard, Lang shows that the ironist is, in the end, a very lonely figure despite the number of times he encounters someone who agrees to talk to him. In his effort to get behind appearance into the world of truth, the ironist becomes more firmly rooted in appearances:

> While his entire existence is a strategy calculated to free him from the constraints of the phenomenon—actuality—he is in fact utterly bound by it, since he must perpetually fend it off. Dwelling in a self-imposed exile, frenetically poetizing each moment into an aesthetically pleasing experience, he knows no continuity but "boredom: this eternity void of content, this bliss without enjoyment, this superficial profundity, this hungry satiety." (Kierkegaard, *Concept of Irony*, 302)[18]

Don't forget how B's fine presentation began and ended: He started by talking to himself and he finished by taking no questions. And he concluded with that provocative, even challenging "perhaps." Perhaps—but only perhaps—you will be able to learn something from Plato's ironic Socrates. It is, after all, no coincidence that the romantics, who held the individual in such high regard (who, some say, invented the individual for our times), reinvigorated irony. If Socrates did value conversations that require the harmony and fellowship of community—and I think B is right to say he did—he had a funny way of trying to get there, because the life of the ironist seems to me a socially arid one.

I hope you are tempted now to consider an alternative to the ironic Socrates. Let us consider him a comic figure.

To understand Socrates as a comic figure, we would do well to invert B's strategy. Instead of focusing on the action, let's focus on the words. Perhaps there is, in truth, no human meaning of virtue. Perhaps it is just "a gift of the god to those to whom it comes" (100b). Perhaps there is nothing to be learned from dialogical inquiry, except of course that there is nothing to be learned. Perhaps Socrates really is ignorant. That would be very funny.

I don't want to fall into the trap of what B called the standard interpretation of the *Meno* and suggest that this dialogue consists of many "fruitless attempts" to define virtue with the implication that if Socrates were a better teacher or Meno a better student, their efforts would have borne fruit. But neither do I want to fall into B's more subtle trap and allow that if we understood the true nature of Socratic/Platonic irony, we would be in an educationally favorable position. I want to suggest, instead, that the failure to define virtue may be all there is. The purpose of Socrates' questions may not have been to penetrate common sense and rise to the level of formal knowledge, but it may have been instead, as Kierkegaard put it in *The Concept of Irony*, to "suck out the apparent content [of an idea] with a question and leave only emptiness remaining."[19] As Lang puts it, following her reading of Kierkegaard, perhaps Socrates' rhetoric held no positive content. Perhaps his work involved a "non-dialectical negation of existing modes of thought" (a negation of the thesis with no third moment in view; simply negation). Perhaps Socrates' words are not "a phase in mankind's progressive acquisition of the truth"; and perhaps, finally, there is no message in the words.[20] Wouldn't *that* be funny! If there is no message in Socrates, that would be the greatest joke in the history of the Western world, for just think of the amount of effort that has gone into interpreting Socrates to find a message that is true about the way life ought to be lived. Think of the time spent trying to apprehend the intended meanings of the dialogues on virtue, beauty, goodness, love, piety, and so on. What if, in fact, there is nothing there? You'd just have to laugh. And Socrates would take his place as the world's greatest comic.

By saying this, I am not disputing the god's assertion that in truth, in this life, there is no one wiser than Socrates (*Apology*, 21a). I would not be that impious. But we must follow Socrates' illumination of this divine revelation. He is wise in human, earthly knowledge *and* wise in the fact that he knows that this "human wisdom is worth little or nothing" (*Apology*, 23a). Socrates' wisdom lies in the fact that he does not assert knowledge of moral truths when he has none. He is wise in his decision not to presume to found a moral order or its earthly form, the state, without knowledge of the moral good, which is inaccessible to him. As Nietzsche puts it, the "problem of Socrates" for which he had to be condemned by the good citizens of Athens was that he used his humor to shake his auditors' faith in the earthly grounding of their actions, the *polis,* and he supplied them no political alternative.[21] It is not that Socrates was a "moralist pure and simple," as B would have it. He was a humorist pure and simple. He had no intentions. The problem Socrates faced was that people came to understand the threat of his joking. He got himself taken seriously. As Daniel Conway has put it so well, "Although [Socrates] posed no direct threat to anyone, his life as a fool constituted an indirect challenge to the accepted model of political organization."[22] Presuming to teach virtue, however you try to do it, by whatever level of indirection you think you might achieve it, is, in itself, a joke: "The teacher of virtue must either embrace the utter folly of his enterprise or renounce the enterprise altogether."[23] Socrates, the teacher who does not teach, is at root a comedian.

Candace Lang has done us a service in carefully separating irony and humor as two distinguishable rhetorical forms. They are often lumped together. Indeed, *Webster's* says irony is often a method of "*humorous or sarcastic* expression." And, indeed, those who see Socrates as essentially ironic often see the humor in him too. But I think it is valuable to think of the two as separate. Irony and humor have separate aims.

Irony aims high. It aims ultimately at the apprehension of truth, the Forms, eternal, unchanging Good. Humor is base. It aims at the earthy. It aims to puncture all aspirations to higher, more divine thought and to bring us back to earth, just like Socrates' watercress. Just think of your favorite comic. He or she never has any high level message to deliver. He or she just calls into question the seriousness of high level thoughts. (I won't succumb to the temptation to give examples from my favorite comics because they always fail and often offend.)

To appreciate the low-level aim of humor, just think about the words, "humor" and "comedy." "Humor" often referred to bodily fluids, and much serious thought—religious, political, scientific—has been devoted through the centuries to what one is supposed to do with bodily fluids, how they are to be used, where they are not to be spilled, and so on. The humorous has always been opposed to and the target of serious thoughts, a notion I will return to in a moment.

"Comedy" comes from the Greek words "komai," the peasant villages, and "odeia," songs. Comedy reflects the songs of the villages, the joyful celebrations following feasts. Comedy does not consist of the speeches of the senate or the solemn deliberations of the councils of state. It is baser than such high-mindedness. Dante said he called his major work the *Comedy* because it was "in its style lax and unpretending, being written in the vulgar tongue in which women and children speak." Comedy and humor aim low, but they have no goal whatsoever except to destabilize everything that might become serious. Comedy, the celebrations of the peasants, is essentially destructive and disruptive, destructive of reason and disruptive of the reasonable. It is rude.

I prefer my Socrates to be a comic figure, and I value him for that. His targets, let us not forget, were the high minded, those who thought they were wise. His targets were those in positions of power, those who were in positions to impose their truths on others, those, like Meno, who lived lives around a will-to-power. I think of Socrates' project as essentially humorous and, because of that, it is also essentially political, but in a very different way than B would imagine that term. Humor produces the possibility of making meaning. Humor is fecund but without certainty of outcome or positive content. (We say good jokes are pregnant with meaning.) Humor clears the field of imposed meanings and the truths that have come to be true and on which government and the good conduct of people rest. It makes room for the peasants to have their say. It allows their lives and their celebrations to stand on the same ground as the solemn rituals designed to display state power. It is not a coincidence that the Socratic project of Plato opens with the death of Socrates. The premise of the *Apology* is that reason, embodied in the reasonable men of state meeting in an assembly of reason, will have its way with those who, like Socrates, take it as their job to call the reasonableness on which the state rests into question. Reason will not tolerate those who take it as their job to laugh at the truth, to make truth laugh.[24]

Socrates' jokingly entrusting Anytus to the poor specimen Meno is a joke of a high order. Socrates does not pretend to have a better way to govern Athens. He leaves the decisions on how to govern to those who would govern. He has a kind of ribald faith in people to do the best they can. But he cannot take the workings of the state seriously, even when his own life may be at stake. He must leave the scene without any enduring faith in the value of his own work. He leaves, I imagine, with a good laugh at the prospect of Meno's trying to talk with Anytus about virtue.

Don't forget: the jokes continue right through Socrates' condemnation. His proposal for punishment after he has been convicted is, "free meals in the prytaneum." And why? Because "I make you happy" (*Apology*, 36e). Because his incessant questioning could make Athenians laugh at their high-mindedness, the high-mindedness that requires victims to insure itself of its correctness. Socrates knows that he is the victim of "that prejudice and resentment of the multitude which have been the destruction of many good men before me, and I think will be so again" (*Apology*, 28b). The many will conspire against the one in a serious state. But Socrates' joke about going on welfare says that for life on this earth to be well lived, the particularity of the one must be protected from the mass of the many. The jokes must be allowed to continue right there in the prytaneum; people must be made happy (not complacent); conviviality must reign if conversations are to continue. Otherwise, the operations of reason will make victims of all thoughtful people who would try, by acting as a gadfly, to animate life in the state.

Instead of searching for Truth, my Socrates has us focus on the *operations of reason* as they play themselves out on people. My Socrates incites an interest in the human implications of searches for truth, because a search for truth usually results in discoveries of truth, and discoveries of truth usually create victims out of those who, for one reason or another, do not or cannot believe the truth or accommodate themselves to it. My Socrates encourages us to attend to relations between the operations of reason, on the one hand, and violence, on the other.

To engage in this kind of investigation we must keep our heads out of the air and keep our eyes on the ground. We have to talk cases, earthy, empirical cases. Not Truth, but the effects of truths. We may even have to talk about what is happening here, right now. What am I as a teacher doing to you (not "with" you or "for" you; at least we can insist on honesty in prepositions) as students? What is my friend B doing as he, he says, talks to himself? I am personally coming very close to refusing to talk about anything else besides what we are doing to you here in this classroom—and I want to talk about it in terms of the violence involved in those nice, well-meaning, probing, penetrating questions like, "What do you mean by that?" and in those pedagogical strategies like, "That's obviously not right. On that we are agreed. So let us begin again, and let us try to get it right this time." B would like you to examine yourself and ask if you have sufficient character to enter into conversations about serious things that matter. I would like us to consider what we are doing here together. If we can see the humor of our many efforts to be high-minded and serious, we might decide to do things differently.

Doing things differently involves, for me, simply but surely continuing the conversation.

It is time to return to the beginning of the lecture so I can end it. There is something conservative, something conserving, about conversation. Conversation works against the forces that split and divide, the forces that would create the conditions for organizing the true in relation to the false, the good in relation to the bad. George McFadden, in *Discovering the Comic*, writes of *The Canterbury Tales*, a good comic work, that the Host of the Tabard Inn, Harry Bailey, "organizes everything for the tale-telling sport, and later serves to keep the group in harmony whenever the highly individualistic figures threaten to fall out of discussion with one another."[25] Just keeping people together, keeping the conversation going, is fun; it is enjoyable. There is something about the comic that helps the conversation continue. That which is serious always contains the threat that it will finally *get* serious and end the conversation. The comic, in contrast, helps us see new possibilities, it opens new vistas, it give us something more to talk about. The comic can keep the conversation going.

Finally, I return to Socrates suspended in his basket between heaven and earth. This is the same Socrates who at the end of the *Apology* says, "But now, the time has come, and we must go away—I to die, and you to live. Which is better is known to the god alone" (42a). Certainly I don't know which is better in the End, but I will say this about one of the choices: If you want to lead a serious life, you should kill Socrates. Join with Anytus and send him on his way to heaven. Don't dare let him stay around. He may make you laugh, even at yourself. If, on the other hand, you want to lead a vital life, a life filled with good company, the drink that is necessary to keep you at the table when you might be inclined to leave, and the friends that give you a future, go cut old blathering Socrates down. Bring him down to earth. Talk to him.

You may appreciate the humor if I say I will take a few questions before I leave.

Two Harsh Disciplines: Solitude and Community

The tragic educator, for whom the humorous Socrates is a model, and the progressive educator, who follows an ironic Socrates, have different educational ends in mind. The tragic educator takes it for granted that humans are fundamentally alone. For him, society is always coming between a person and himself. It cannot be otherwise, for humans need society to survive. Consequently, education should teach us to disengage, as best we can, from the social, to examine it carefully, and to confront it critically, because education's ultimate aim is to allow us to face the solitude with which we are left once we have mentally and emotionally removed society's hooks from our bodies. This solitude is our fundamental condition. Society does everything in its power to distract us from it, and education's task is to teach us to see it, to acknowledge it, and to live it—an impossible task, but one that nonetheless must be undertaken. To undertake an impossible task with full conviction requires a tragic educator—full of humor.

The progressive educator, by contrast, takes it for granted that humans are fundamentally with others. The task we must learn, therefore, is not to live alone, for we delude ourselves if we believe we can. We need to learn to live with others as best we can. The problem with society is not that it comes between a person and himself, but rather that it comes between every human being and his fellows. It convinces us we ought to live for ourselves alone. Society masks from everyone the condition of human mutual interdependence that *is* the human condition. Education, thus, must teach us to disengage from society, to examine it carefully and to confront it critically, because its ultimate aim is to allow us to reconstruct a better society, one that permits humans to face each other genuinely, to aid each other generously, and to produce and enjoy together what no one individual could produce or enjoy by himself. Interconnectedness is our fundamental condition. Society does everything in its power to distract us from it. Education's task is to teach us to see our interdependence, to acknowledge it, and to promote it. This is a challenging and difficult task, but not an impossible one. To undertake such a challenging and difficult task, and to do so with full conviction, requires a progressive educator—with a capacity for irony.

Turning Toward Collegial Teaching

The paradox of pedagogy confronts the tragic educator and the progressive educator with equal force. Whether, like B, we start from the view that education is ultimately for society, or like A, we start from the view that education is ultimately for the self, we are led down the same path. The *difference* between A and B does not put either in a favored position with respect to the paradox. But the difference between these two may give them an unusual way to confront the paradox of pedagogy. *A's and B's responses to the paradox of pedagogy can be juxtaposed in front of students.* If students were taught by both A and B at the same time, students would be confronted with the paradox of pedagogy, not as some intellectual formulation, but as a directly embodied presence in their own education.

There are two ways A and B can come together to teach.

First, one individual teacher could allow herself to be torn between these two orientations. She may feel at times like A and at times like B. Rousseau himself was torn in this way. As a writer and thinker he seems to have lived with an elegant tension between the social aim and the solitary aim we have discussed. Peter France claims that "the tug-of-war between solitude and society" was Rousseau's central theme.[26] Having someone like Rousseau as a teacher[27] would provide a most interesting means of manifesting the paradox of pedagogy to students. It would be quite difficult for Rousseau's students ever to settle clearly on a single path with a clear aim (society or solitude). Whenever one path seemed to students to be the one down which their teacher was beckoning them, it would not be long before the other surfaced as the more important path.

The second way of responding to the paradox of pedagogy is more interesting. This pedagogical arrangement is simple, yet somewhat shocking: Why not have A and B team up to teach a common group of students together? In this arrangement the points of view of A and B are bodily present to the students; the two perspectives do not have to alternate or be present only partially. The *difference* between A and B will be palpable. This difference, which might seem a source of pathology in a single teacher torn between orientations, now becomes explicitly a moral and educational object for students' attention.

But putting A and B together in a classroom is difficult because there is a gap—a silence—that separates them. A and B must teach together across a nervous silence. Each has a point of view that is stable and reasonable. Each acts in a way conditioned by his point of view. But when A and B come together, they meet at an impasse. That there are two "sides" is obvious. It would seem that the only question for their students is which side to take. If one could only decide, then no one would have to be nervous anymore. But A and B insist on maintaining their silence, which they break only when someone chooses a side, or when someone tries to get them to engage in combat. They speak only to insure their silence.

The silence across which A and B speak to one another is analogous to Robert Frost's "Mending Wall." Frost's fence makes good neighbors by providing a meeting place for those the fence separates. It is across Frost's wall that one neighbor calls to the other. It is along the fence that the two walk the dividing line that they have in common. It is at the wall that they work to make repairs that importunities beyond their control have necessitated. In re-placing in spring the stones winter dislodged, two people work together to repair that which they have in common that separates them. It is across the fence that the call of one person is answered by another.

In part 2 we turn away from the promise of pedagogy that we have found so paradoxical. We imagine a pedagogy that *begins* with pedagogues turning away from the student-teacher relationship. We imagine a pedagogy that, because of its seeming indifference to the student-teacher relationship, leaves room for colleagues to answer one another's call, a pedagogy that permits colleagues to meet at the boundaries of their thought so they might work together in the place marked by the nervous silence between them. In the turn away from a pedagogy based on some permutation of the student-teacher relationship, two colleagues may find themselves facing one another. In that place, at the boundary they have in common that separates them, they may feel moved to act.

Team teaching as it is practiced most commonly has almost nothing to do with the collaboration we are describing. We prefer the term "collegial teaching" since it suggests we are talking about something unfamiliar to most teachers. What is crucial to collegial teaching is that the two (or more) teachers join together out of a common intellectual interest. What brings the colleagues together must be a genuine *interest,* not an interest invented as a pretext for creating a course. And there must be some *common* ground in their intellectual interests so together they can formulate a question or project the joint pursuit of which will be genuinely interesting to each—though not necessarily for the same reasons.

For A and B to teach well together, each has to be able to identify with and take the point of view of the other. The mutually enhancing quality of collegial teaching has its source in an ability to identify sympathetically with an absolutely opposed position. In some sense, then, each teacher involved in such a project will suffer the split of the single teacher torn between A and B that we mentioned earlier. A will have a subordinate B within him, and likewise B will have within him a subordinate A.

So far collegial teaching sounds like a collaborative research project (which it is). But where do students fit in? We wish we could simply permit ourselves the luxury of saying students enter the project of collegial teaching because the colleagues have invited them to enter. The spirit of generosity and openness that endemically informs research and intellectual inquiry sparked by curiosity and human interest should lead naturally, or so it would seem, to the proffering of this invitation. Students join with their teachers because they seek an education, and what better way to get an education than to participate in intellectual inquiry along with those who are more knowledgeable and experienced?

We wish we could say that students become colleagues because they are invited to do so, but we are aware that most teaching occurs in institutions. The spirit that nourishes collegial teaching is dampened by institutions. That is why teachers must, in a sense, turn away from students. The invitation they issue is, in fact, an invitation for their students to give up being students. It is an invitation to colleagueship.

In the turn away from students *as students*, in the turn away from the student-teacher relationship, colleagues (which may include one's students) may find one another. *Under the arrangement of collegial teaching, the personal relationship once again becomes the central supporting, determining, and founding fact of pedagogy.* But now it is the personal relationship between colleague/teachers rather than between teacher and student that becomes the matrix for education. At the heart of collegial teaching is a relationship between people who are equals in all important respects. In that relationship, without obvious entrées to relationships of domination, without obvious rules for forming their interactions, the colleagues must invent, from A to Z we might say, what is to happen between them before their students.

In suggesting that colleague/teachers "turn away from the student-teacher relationship," we are not recommending that teachers care less about their students' educations. On the contrary, we think such a turn will create conditions that will make possible a better education for their students. "Turning away" in no way implies rejection. Instead, it opens up a potential for *accepting* students in a way that is rare in most educational institutions, namely, as intellectual colleagues.

As almost all teachers know, teaching is a lonely profession. Despite all the pedagogical associations, in-service workshops, and faculty development efforts that are now the vogue (and which only serve to reproduce and reinforce the master-pupil relationship), the vast majority of teachers know that what really counts happens when they are alone with their students in the classroom. Given this common condition, most people will find it hard to entertain the idea that the most important personal relationship in the classroom could be the one between two colleagues who are teaching a class together. Yet we have found it to be so. Although there may be no perfectly suitable response to the paradox of pedagogy, the *best* response, we think, is to have two pedagogues who differ (as A and B differ) get together out of (*a*) common intellectual interest, (*b*) mutual respect, and (*c*) an openness to the potential of friendship between them, and plan and teach a course together for a common group of students.

Under these conditions, the relationship they form will inevitably be erotic. Eros will fuel all that transpires in the course. The relationship between colleagues will not follow the model of a romantic or sexual relationship, but will be based in *homophilia*, the friendship that occurs between people who can each perceive a "likening" in the other. Perceiving a likening in one another does not mean perceiving a likeness; it means sensing a shared impulse to *become* more like one another. In the turn away from the erotic bond between teacher and student painted so vividly by Rousseau, and unmasked so dramatically by Freud, love has entered the classroom in a form where its very presence is *not* dedicated to undermining the development or the liberation of pupils.

We are not describing some kind of utopian fantasy, but rather a kind of teaching we have both experienced in an educational institution that has existed for over twenty years. Our experience shows that when A and B become colleagues and teach together, they can provide more and become more than the sum of what each could do were they teaching separately. A can become more of an A when he teaches with B, and likewise, B can become more of a B. At the same time, A can permit himself to be a B at moments, and B can try on the persona of an A. The limitations of each orientation can be transcended by working together. There is a mutual enhancement that arises from such a collaboration, an enhancement that arises not from compromise or intellectual accommodation, but *from the public, rigorous, persistent, relentless articulation of the differences between A and B*. Difference becomes the moral and intellectual object of awareness for the students, and for A and B as well.

The point of articulating the difference between themselves is not to have students choose sides. It is rather to raise for the students all the issues we have written about in this book. It is to let them see how paradoxical their position as students is, and to permit them to articulate, responsibly and authoritatively, their own responses to this paradox.

Finally, it needs to be understood that the friendship, the collaboration, the respect, and the love between the two colleagues is not going to end when their common course concludes. There is no way to predict what will become of it. Continuing collaboration can take many forms. On most occasions, it will lead the colleagues to continue the conversation they have started in the presence of their students. They may decide to write a book together, but they need not write together, nor even converse with one another. Even in the absence of words, even in silence, friendship is possible. Indeed, some forms of friendship thrive best in silence (recall the comments by both Illich and Foucault). Whether the continued collaboration of the colleagues aims toward social acts of conversing and writing or toward solitude and silence, friendship has the last word. This fact, it turns out, is what informs collegial teaching from the start and has the deepest impact on the students, though they may never know it.

6

COLLEGIAL TEACHING

> So a person ought to be conscious of his friend's existence, and this can be achieved by living together and conversing and exchanging ideas with him—for this would seem to be what living together means in the case of human beings; not being pastured like cattle in the same field.
>
> —Aristotle, *Ethics*

IT IS ALMOST SCANDALOUS to talk about love and friendship between colleagues being the grounding for teaching and learning in a college. This is an age of accountability, of assessable student outcomes, of individualized instruction, of teaching by objectives, and so on. To say one should turn away from students and toward one's colleagues is to invite censure for a dereliction of duty. But we see this turning toward colleagues as a *more* responsible way to fulfill our duties as members of the faculty of a college. We have in mind the possibility of teaching in such a way that students might stop being "students" and become, instead, colleagues of their teachers. The turn toward colleagues can create an intellectual environment conducive to a stimulating and exacting education.

Our work at The Evergreen State College has allowed us to experience the pedagogical power of this scandalous turn away from students. Describing some aspects of our experience at this college will give a sense of the possible in collegial teaching.[1]

At Evergreen most teaching occurs in Coordinated Studies Programs. One such program constitutes the entire "course load" of any student who takes it and the entire teaching load of the two- to five-person faculty team who teach it. Coordinated Studies Programs are thematic. They center on a problem or question. Faculty members from different disciplines—each of which is expected to shed some light on the program theme—constitute the teaching team. There are only a few expectations of every team. There must be a weekly faculty seminar; faculty must write timely narrative evaluations of each student, and there must be a process of self-evaluation and colleague evaluation at the end of the program. Virtually all the details of student and faculty work and of their intellectual life together for the duration of the program are decided by the faculty team (perhaps in consultation with students—but that too is up to the faculty team). Team teaching is thus the norm at Evergreen. Everyone expects to teach on teams about 80 percent of the time. Many teach on teams all the time.

But "collegial teaching" is not synonymous with team teaching. Indeed, many of our own colleagues at Evergreen may find the concept as strange and unfamiliar as would teachers outside the college. Collegial teaching is a particular form of team teaching. In this chapter, we first suggest a set of criteria that differentiates collegial teaching from other forms of team teaching. Then we present a few "moments" from the life of a collegial teacher. Finally, we answer questions that inevitably arise when people try to imagine themselves turning away from the student-teacher relationship and toward a colleague.

Criteria

Five criteria distinguish collegial teaching. The first two are inseparable.

1. The faculty colleagues must be *equal*. This is one way of saying they must respect one another. It is not a way of saying they must have equal rank or status, unless in their particular environment, rank and status affect respect. It means, rather, that the faculty colleagues must experience themselves as equals, and must, as a consequence, be able to act as equals before students.

2. The faculty colleagues must be *different*. This is one way of saying that they must be *interested* in one another—in how each other sees things, thinks about things, construes problems, poses questions, responds to dilemmas. It means there must be genuine intellectual differences between the colleagues.

In her analysis of political action, Hannah Arendt specifies the human condition of *plurality* as the fundamental prerequisite for political action. Plurality she defines as the simultaneous presence in a group of equality and difference: "Plurality is the condition of human action because we are all the same, that is, human, in such a way that nobody is ever the same as anyone else."[2] The first two of our conditions correspond to Arendt's plurality. It is essential that people engaged in collegial teaching be able to speak with their own authority (i.e., be different) and yet be radically open to hear others (i.e., be equal).

3. The colleagues must function *primarily* as colleagues—intellectual colleagues—and *not* as members of a team whose joint responsibility is to deliver a curriculum or administer a program. We emphasize "primarily" because the colleagues will not be able to avoid sharing the responsibilities of administering a program. This, somewhat ironically, is what we are paid for. We must "deliver the goods," and there is the inevitable burden of making sure that space is scheduled, syllabi are printed, and so on. The paper must be pushed. Some team teaching at Evergreen and elsewhere consists of nothing more than administering a program. But when the colleagues envisage their work in this way, what typically results is team teaching by "division of labor." Collegial teaching is far removed from this conception of team teaching. Collegial teachers will responsibly share the work of making sure the program runs, but they will not see that dimension as the primary focus of their work.

4. Collegial teachers will *not* conceive of their program as a curriculum at all. They will *not* see the program as consisting of some domain of subjects, topics, or methods that have to be covered. They will instead view the program and all its activities (assignments, lectures, seminars, tests, etc.) as a way of carrying on a conversation among themselves—a conversation about *something* (where the program theme usually supplies the something). Since they are intellectuals who respect one another (are equals) and are interested in one

another (are different), the conversation they intend to have will be a collaborative inquiry.

5. Finally, the faculty colleagues must conceive of the students in a way that differs from the way most faculty view most students, whether teaching in teams or alone. First, students are taken to be interested auditors to the ongoing conversation among the faculty colleagues. Second, they are viewed as potential participants in the conversation, should they decide to enter it. Each of these notions is liable to misinterpretation.

To view the students as auditors does not in any way entail making them passive recipients of knowledge delivered by expert faculty. Indeed, the notion of collegial teaching threatens the concept of expertise as it has come to be understood in the academy and transforms the notion of knowledge away from anything that could be "delivered." By calling the students "auditors," we are not referring to what specific activities they are called on to do in class; we use the term to characterize the more general relationship between the students and faculty. Students may listen to a conversation. There are no demands placed on them. An auditor occupies, some think, an educationally privileged position (see B's lecture, chapter 5).

To view the students as potential participants in the conversation does not mean they must be judged by the faculty as having realized some potential before they will be allowed into the conversation. It does not mean they are required to have some prerequisite set of experiences before they are permitted into the conversation. All any one student has to do is decide to join in the conversation, and she will be welcomed to it. But this, too, is a slippery point. It will not do for the student to enter the conversation *as a student* because the conversation by definition can only take place among equals, and a "student" is not the equal of a "faculty member." The student who tries to enter as a student will find her entry into the conversation barred. A student can only enter the conversation by renouncing studenthood—with all the privileges of that role—and by assuming the stance of an equal and different participant. She must enter under the condition of plurality. Thus, to say that students are *potential* participants in a conversation is crucial. This potentiality marks the possibility to cease acting like a student and to start acting like a colleague—not an easy achievement for most students.

Moments

Can collegial teaching really occur? These criteria make it clear that the task is demanding, both for faculty and for students. But we know that it can occur. Here are some specific *moments* in the work of a person engaged in collegial teaching at Evergreen.

1. It is the first day of class. You confront a sea of faces as you stand before the class. There must be one hundred young men and women—students—staring at you, wondering what you are going to say to them. There is one thing that makes this scene fundamentally different from the way it usually occurs in almost every college or university. In addition to the hundred students are a few colleagues. They may be seated among the students; they may be seated at a table in front of the class alongside where you are standing; they may be standing around the perimeter of the room. Their presence as colleagues—and as fellow teachers—makes typical relationships to the students impossible. Their presence makes the experience of that moment before speaking to a classroom audience fundamentally different from the typical first encounter with a new class.

Every teacher knows the way this scene usually plays itself out. When I teach alone, my students and I exist in a pair-bond. We occupy complementary roles in a two-role structure: student-teacher, each defining the other. We depend on each other for social existence, and we depend on each other for behavioral coherence. I cannot function as a teacher unless my students perform the expected student behaviors and they cannot become students unless I do my part. We are locked in a dance that the school brings into being. We may arrange to have a lovely dance together; we may have a miserable time together. But we must dance and we cannot dance without a partner.

When I stand before my own class in that brief moment of silence that precedes my speaking, I dimly feel the force of the pair-bond. I know that a great deal depends on my performance, on what I am going to say. I know that my students are hoping that I will be a good teacher. I, too, hope that I will be good, just as I hope I will have good students. The having of these hopes may put one in a thrall, just as the opening strains of a dance band put one in a kind of spell. I may, in the end, satisfy my students, or I may disappoint them. Either way I am the creature of my students. They may satisfy me or disappoint me. Either way they are the creatures of me, their teacher.

In the version of the scene with my colleagues present, everything is different—at least for the teacher. I know the students are waiting for my words, but I am not primarily speaking to them. Regardless of what pedagogical function I am filling, I am at the deepest level speaking first to my colleagues, and only second to the students. My colleagues are the ones I wish to touch with my words. I am concerned with the next step in our ongoing conversation. It is up to me, right now, to keep the conversation going. But this is different from the typical situation alone with my students. My colleagues are not defined simply by their institutional roles. They are specific individuals I respect and in whom I am interested. They are not professors; they are Paul, Jane, Sarah, and Bill. They are colleagues and potential friends, and I care what they think about me in a way that differs from how I care about what my students think of me. I am not trying to satisfy them, I am trying to contribute to the conversation in which we are engaged together. I am trying to talk to them.

The students are there, too, of course, and I am talking to them, too, of course. But that sense of utter dependence within the pair-bond is gone. Their eager expectations or their sullen indifferences do not create the space in which I speak. I am no longer the creature of my students, and they are no longer "mine." I do not have a contingent identity. No more dancing. I have room to breathe.

2. It is Tuesday afternoon and you are about to open a student seminar on Hobbes's *Leviathan*. That morning you and your colleagues had held a *faculty* seminar on *Leviathan* in Paul's living room.

The faculty seminar is never routine since it operates by no rules. The teaching team simply gathers to discuss the book they have all read. Each team has to invent its own way of talking together. They improvise. They discover who each other is and how each other thinks simply by talking together in a protected space. The space is protected in a double sense. It is protected from students, and it is protected from administrative planning and decision making.

This week Sarah, a feminist theater instructor, surprised you by being uncharacteristically silent. She asked some specific questions about the text, but did not offer her own views on it. Paul, a political theorist, was helpful in connecting Hobbes's views to the rise of science in Europe. In explaining to the others the psychological dimension of Hobbes, you discovered that Hobbes could be seen not only as an early associationist, but even in some ways as a progenitor of Freud. This insight pleased you, for it helped you see there was a much greater political component to psychoanalysis than Freud had realized—a suspicion you had been harboring for quite some time. Bill, a sociologist, never mentioned Foucault, though his usual perspective was obvious in his brief "debate" with Jane, an English historian.

Now, you are about to start your book seminar (twenty students who meet with you to discuss *Leviathan* at the same time your four colleagues meet with their student groups to do the same thing). You pose a question about the difference between Hobbes and Plato. You all read *The Republic* six months ago, early in the program. Your earlier ruminations about the latent political content of Freud's writings have led you to think about the different ways to conceive of the proper relationship between human nature and political organization or government. Hobbes and Plato, you sense, have opposite notions about how this relationship should be conceived. You intuit that Hobbes's notion might be termed "negative" and Plato's "positive," but you are not sure what these terms mean, or why you think they apply. You hope your question to the students will stimulate a discussion that will help you sort this out; at the same time, you know that prodding them to think about the present reading in terms of the earlier text is good general practice, and is likely to lead somewhere fruitful, even if it is not in the direction you are anticipating.

In this moment, there are no colleagues in the room. But this moment is not the same as the usual moment before the beginning of a seminar. Now, you are about to engage in conversation with your students not primarily as an expert trained in one of the academic disciplines (psychology) but rather as a person who is a member of a faculty seminar that has just discussed the text your own seminar will now discuss. Your thoughts, your questions, your orientation to the text have all been colored by the sustained discussion you had with your colleagues on *Leviathan.* This new seminar will be another point in your sustained conversation with your colleagues.

Collegial teaching changes the normal stance of member of a discipline. In this moment you face your students not as someone who knows something important about this text that they do not know, but as someone engaged in a serious inquiry *with others* about this text. Your conversation with them is in some peculiar and indirect way, a "spillover" from that primary conversation. But this new stance does not eradicate your discipline's perspective in you; it merely subordinates it. Your question about Hobbes and Plato with its emphasis on human nature is directly connected to your interest in psychology. Your question is a psychologist's natural question and the fact that you formulated this question has everything to do with the fact that you have been trained in the discipline of psychology. At the same time, however, you probably would not have made the connection or formulated the question had you been a psychologist teaching alone. Indeed, you would never have been reading Hobbes with your students in the first place! It is only the collaborative inquiry, the collegial conversation, that has made these thoughts and questions possible.

Your students then are left with a set of possibly inchoate, possibly dawning set of questions about how they might fit into this inquiry. But the fundamental question is how they might relate themselves to this *conversation among others,* not how they might relate themselves to this *one special person,* their teacher. And you are left happy to welcome them into this conversation. It is rather like having, along with your three children, another adult at the dinner table. The children will still get to converse, you will still speak with them and respond to their questions and stories, but the dynamics of the conversation will have altered entirely.

3. It is the end of the academic year. After writing narrative evaluations of each student's accomplishments comes the program's final piece of work: a self-evaluation and colleague evaluations.

Your self-evaluation was a free-form essay reflecting on your work over the past year. By Tuesday morning, you had copies of your self-evaluation to each of your faculty colleagues, and you had received copies of their self-evaluations. Then you wrote evaluations of each of your colleagues. These were frank letters addressed directly to each person. You wrote about the quality of their work as colleagues and teachers in the program.

Now, you anticipate the final evaluation conference. At the conference all the evaluations are read, and all are discussed. Once again, it is up to the team to decide how to proceed.

You wonder what your colleagues will say about you. You are not worried. You know you have done good work this year, and you are well aware that your colleagues have appreciated your contributions. Beyond this broad feeling, you are curious: What specific words will each of them have committed to paper to characterize your work? You can only expect to be surprised, for it is always a surprise to read such letters. You realize how rare is the occasion you are about to participate in once again, as you have for fourteen years. It resembles an annual ritual, yet its specific content is anything but ritualistic or predictable. You can expect civility and courtesy, but you never know what will be written in the letters or said in the discussions.

What is rare is receiving the concrete and careful attention to your work from a peer that is demanded by the writing of a colleague evaluation. Letters might contain sentiments like these.

You might receive careful attention to one specific piece of work:

> Dear ———,
> Of your several workshops, . . . the one on Nietzsche turned out to be the richest and most provocative. It helped the students sort their way through, among other things, Nietzsche's key distinction between genealogy and definition, which, if only they knew, lies close to the heart of much of the recent philosophical debate in the human sciences.

You might receive some blunt criticism:

> One other aspect of your teaching I want to critically question is your way of talking to some students, some of the time. I haven't seen you interact with students in seminar or in your office, but I have heard you talk *about* students a great deal, and I have heard and read about (in student evaluations of you) a number of cases where students feel you have been unduly judgmental and downright unkind to them through things you have said. I know that you care very much about students and that you also work

very hard at being fair and honest. But you have a psychologist's tendency to categorize and diagnose. I fear that you inadvertently trample on some students' feelings, some of the time, more than is necessary or educationally useful.

You might receive praise that is more personal than professional; these letters can sometimes be "professional love letters":[3]

Dear ———,

As you must know by now, I judge a colleague not only by his intelligence, education, initiative, etc., etc. I am old-fashioned. I look out and I see a person, and it is the person I seek to give an account of, not merely his qualities. I want to say something about who you are, and only secondarily about what you are. And so I say: You are a *mensch*. The students and we were fortunate to have had you for a year.

Sometimes the affection is expressed in a different tone:

You're a smart son of a bitch, too, a fair Frisbee flipper, and the very antithesis of Yossarian. If only you could sing.

Let's do this again sometime.

Sincerely,

———

Or you might find a teacher showing, through her own expressive and distinctive style, that she has been watching her colleague from the very first day of the program.

Dear ———,

. . . When you came into NAS [Native American Studies], you seemed a veteran to waiting, wondering, and accepting what was. You didn't struggle as I did upon entering the program. You came to Monday meetings. You prepared and delivered a terrific lecture. You waited in your office for students who needed your assistance. You took your share, you said "yes," and you seemed to love all of it. You were non-judgmental, supportive, and listened carefully to everything said on Mondays. Your attention (at least it seems like attention, you may be body traveling or hypnotizing yourself to do something or other, or not do it, or memorizing lines for a play; silent attentiveness, focused eyes, a rarity) was fascinating, perhaps even curious because I lost mine easily (attention) and wondered "what in the world is ——— so busy puzzling over, nothing at all has happened for at least an hour now."

The letter, written by a painter, is accompanied by a black-and-white sketched portrait. The portrait is an integral part of this evaluation and demonstrated to its recipient that he has had perspicuous attention paid to him for the entire quarter.

These excerpts suggest what a faculty member has to anticipate as he waits for the faculty evaluation conference to begin. *This* moment of silence does not include students. In collegial teaching the most telling moments are not *fundamentally* driven by the presence of students.

4. I am seated in a lecture hall. I am one faculty member among one hundred students. One of my colleagues, A, is about to deliver a lecture on Plato's *Meno*. Sarah, Jane, and Paul sit scattered around the room. Three days ago, I had been at the lectern, and I, also, had lectured on the *Meno*. A's lecture, he has told me, will be a direct response to what I said. I had presented Socrates as an ironist; he wishes to show that Socrates may be seen as something very different: a comic figure, a humorist.

One hour later he has completed his lecture. While he takes questions, there is, for me, a profound moment of silence. In this moment I am allowed to savor my immediate visceral reaction to my colleague's lecture.

Really, it is an extraordinary moment.

On the one hand, I couldn't feel more flattered. My colleague has spent a sustained period of thinking and writing for the sole purpose of responding to what I said in my lecture. None of this marvelous lecture would have come into existence had A not taken my words and thoughts seriously enough to want to respond to them in a serious and sustained way. This respect has made itself felt publicly in the intellectual air of the program.

On the other hand, I am startled by how different his view of Socrates is. A's response to my lecture is not some assistant professor's picky academic critique, nor is it in any way an attempt at some kind of intellectual one-upsmanship. It is an alternative vision. This different vision makes my own view sharper. It outlines my own thoughts by showing me, and anyone who listened, the limits of that thought. It helps distance me from my Socrates. I begin to hear—in my memory—my own lecture as a student might have heard it.

As I think once again of A's Socrates, his view becomes plausible. Perhaps A is right, perhaps we should take Socrates more at his own word; perhaps he does know nothing; perhaps we should assume he means just what he says. What a radical idea!

But no. There is, finally, no good reason to give up my Socrates so quickly. But there is a touch more humility now in my interpretation, just as there is more clarity in it. I know why A would have just the Socrates he does, given what I know about his intellectual commitments; consequently, I begin to consider why I would have the one I do. I see now that more than "careful reading of the text" has produced my Socrates, a lot more.

Finally, I wonder what the students will make of two incompatible Socrates. They will be on their own now to work out their own ideas in seminars, in informal talk outside of class, in responses to essay assignments, and perhaps in responses to exam questions. I hope these two sharply differentiated figures of Socrates will stimulate them not to choose one or the other—though there is always that danger—but rather to develop a third equally sharply different Socrates of their own. If any individual student goes so far as to do so, and also has the gumption to find a way to make his Socrates public in the program, I stand to gain still more in my own understanding of my Socrates. But if no students do that, there is always A. He and I have a lot to talk about.

Questions

1. What actually happens in a collegially taught program? What would I see if I observed such a program for a week?

You would see lectures, you would see seminar discussions, you might see workshop exercises or science labs, you would see students reading books in the library or in their rooms, writing papers or doing problems and exercises. You might see students studying in preparation for an exam or writing the exam. If you looked behind the scenes, you would see a faculty seminar and a faculty planning meeting. With the exception of the last two items, what you would see is not very different from what you might see in almost any college course.

There is no special *technique* that makes teaching collegial. What is distinctive about collegial teaching is the stance taken toward one's colleagues. Collegial teaching is primarily dependent on how you relate to your colleagues, which, not incidentally, affects the stance it is possible to take toward your students. Such a shift creates a different spirit in the classroom, a different ethos. We presented our view of collegial teaching through a series of moments because there is nothing directive or technical to say about collegial teaching. Paraphrasing Tussman, if we could make an ethos for you, we would; as it is, we can only help you think about creating one for yourself.

If you observed a collegially taught program for a week, you would begin to feel this spirit of collegiality, but the activities you saw would, for the most part, not be very different from what you might see in any other classroom.

2. There must be something you could actually *see*, without having to "feel a spirit."

There are a few things you might see that could directly reflect the collegial nature of the teaching, and these might be somewhat different from what you would expect to see under normal teaching conditions. For instance, at a lecture, you might hear a professor raise a question from the floor—a rather sophisticated question, perhaps—and you might hear five minutes of dialogue back and forth between the lecturer and the questioner that wouldn't resemble the normal pattern of question-and-response at normal college lectures.

You might hear a lecture that was, to your ears, too sophisticated for the students. In a collegially taught program, this would not be the result of an overestimation of the students' abilities. It would be due to the fact that the faculty member was speaking principally to his colleagues. Auditors have the chance to listen, but they are not taken into consideration so very much by the parties to the primary conversation. And there is certainly none of the "speaking down to" or pandering to students that you sometimes see in colleges.

You might show up at the lecture hall one day to find a "faculty panel" instead of a normal lecture. The faculty panel would consist of the whole faculty team seated behind a table, each with a prepared talk of ten to twenty minutes. Faculty panels are often the occasion of pleasant surprises. Given the ground rule that there is no previous discussion among presenters, it is usually startling to discover how well the talks "go together" in one way or another. It often seems as if they had been planned as a whole rather than independently of one another. By saying they "go together," we don't mean that the presenters agree with one another, but rather that there is a coherence in the presented material—as if all the participants were involved in the same conversation.

And that is the point. The "surprising coherence" is not really surprising at all, because the colleagues *are* all involved in the same conversation. They have been reading the same books, discussing the same questions, formulating topics and exams, and listening to one another for the duration of the program. The fact they did not speak to one another about this one panel is a small fact in the face of their ongoing work together. Of course there is coherence in their talks. They *are,* over the long run, having a coherent conversation.

Finally, if you showed up to observe a normal lecture, you should not be surprised to hear it peppered with references to ideas, insights, and questions from previous talks by the lecturer's colleagues. You might also find the occasional essay assignment or exam question referencing the differing points of view of specific colleagues on the team. In other words, *the intellectual content of the collegial dialogue becomes one of the texts of the program.*

3. You say collegial teaching requires a "turning away from students." Don't the students feel rejected? Don't the students need attention and care to become properly motivated?

The simple answer to the question about feeling rejected may be simply no, they don't feel rejected. In one collegially taught course one of the two faculty members introduced himself to the students on the first day with the blunt statement that he was there for the purpose of continuing an interesting conversation to be had with his colleague. He hoped, he told the students, that they might profit from this conversation, but he really didn't care all that much whether they did or not. His alarmed colleague, who had been sitting in the front row during this announcement, was quick to express his fears after class that their enrollment would surely drop precipitously as a result of this introductory statement. "You don't keep students by rejecting them at the outset," he said. In fact, enrollment increased by 15 percent by the end of the first week. The fearful colleague concluded that "greed" was responsible: The students sensed that something special and vital was going on and they were greedy to be in on it. Real conversation, genuine inquiry, friendship (which often involves a certain exclusivity)—these are not the normal fare served up by modern colleges. Students are usually appreciative of these things when they see them; they want to be as close to them as possible for as long as possible once they come into contact with them. Collegial teaching gives them that opportunity.

But beyond psychosocial dynamics, there is something more to say about this "turning away." Turning away from students in no way implies not caring for students. It is a *way* of caring for students. Think about the single parent at the dinner table with her three children. As the sole adult present, her primary orientation will always be toward the children. She will attend to them and her care will be obvious. But what happens when a second adult becomes a member of the dinner table? The first adult takes a spouse and suddenly two adults who care about each other are dining with their three children. Does the fact that they attend to each other and care about each other mean they no longer care about their children? Of course not. On the contrary, their care for each other becomes one mode of manifesting care for their children. Moreover, the fact that their attention is not focused entirely on their children gives the children some breathing space, some room to grow in; it gives them the opportunity to listen to adult conversation and notice what adults are like. It lets the children appreciate the adults, not just the other way round. Turning away from students, thus, in no way entails ceasing to care for them. It does mean that the care will be manifested in different ways and that it will be experienced in different ways.

It is important to add that turning away from students is done by the *team* of colleagues. But each member of the team continues to be an individual as she teaches. One must distinguish the teaching done by the individuals from the "teaching" done by the collegial team. Individuals on the team will teach as they teach. Some may be nurturing and attentive of students; others may spend less time and energy on students. Some may be supportive and warm, others may be distant and cold. All this is a matter of temperament, teaching style, and individual inclination.

The turning away we are stressing is done by the team. The students' experience in a collegially taught program has at least two facets. It is an experience of a team and also an experience of individual teachers. An individual student can feel supported, nurtured, and attended to by a single teacher and at the same time be an auditor of a team of colleagues who clearly care more about their work together than they do about the collectivity called "the students" who are outsiders to this work.

4. OK, you sustain a vital conversation with your colleagues and you make this the center of your work. But do you actually teach your students anything? Do you care if they learn anything?

One must distinguish, once again, the "you, singular" from the "you, plural." The individual teachers may teach a great deal. It is a separate question whether the team of colleagues *as a team of colleagues* teaches anything. It is possible that they do. It is also possible that they will *teach* nothing, and yet that the students will still learn something. It depends on how you construe the word "teach."

The principal question is whether students can get something of value by becoming auditors to a collegial team. We feel they can, just as children can get something of value listening to adult conversation at the dinner table. We are not interested in trying to prove that they do, because, in part, that would require us to turn back toward the students and take an uncollegial interest in them as the bearers of "student outcomes." It is sufficient that we think they can get something; that thought alone is the basis of our actions.

The secondary question is *how many* students can get something of value by participating in a collegially taught program. This too is an empirical question and there is no way we can answer it. We respond to this question with another question: If we knew at the outset that only 10 percent of our students would get something of long-lasting value by participating in such a program, would we still go ahead with it? If we asked this question of ourselves, one of us would answer yes, the other, no. This approach, again, seems not very useful.

Another approach to this question is to return to the point of view developed by Foucault and Illich. Illich, remember, criticized schools for equating learning with teaching, that is, for making it an axiom that no one learns anything without being taught it by an institutionally certified teacher. We, who are called teachers by our institution, have been trying to find ways to continue our own learning while working within the confines of the institution called a school, and at the same time we are trying to provide a different kind of opportunity for those the institution calls students—an opportunity in which they may learn something through means other than those the institution defines as "teaching." This seems to us worth doing regardless of how many students take up this opportunity. On the other hand, we must add that we have been encouraged, not discouraged, by our students' responses—and the more time that elapses between the experience itself and when we hear from them, the more encouraging are their responses.

5. You may feel encouraged by student responses, but don't the students feel discouraged? Don't they get confused by hearing so many different views of the same subject?

Thank you. That's it exactly! We *do,* in fact, teach our students something. We teach them confusion. We do not give them the opportunity to become unconfused by making themselves dependent on the authority of institutionally recognized authorities. By having colleagues speaking authoritatively *to one another,* but doing so in front of the students, the students would—of course!—become confused. They would have to develop, in consequence, their own authority if they want to find any truthful answers for themselves. We do not deliver to them any unchallengeable thought. Everything is disputable (and disputed) in collegial teaching. If the students learn anything, they learn that if they are going to have any thought whatsoever, *they* have to do *all* the thinking.

6. Let's be clear. You *are* teachers. As you yourself admit, you still evaluate students, you still award and deny credit, you still are a cog

in the credentialing process carried on by your institution. Maybe all your fancy talk is just a way of kidding yourselves into thinking that you're not doing what, in fact, you *are* doing. Isn't this all an elaborate justification for your own decision to live your lives in an institution?

Maybe. Without question, we contribute to the institution's functioning as an institution. And this institution is a functional part of the larger institutional framework of modern society. We do, however, deny the implied charge of being blind to this aspect of our work. We have our eyes wide open to it.

Beyond that, we can only say that for reasons we cannot explain, we have experienced our teaching together as human interaction of the type that institutions *automatically* erode and eventually eradicate. We cannot prove this claim. We chose instead to write about the experience.

7. There is an unresolved tension about the number of people who can teach as colleagues. You describe teams of four and five colleagues in many of your examples, yet the experience you speak of involves *two* colleagues. Can more than two colleagues really act together in a way that satisfies your conception of collegial teaching?

The metaphors we have used are distinctively based on two. This is probably not a coincidence. It is certainly a reflection of our experience. But the nature of our experience says nothing about what else is possible.

Perhaps the image of Socrates in conversation is more useful a metaphor than dancing or dinner with a spouse and children. Socratic dialogues typically start with two people in conversation. However, the conversation itself creates opportunities for others to join in. This can happen in many different ways, and does happen in different ways in different dialogues. The important point is that what starts out as "naturally" appropriate for two can become appropriate for three, or four, or five, or many. The image presented in the *Phaedo* of a *group* of friends gathered for a final conversation with Socrates before his death suggests with great force that what begins with two need not be limited only to two.

Perhaps it is best to think of two teaching colleagues *starting* a conversation. Early on, the other colleagues stand in somewhat the same position as the students. They have the opportunity to join in if they choose. Nothing forces them to, but nothing prevents them from doing so either. Of course, they have it easier than the students, because they don't have the institutionally imposed label of "student" to overcome. They are already by definition "colleagues," and the only question is whether they will really become colleagues.

8. Can I learn to do collegial teaching at my institution?

The two key words in your question are "learn" and "institution"? Can one *learn* to be a colleague? Have we been interested in *teaching* anything by our writing? Our A and B had different answers to what flowed from questions such as these, and so do we. Beyond that, this is a question quite similar to Meno's opener, "Can virtue be taught?" It seems one must be a colleague before one could even think about becoming one.

With respect to the word "institution," the question is about the possibility of working against the grain of modern institutions. Many contemporary institutions might well approve of and foster collegial teaching. But in so doing, they will inevitably make a *program* out of it. They will issue memos promoting it, offer workshops to help faculty learn how to do it, appoint administrators to support it, appropriate funds to study it, implement it, and above all else, evaluate its effectiveness. An Office of Collegial Teaching Support is easily imaginable. In doing all these things that institutions do so naturally, they will be making it difficult for collegial teaching to happen. But probably not impossible. We would guess that most colleges and universities are not yet so thoroughly administered that two colleagues could not get together and try to put a conversation between them at the center of their teaching.

CONCLUSION

> But for all that, it was still a school.
>
> —Michel de Montaigne, "On the education of children"

> My contribution is to ask for a paradox to be accepted and tolerated and respected, and for it not to be resolved. . . . It is possible to resolve the paradox, but the price of this is the loss of the value of the paradox itself.
>
> —D.W. Winnicott, *Playing and Reality*

THIS BOOK IS A report on a conversation between two college teachers. Our focus, by force of circumstance, has been higher education. But our topic has been freedom. What can freedom mean in the relationships that colleges require and make possible? How might we respond to that question in contemporary institutions of higher education?

Our focus was narrow but our topic is, in fact, broad because we live in a time when what might be generally called "pedagogic relationships" are at once widespread and in crisis. Such relationships include child-parent, patient-doctor, client-professional (including such professionals as lawyer, architect, accountant as well as the more obvious "helping professionals"), army recruit–sergeant, toddler–day care worker, member of congregation–minister, worker-manager, and so on. These relationships are all characterized by the dependence of one party on the authority of another. Such relationships structure the texture of everyday life for most of us.

The present crisis has called into question the authority on which these relationships are based. We cannot imagine a life without such relations, yet today our society seems incapable of imagining that such relations could ever be, *or ever were,* satisfactory. This crisis is manifested most obviously in the current discovery of "abuse" in all of these relationships. It is obvious that a crisis of the legitimacy of authoritative pedagogic relationships is one of the defining factors of our time.

Responses to this crisis so far have been of one sort: attempts to manage, control, or discipline the pedagogic relationship, or to find ways of doing without it altogether. In education, the emphasis is on new and more innovative forms of curriculum, alternative models of management, and alternative institutional arrangements for monitoring behaviors of everyone. Schools *as institutions* feel it essential to take over almost all the tasks that parents *as individuals* used to feel responsible for. The promotion of health has moved from the hands of the family and the family doctor to "systems" of health care, interlocking networks of insurance agencies, clinics, and "practitioners" of every sort, a vast impersonal system designed to "meet people's health needs." The courts overflow with cases involving every sort of abuse; they attempt both to compensate people for the damage done them and to place people in "settings" where the chances of further abuse are lower than in their present settings. Personal authority exercised in pedagogic relationships is being undermined and dispersed while the power of institutions over individuals grows more specific, invasive, and pervasive.

There have been too many efforts to resolve this crisis too quickly. We believe a thoughtful and deliberate attempt to understand the pedagogic relationship itself, in its complexity and depth, ought to precede any attempts to "fix" it or do away with it. In this book, we have taken a long look at the pedagogic relationship in one particular manifestation: the student-teacher relationship. We have seen the paradox in which it places both members of the relationship. And we have examined our own attempt, not to deny, control, fix, or do away with this relationship, but simply to subordinate it to a fresh and invigorating human relationship of another sort. This new relationship between teacher/colleagues is, like the student-teacher relationship, still personal, still erotic, and can still provide a matrix for learning and development. But it is no longer asymmetric; it can exist only between equals. It does not replace the need for student-teacher relationships as part of learning and teaching in institutions. Rather it displaces them in a landscape that is emotionally dominated by the collegial relationship.

Our response to the set of issues surrounding the crisis in higher education has not been to further dehumanize the classroom by trying to monitor, control, and manage the personal relationships within it. Our effort, rather, has been to further complicate the educational environment by centering the classroom on a new personal relationship. This move creates more personal dynamics, not fewer; more unpredictability, not less. But it does relieve some of the burden on the student-teacher relationship by making it secondary to an exemplary relationship to which a student can aspire and possibly achieve. To achieve it, to achieve colleagueship with her teacher, a student does not have to "kill" her teacher, sleep with him, or prove herself to him. She just needs to talk with him. She needs only to join in the conversation that is already going on between or among her colleague-teachers.

At moments in this book, we compared college students to children at a dinner table. It is well known that teachers function in loco parentis and that the student-teacher relationship stands in the shadow of the more primordial child-parent relationship. It is thus somewhat surprising that no one has seriously thought about the implications of having more than one teacher in the classroom, just as children in most places have more than one parental figure in their lives. By "more than one," we mean not just a series of teachers "taken" serially, but teachers who work together and whose *interactions* are part of the everyday experiences of their students. In this book, we have thought about those implications and more: We have described and documented them. We conclude that teaching may be done more robustly by two teachers than by one.

Taking on a colleague to undertake collegial teaching will change a teacher's relationships with her students. It will not eradicate or diminish those relationships, any more than taking a spouse will diminish one's relationships with one's children. In both cases, the authoritative partnership *enhances* the relationships with those dependent on it. More important, such an arrangement attenuates the force of the relationship of dependency in which "abuse" seems to thrive, and enhances the possibility for the exercise of effective pedagogic authority. Changing the structure of the pedagogic arena may turn out to be one fruitful response to the current crisis in pedagogic authority.

Equality and Authority

Collegial teaching is more than just a novel approach to running a college course. It is a distinctive and very pointed response to the paradox of pedagogy.

In chapter 3, we saw how much emphasis Freire placed on the concept of equality. He appreciated how readily the unequal relationship between student and teacher—that pedagogical crucible so carefully cultivated by Rousseau—could turn into an instrument of domination, and thereby into an instrument that perpetuated an already-dominating political order. Freire made the culture *of his students* his privileged object of study and he insisted the teacher had much to learn from the students. These were fundamental moves in Freire's attempt to restore equality to education. He tried to crack open the tight asymmetrical bond between student and teacher, but without abolishing the teacher's authority as a pedagogue. We saw how difficult a line this was for anyone, including Freire, to walk, and in what ways the success of such a project must be qualified. Let us look at collegial teaching from the perspective of Freire's much hoped-for ideal of equality.

Equality is central to collegial teaching. Without equality there can be no collegial teaching. But the application of the concept has shifted from its use in Freire. Collegial teaching demands, first, equality *among the teachers*. This must be an equality in practice: the colleagues must respect one another and be able to converse before their students as already established intellectual equals. Here there is no claim that the students and teachers are equals; indeed, there is a recognition that the inevitable institutional setting of their work together makes student-teacher equality all but impossible. But a second version of equality is equally important in collegial teaching and this equality *is* between the students and their teachers. This equality is potential and presents itself in the *invitation* to join the conversation among the colleagues, a conversation that is, a fortiori, among equals. This equality is embodied in the invitation to renounce studenthood and thus to break out of the institutional definitions that demand and constitute a fundamental inequality. But there is no pretense that this potential equality is easy to establish. There is a frank acknowledgement of the unlikelihood of student-teacher equality and of the many obstacles that stand in its way.

Collegial teaching does not overlook Freud's insight that authoritative relationships are inevitably colored and distorted by transference, and thus are unequal in the deepest sense. At the same time, collegial teaching heeds Freire's insistence that a liberating pedagogy cannot be based on inequality. To have it both ways, collegial teaching *partitions* equality so that it can be experienced in distinct ways in diverse arenas. Equality is a complex and differentiated concept in collegial teaching.

Equality between colleagues is a constant reality; it is a palpable part of the daily environment effected by collegial teaching. Students breathe an atmosphere in which learning and equality are constantly conjoined. They see before them two or more people pursuing understanding through an intellectual conversation among equals. Students are never given the opportunity to imagine that learning results from an authority's imposition of knowledge from above.[1] Dialogue is the vehicle of their education, and Dewey's conjunction of democracy and education is part of the reality of the collegial relationship that is the center of their education.

Equality between colleagues does *not* substitute for student-teacher equality in this venture; collegial teaching does not replace one ideal for the other. But because (potential) student-teacher equality is so clearly and publicly distinguished from colleague equality, the former becomes a clearer concept and a more potent ideal than in most educational settings. Typically, equality between student and teacher is treated in one of two extreme ways. Most commonly, it is repudiated. The obvious inequality between student and teacher is taken as the basis for pedagogy, and any possible equality is relegated to some distant, possible future. On the other hand, so called "humanistic" education often insists on equality from the start, and acts as if it could make such equality real by declaring it. Often, this declaration is amplified by such simple-minded techniques as letting students grade themselves, giving students all A's, allowing them a hand in choosing assignments, or similar technical superficialities. This "humanistic" approach, aside from being intellectually dishonest, blurs the concept of equality, and makes it even easier for teachers to manipulate students than arrangements where power relations are explicit and above-board.

Although collegial teaching does not pretend that students and teachers are equals, it insists that equality is a prerequisite for intellectual work among people and, in the colleague/teachers, it provides students a genuine example of such work. This relationship among equals trying to learn together is "in their face" whether they like it or not—from start to finish—and there is likely to be much public talk about it. Still, at the same time, collegial teaching insists on the *possibility* of equality between students and teacher—not at some remote "later moment" when the students have grown up and proved themselves, but right now, or at any time, just as soon as the student is willing to enter the conversation as an equal. Most students, for one reason or another, will not accept this invitation. Many will not want to; some who want to will not know how to achieve it. But the invitation itself has a potent educational impact. The invitation stresses that the inequality so obviously felt between student and teacher is not an ineradicable fact of life, but is instead an institutional creation.[2] And the visibility of the one or two students who inevitably do accept the invitation makes the educational impact of the invitation to collegiality all the more potent.

Another way to understand the educational utility of the partition in equality under collegial teaching is to appreciate the way "difference" is correspondingly partitioned in this environment. In a typical educational environment it is very easy to confuse equality with sameness, and to assume that difference is always the source of inequality.[3] Under collegial teaching, the students experience difference in two ways. First there is the obvious difference between themselves and their teachers. But then there is the always-stressed, always-apparent difference between the teachers themselves. These differences between teachers do *not* produce inequality. So students have an opportunity to conclude that if the first kind of difference is the basis for inequality, it must be because of the specific nature of the differences between students and teachers. This insight opens the door for some interesting investigations. The difference between difference-cum-equality and difference-cum-inequality becomes part of the implicit curriculum of any collegially taught course.

With collegial teaching we are still in the spirit of Rousseau—but with a difference. We remove the students from everyday life in society and place them temporarily in a protected space. Right in the heart of an institution of learning a space is created in which a personal human relationship becomes the central emotional reality of the space. This personal relationship is not institutionally stamped, yet it energizes and animates everything else that goes on in this space inside the institution. And just as Jean-Jacques relies on necessity and utility for Emile's learning—just as he does not expect Emile to learn by being told but expects him to learn by running up against the "thing-ness" and the resistances of the world—so too in collegial teaching we expect the students to learn from encountering the collegial relationship of their teachers in this same way. What is said about this relationship is secondary. What will matter is that this personal, collegial, intellectual, erotic relationship is a fact of their world, one they can't manipulate and one that fundamentally alters the kind of relationship they are used to having personally with their teachers (most of all, if they are used to having either especially hostile or especially friendly relations with their teachers). The collegial relationship is a reality they "run up against" in some way or another almost every day in the collegially taught course.

We think we teach in the spirit of Rousseau. Yet we have broken the "folie-à-deux" and turned the teacher's primary attention away from his Emile and toward another teacher. Our decisive difference from Rousseau is that pedagogic authority is neither abandoned nor weakened under collegial teaching, but is multiplied and made plural. Less monolithic, less abstract, and less familiar, pedagogic authority becomes differentiated, and thus more knowable. Two experts who occupy the position of "professor" and yet who disagree[4] cannot be seen as pure embodiments of the truth to be learned by the students. And if they do not possess the truth, then what gives them the authority to be teachers? Or who does? What role does the institution have in creating pedagogic authority? Can different sources of pedagogic authority be distinguished and are some more legitimate than others? These are questions collegial teaching gives students the chance to ask. Once they are asked, traditional pedagogical authority becomes problematized. Once monolithic authority is fractured, such questions cascade. These are questions unlikely to occur to Emile, because Rousseau has made Jean-Jacques a virtual god over him. The multiplication and pluralization of authority marks a decisive advance over Rousseau's conception, we believe, yet does not fundamentally violate Rousseau's insight that education, at its core, must be personal.

Not only have we introduced a colleague for Jean-Jacques, but in the spirit of Freire, we have also brought along peers for Emile. Here we have yet a third incarnation of equality. The students have their own equals in the environment, something Emile does not have. They thus have people with whom to engage in their own conversations, people they might feet equal to and separate from, even while they are not yet engaging in "the" collegial conversation. The introduction of peers for each student is not novel to collegial teaching, but under collegial teaching it is not an economic necessity to be tolerated but rather a virtue of the teaching-learning arrangement. It represents a second blow to the binding student-teacher bond that collegial teaching seeks to "turn away from." Once students discover that their teacher's primary erotic energy is focused elsewhere, they can turn to their peers with an interest and curiosity quite uncommon in normal teaching arrangements. Thus peer-bonds allow *students* to "turn away" from the student-teacher relationship, too.

Transference is not "finessed" in this setting, nor are Freud's insights regarding transference devalued. Instead, the erotic landscape is transformed by the introduction of peers for both student and teacher. The key factor here is the multiplication of the transference-figure (the teacher) in the setting. As long as the single, lone teacher is the sole object of transference, he is a sitting duck for transference reactions, regardless of what he does. He becomes a magnet for emotional attachments, conscious and unconscious, affectionate and hostile, which, along with the inevitable counter-transference, create all the "problems" we examined in chapters 1 and 2. Collegial teaching, without suppressing eroticism, creates a somewhat safer setting for the erotic relations necessary to learning and teaching. Although both teachers remain attractive to students, they are less emotionally accessible to them, because they are so focused on each other. In some ways, then, collegial teaching replaces the emotional dynamics of the single-parent family with the emotional scenario of the two-parent family. Transference can scarcely be expected to vanish in this setting. But transference reactions will be less intensely focused, more diffuse, complex, and fragmentary. Everyone will have more room to maneuver.

Finally, in praising collegial teaching, we deny no power to the incisive analyses of Illich and Foucault. Collegial teaching is only a *response* to the institutional realities Illich and Foucault have analyzed so compellingly. Collegial teaching presents an *example* to students, to one's colleagues in the institution, and even to oneself that despite all the strictures and confining disciplinary mechanisms of the institution, two people can still come together as friends and learn together—and do so *in the institution*. A and B have to function as agents of institutional power, but when they are together in the classroom it is clear that they are doing something else too. Their students can see that there is more to the authority they are subjecting themselves to than institutionalized authority. They can see that their teachers' work involves more than keeping the institution running smoothly. Students can learn something vital from this exemplar. They can learn that such human responses are still possible within institutions. They can follow their teachers' example—now or later.

The Inevitable Institutional Setting

The moments in professors' teaching lives described in the previous chapter could not have happened at most colleges or universities. The common institutional structure of most colleges and universities is (1) dominated by the notion that the center of a college education is specialized knowledge in one of the traditional academic disciplines (a major), (2) constituted by departments dedicated to offering courses taught by single teachers to cover traditional subjects in their discipline, and (3) maintained by demands on faculty to publish and advance up the ladder of academic success. The kind of teaching we are calling collegial requires a completely different institutional structure. The Evergreen State College provided this alternative structure.

In 1978, Richard Jones, a member of the founding faculty of Evergreen, wrote in an evaluation of Don Finkel: "For a while, there, I thought that Evergreen would, like other colleges, get around to running itself. I was wrong, and I'm glad to have noticed it. Evergreen isn't going to run itself, ever. If it ever does, or if it is ever allowed to, it [will] be the Evergreen that has this joyous whammy on you no more." It was almost inevitable that Jones (who died as we were revising this book for publication) would be wrong and that Evergreen would get around to running itself. Such an institution will almost always become routinized as the founding fervor subsides and as the larger institutional order begins to adopt the changes that, when they were first tried, were revolutionary.

Changes over Evergreen's first twenty years have threatened the possibility of collegial teaching. It is ironic that the very institution that encouraged such teaching would make it less likely. The college has responded to pressures, some internal, some external, some old, some new, to provide *assurances* on matters on which, in our judgment, it would be better simply to take one's chances. Assurances were demanded concerning faculty reappointment, a stable curriculum, a multiculturalism agenda, and college-wide assessment. In each case the college responded affirmatively by instituting a series of structural shifts.

It is surprising that just when its innovative and alternative methods were receiving national recognition, the college should engineer a pattern of shifts that would endanger the vital center of its innovative and alternative approach to college education. But it seems to be in the nature of modern institutions to shift in just these directions.

The genius of the college's founding lay in its negativity; negative responses to demands for assurances were and are needed to sustain the college's potential for collegial teaching. Modern institutions seem incapable of responding to "rational demands" with a simple "no." Evergreen, of all places, should have been capable. Providing assurances in response to new and old anxieties, from within and without, in the end may lead to the loss of what was most important about this institution.

In recent years, as we have discussed what we may be losing, we have found a term that has helped us name our fear. The German word *Schwund* refers to a loss that occurs through a draining away. The draining away has the peculiar quality of not being noticeable until everything is gone. "Think of a pond," said the person who explained the word to us:

> Everyday, you return to the pond and it is still there; "it's a pond," you say. You may be a little uneasy because it seems to be changing, but you cannot articulate your uneasiness. You reassure yourself that everything is fine; "it's a pond." One day you come back and the pond is gone. As you think back, you can reconstruct the history of the loss of the pond as a gradual, incremental phenomenon, but there was no way to do so as the process was going on. And, what's more, you can't get the pond back. *That* is *Schwund*, that loss.

We are concerned about the loss of many of the conditions of collegiality that Evergreen's founding in negativity provided, and we have written elsewhere about those specific concerns.[5] However, we are cognizant of the fact that collegial teaching is dependent also on the collegiality of the colleagues who teach together. We are optimistic enough to believe, as we put it above, that genuine human intercourse can happen in modern institutions and that students can learn from such exemplary relationships. We are concerned about the losses, in the sense of a *Schwund*, that we suffer as we gain all that the regularization and routinization of Evergreen has to offer. But finally, we know that collegial teaching can occur under even the most arid institutional arrangements.

Beginning Again

> No guarantees, no clarity, a life beyond contract. It sounds impossible, until we remember that this is the life most people have lived. Always.
>
> —Nils Christie, *Beyond Loneliness and Institutions*

The possibility of freedom within an institution can only be investigated with respect to the particular conditions of a particular institution. At Evergreen in 1991 we had concluded that shifts in the college were making collegial teaching less likely to take place. Yet in 1992, we both found ourselves free to teach as we saw fit, which meant teaching together again—beginning once again the activity of collegial teaching. Despite the changes at Evergreen, there was nothing to stop us from teaching just the way we wanted to teach.

Our imagined reader who, at the very end of Chapter 6, asks, "Can I learn to do collegial teaching at my institution," must be warned that there are two different ways to understand "doing collegial teaching." The first construes "doing it" to mean achieving some end, attaining some pre-figured end state that is taken to be desirable. The second, radically different, construction understands that "doing it" signifies *starting something new,* and nothing more. Hannah Arendt, in describing human action, says, "It is in the nature of beginning that something new is started which cannot be expected from whatever may have happened before. This character of startling unexpectedness is inherent in all beginnings and all origins."[6] To embark upon collegial teaching is to make just such a beginning. No guarantees come with the project. No contract can insure its success. The desired end may not come about. But teachers who undertake such a venture—and their students too—are likely to be surprised by what the venture brings (as we were, during our third round of teaching together in 1992—93). Indeed, according to Illich, it is just this openness to surprise that lies at the center of any truly educational enterprise: "It is precisely for surprise that true education prepares us. . . . [Education] presupposes a place within the society in which each of us is awakened by surprise; a place of encounter in which others surprise me with their liberty and make me aware of my own."[7] Collegial teaching, whatever its institutional setting, is predicated on openness to surprise and the willingness to begin "doing it" in the face of improbabilities and uncertainty.

Certainly, the educational institution can makes things easier or harder. But it is a mistake to look to the institution to "make collegial teaching happen." To do so is to miss Illich's point about true education; it is to blind oneself to Arendt's insight about human action. Institutions cannot "act," in Arendt's sense, and it is not in their nature to welcome surprise. It is humans who must act freely within and *despite* their institutional settings. If their institution does not get in their way, so much the better.

We began by asking what kind of a relationship a student enters when she enters the student-teacher relationship. We saw in part 1 that this relationship, powerful as it may be, is inherently problematic; no matter how much you tinker with it or how much you "facilitate" it or how much you manage it, the student-teacher relationship must remain paradoxical. Illich and Foucault have shown us that we must be especially wary when we invite institutions to facilitate or manage this relationship. We suggest, therefore, turning away from the expectations fostered by institutional facilitation, from the promises of grants, programs, and institutes. We suggest simply embarking on the project with a colleague as an act of potential friendship. There is no better way to begin. And from such a beginning "something new is started," something that has never happened before.

Ending

Even as we began to teach collegially together again in 1992, we agreed that the future of collegial teaching at Evergreen was problematic. In 1994, we still agree. Yet our agreement only goes so far: one of us is more hopeful, the other takes a bleaker view. Such diverging outlooks should not be surprising by now. It would be strange indeed if, at this point in our work, we did not have at least two interpretations of our common situation.

We have cycled three times through hopefulness and despair over the promise of pedagogy. We have found three scenes—the intimate, inspired, one-on-one pedagogy of Rousseau, the culture circles of Freire, and the negatively defined Evergreen State College—in which a liberatory, humane education appears possible. Freud darkened the scene of Rousseau's scheme and Foucault and Illich pulled a blanket over the scene engineered by Freire. Now, with the regularization of Evergreen, clouds are gathering over this relatively new, rather hopeful situation. Once again, though, there are two very different ways to react to the gathering of these clouds.

It would be easy to think that we are at the end, that there is little hope for finding our way out of the paradox of pedagogy. Every instance of pedagogical promise, A points out, eventually devolves into a scene too cluttered with psychological or disciplinary or managerial mechanisms to permit freedom to flourish. But it would be equally easy to think ourselves at a new beginning. B reminds us that every dialectic has its third moment. The promise of Evergreen might go as unfulfilled, finally, as did the promise of the student-teacher pedagogy framed by Rousseau, but that is no reason not to expect that out of the present Evergreen might come another set of possibilities for the education for freedom. Behind these two interpretations of our common institutional situation lie two views of freedom.

One view of freedom has it that people must actively engage in clearing a space for their freely chosen life together. It is only in these empty, purposefully cleared spaces that freedom can be enjoyed. Evergreen, at its founding, was a relatively empty place. People worked hard to insure that the place would not become filled with the usual academic apparatuses. The empty Evergreen promised to be a place where people could act their freedom—freedom of thought, freedom of political engagement, freedom of association. It was a place that enabled collegial teaching. It was a place that encouraged students to throw off the bonds of studenthood and become colleagues as well. It was a place where traditional forms of authority were renounced in favor of the possibility of people's becoming authors of themselves. Evergreen *was* the possibility of freedom in the teaching/learning encounter.

The first reading of our account of Evergreen would have it that this possibility of freedom is gone. The possibility that collegiality can continue to inform the work of the college becomes less likely with each succeeding year. Such a change would constitute a loss of a high order, the loss of the possibility of freedom as the College comes to be, simply, yet another institution of higher education.

But the second interpretation of our common situation points in a different direction. It is possible that our current circumstances might open up new forms of teaching and learning that could lead to the freedom we desire for ourselves and our students. Freedom, according to this interpretation, does not owe its existence to a place. Freedom is *action* in a set of historically given circumstances; it is conscious, deliberate thought and action in situations, as Dewey said, "in which we find ourselves." This freedom requires an active awareness of imposed limitations, of obstructions to new possibilities. As Maxine Greene put it, "The ones who have an awareness of freedom . . . take the obstruction personally; it is the way in which their lived situation speaks to them."[8] So although we might lament the loss of a certain kind of openness that was Evergreen, we need not succumb to nostalgia. This interpretation suggests that people who want a pedagogy of freedom should recognize the multidimensional nature of their embeddedness in their situation and act on that. This understanding would claim as its pedagogical material the very constraints one faces in, for example, institutions of learning and would encourage people to aim at surpassing those constraints. Such action might lead to transcendence of the situation "in which we find ourselves." In that transcendence is the freedom we all seek. So says the second interpretation of freedom.

Although one of us gravitates toward the first interpretation of freedom and the other gravitates toward the second, we each experience sympathetic responses to both points of view. When pushed, however, each of us comes down on a different side of the fence (because we begin on different sides). We are two and we disagree. There are two interpretations and each of us is pulled toward one or the other. It seems time to stop, for we are either at the final end or we are ready for a new cycle to begin.

But it would be surprising if there were only two interpretations of our situation. There may well be a third.

The first two interpretations share a common problematic: What is *one* to do in the face of the paradox of pedagogy, which is also the paradox of teaching freedom? How is *one* to become the author of one's own world? How is *one* to act in the face of constraints that relentlessly take shape in previously open situations? One, one, one. . . .

But *we are two*. It is in that thought that we have found *our* response to the paradox of pedagogy.

Posing the issue as one of holding a spatial view of freedom *or* holding a dialectical view can blind us to the issue at hand. Posing the issue of the aim of education as being for solitude *or* for community can blind us to the issue at hand. Posing the issue of assuming a posture of political critique as one based on irony *or* humor can blind us to the issue at hand. We had each, in our own individual ways, settled all these issues before we started this project. And being settled on these sorts of questions blinded us to the issue at hand.

We have found our response to the paradox of pedagogy not in any simple either/or. We found our response in that chasm that opens between the two lectures by our A and B, the lectures that appear at the center of this book, between our sections on a pedagogy organized around students and a pedagogy organized around colleagues. We found our response in the space that opens silently between the two of us as we converse with one another about those things that seem important.

We may not be able to agree on where we are, but this exercise has helped each of us understand better the place where each of us is. Each of us can say, "My colleague has called me in friendship to the limits of my thought." We have each better surveyed our own territories. We have accompanied one another from beginning to end.

NOTES

Introduction

1. Joseph Tussman, *Experiment at Berkeley* (London: Oxford University Press, 1969), 29.

2. Ibid., 31.

3. Ernest Boyer, *College: The Undergraduate Experience in America* (New York: Harper and Row, 1987).

4. Charles Sykes, *ProfScam: Professors and the Demise of Higher Education* (Washington, D.C.: Regnery Gateway, 1988).

5. See Allan Bloom, *The Closing of the American Mind: How Higher Education Has Failed Democracy and Impoverished the Souls of Today's Students* (New York: Simon and Schuster, 1987); E. D. Hirsch, *Cultural Literacy: What Every American Needs to Know* (Boston: Houghton Mifflin, 1987); Diane Ravitch, *What Our Seventeen-Year-Olds Don't Know* (New York: Harper and Row, 1988).

6. Study Group on the Conditions of Excellence in Higher Education, *Involvement in Learning: Realizing the Potential of Higher Education* (Washington, D.C.: National Institute of Education, 1984), 17.

7. See Faith Gabelnick, Jean MacGregor, Roberta S. Matthews, and Barbara Leigh Smith, *Learning Communities: Creating Connections Among Students, Faculty, and Disciplines* (San Francisco: Jossey-Bass, 1990), for an overview of various schemes and administrative advice for implementing them.

8. Tussman, *Experiment at Berkeley*, 11.

9. In no way is the adjective "negative" intended to be pejorative. We use it to express high praise and gratitude to Charles McCann for his approach to administration.

10. Richard M. Jones, *Experiment at Evergreen* (Cambridge, Mass.: Schenkman, 1981), 26.

11. See Jones, ibid., for an account of the history of this pedagogical idea in the thinking and practice of Alexander Meiklejohn at Wisconsin and Joseph Tussman at Berkeley, and for a detailed description of the structure and functioning of Coordinated Studies programs.

12. There are, in the folklore of the college, many tales of programs "blowing up" or coming to grand crashes that led to much pain for faculty and students alike.

13. We have to insist that this book is a report on a conversation. We are not writing to propose a "model" for teaching or new "teaching strategies."

14. Donald L. Finkel and G. Stephen Monk, "Teachers and Learning Groups: Dissolution of the Atlas Complex," in *Learning in Groups*, ed. C. Bouton and R. Y. Garth (San Francisco: Jossey Bass, 1983), 85.

15. John Locke, *Some Thoughts Concerning Education*, ed. R. H. Quick (Cambridge: Cambridge University Press, 1880), enlarged in later editions.

16. F. W. Garforth, introduction to *Some Thoughts Concerning Education*, by John Locke (Woodbury, N.Y.: Barron's Educational Series, 1964), 16.

17. Robert H. Horwitz, "John Locke and the Preservation of Liberty: A Perennial Problem of Civic Education," in *The Moral Foundations of the American Republic*, ed. R. H. Horwitz, 3d ed. (Charlottesville: University Press of Virginia, 1986).

18. Garforth, introduction to *Some Thoughts Concerning Education*, 16.

19. This distinction is important. John Dewey, in a footnote, discusses Rousseau's inclination to educate (and thereby liberate) *for* society. Rousseau, Dewey writes, "opposed the existing state of affairs on the ground that it formed *neither* the citizen nor the man. Under existing conditions, he preferred to try for the latter rather than the former. But there are many sayings of his which point to the formation of citizens as ideally the higher, and which indicate that his own endeavor, as embodied in the *Emile*, was simply the best make shift the corruption of the time permitted him to sketch" (John Dewey, *Democracy and Education: An Introduction to the Philosophy of Education* [New York: Free Press, 1916], 93–94).

20. Richard Rorty, "Education Without Dogma: Truth, Freedom, and Our Universities," *Dissent* (Spring 1988): 198–204, 198.

21. Eva T. H. Brann, *Paradoxes of Education in a Republic* (Chicago: University of Chicago Press, 1979), 1.

1. The Promise of a Personal Pedagogy

1. Jean-Jacques Rousseau, *Emile, or On Education*, ed. and trans. Allan Bloom (New York: Basic Books, 1979). All page references in parentheses are to this edition.

2. Dewey, *Democracy and Education*, 2.

3. Ibid., 3.

4. In this chapter we shall refer to the author of *Emile* as "Rousseau" and the tutor within the book, depicted by Rousseau as himself, as "Jean-Jacques."

5. Lester G. Crocker, introduction to *The Social Contract and Discourse on the Origin of Inequality* (New York: Pocket Books, 1967), xviii.

6. See Jean-Jacques Rousseau, *A Discourse on Inequality*, trans. M. Cranston (London: Penguin, 1984).

7. Book 1: infancy (ages 0–2)—physical care and training; Book 2: childhood (ages 2–12)—education of the senses; Book 3: age of reason (ages 12–15)—education of the intellect; Book 4: age of passion (puberty and adolescence, ages 15–20)—education of the passions; Book 5: onset of adulthood (age 20 on)—reintegration with society, finding a proper spouse.

8. George Dennison, *The Lives of Children* (New York: Random House, 1969), 4; emphasis added.

9. Ibid., 92.

10. Rorty, *Contingency, Irony, and Solidarity*, 19.

11. Ibid., 198.

12. Jean Starobinski, *Jean-Jacques Rousseau: Transparency and Obscurantism*, trans. Arthur Goldhammer (Chicago: University of Chicago Press, 1988), 302.

13. Michael Oakeshott, "A Place of Learning," in *The Voice of Liberal Learning: Michael Oakeshott on Education*, ed. Timothy Fuller (New Haven: Yale University Press, 1989), 37.

14. Michael Oakeshott, "Learning and Teaching," in Fuller, ed., *Voice of Liberal Learning*, 48.

15. David P. Gauthier, *Moral Dealing: Contract, Ethics, and Reason* (Ithaca, N.Y.: Cornell University Press, 1990), 108.

16. Ibid., 102.

17. Ibid., 100.

18. Dewey, *Democracy and Education*.

19. Lawrence Kohlberg and Rochelle Mayer, "Development as the Aim of Education," in *Stage Theories of Cognitive and Moral Development: Criticisms and Applications*, Harvard Educational Review, Reprint no. 13, 1978, 149.

20. Ibid.

21. To say that development is grounded in a *common* nature is not to say the development is foreordained within us, or is grounded in a preformed *human* nature. It is to claim, merely, that its universality is grounded in the possible structure of interaction between human biology and the natural environment humans find themselves living in.

22. Rousseau, *Discourse on Inequality*, 68; emphasis added.

23. He writes, "Men cannot remain content with what is given them by their culture if they are to be fully human. . . . Nature should be the standard by which we judge our own lives and the lives of peoples. . . . Only dogmatic assurance that thought is culture-bound, that there is no nature, is what makes our educators so certain that the only way to escape the limitations of our time and place is to study other cultures" (Bloom, *Closing of the American Mind*, 38).

2. The Paradox of a Personal Pedagogy

1. We use the term "violence" in a broader sense than Freud's specifically biological meaning of "aggression." Affectionate, loving relationships can be just as violent as hostile ones, as the ensuing discussion of transference will illustrate.

2. Janet Malcolm, *Psychoanalysis: The Impossible Profession* (New York: Alfred A. Knopf, 1981), 6.

3. Sigmund Freud, *Introductory Lectures on Psychoanalysis* (New York: W. W. Norton, 1966), 441.

4. Ibid., 287.

5. Ibid., 454.

6. Sigmund Freud, "The Dynamics of Transference," in *The Standard Edition of the Psychological Works of Sigmund Freud*, ed. James Strachey (London: Hogarth Press, 1958), vol. 12: 99–100.

7. Ibid., 103.

8. Ibid., 101.

9. Ibid., 108.

10. Ibid., 101.

11. Sigmund Freud, "Remembering, Repeating and Working-Through (Further Recommendations on the Technique of Psycho-Analysis II)," in Strachey, ed., *Standard Edition* 12:151.

12. Sigmund Freud, "Observations on Transference-Love (Further Recommendations on the Technique of Psycho-Analysis III)," in Strachey, ed., *Standard Edition* 12:162.

13. Jacques Lacan, *The Four Fundamental Concepts of Psycho-Analysis* (New York: W. W. Norton, 1978), 130, passim.

14. Freud, *Introductory Lectures*, 454.

15. Ibid., 444.

16. Freud, "Observations on Transference-Love," 162.

17. Ibid., 163.

18. Ibid., 164.

19. Sigmund Freud, "Recommendations to Physicians Practicing Psycho-Analysis," in Strachey, ed., *Standard Edition* 12:115–16.

20. Ibid., 116.

21. Freud, "Observations on Transference-Love," 168; emphasis added.

22. Freud, *Introductory Lectures*, 453.

23. See the collection of Freud's papers published as *Therapy and Technique* (New York: Collier Books, 1963).

24. Freud, "Observations on Transference-Love," 159.

25. Julia Kristeva, *In the Beginning Was Love: Psychoanalysis and Faith* (New York: Columbia University Press, 1987), 3.

26. Ibid., 7.

27. Ibid., 7–8.

28. Sigmund Freud, "Analysis Terminable and Interminable," in Strachey, ed., *Standard Edition* 23:209–53.

29. Annie Reich, "On the Termination of Analysis," in *Psychoanalytic Contributions* (New York: International Universities Press, 1973), quoted in Malcolm, *Psychoanalysis*, 153.

30. Freud, "Analysis Terminable and Interminable," 248.

31. Freud, *Introductory Lectures*, 433.

32. Ibid., 19.

33. Ibid., 431.

34. Freud, "Analysis Terminable and Interminable," 233.

35. Freud, "Dynamics of Transference," 99 n. 2.

36. Freud, *Introductory Lectures*, 432–33.

37. At the end of the fifth lecture, Freud speculates on possible outcomes of psychoanalysis. He talks about the way civilization stands in the way of the direct

satisfaction of certain libidinal impulses and suggests that direct satisfaction is the due of every human being. But there is a question of balancing direct satisfaction with the demands of social life. To address the question of balance, Freud tells the story of the "little town of Schilda" whose citizens owned a horse that was very strong but had the considerable disadvantage of eating too many "expensive oats." Freud said,

> They determined to break [the horse] of this bad habit by reducing its ration by a few stalks every day, till they had accustomed it to complete abstinence. For a time things went excellently: the horse was weaned to the point of eating only one stalk a day, and on the succeeding day it was at length to work without any oats at all. On the morning of that day the spiteful animal was found dead; and the citizens of Schilda could not make out what it had died of.
>
> *We* should be inclined to think that the horse was starved and that no work at all could be expected of an animal without a certain modicum of oats. (Sigmund Freud, *Five Lectures on Psychoanalysis* [New York: W. W. Norton, n.d.], 55).

38. Freud, "Dynamics of Transference," 101.

39. The following is taken from Lacan, *Four Fundamental Concepts of Psycho-Analysis;* Stuart Schneiderman, *Jacques Lacan: The Death of an Intellectual Hero* (Cambridge: Harvard University Press, 1983); and François Roustang, *Dire Mastery: Discipleship from Freud to Lacan* (Baltimore: Johns Hopkins University Press, 1982).

40. Roustang, *Dire Mastery,* 19.

41. Ibid.

42. Ibid., 30.

43. Rousseau, *Emile,* 480.

44. Ibid., 84.

45. See Donald L. Finkel, "Democracy in Education: Education in Democracy—An Essay in Politics and Psychology," unpublished monograph, 1986.

46. Near the end of his writing career, Freud reshaped his conception of nature. The final Freudian view of nature (see *Beyond the Pleasure Principle* [New York: Bantam, 1959]) was not the benign, "good nature" of Rousseau. His vision of the nature in which human beings find themselves was a little darker. Writing of his impressions concerning "a force which is defending itself by every possible means against recovery and which is absolutely resolved to hold on to illness and suffering," Freud concluded, "These phenomena are unmistakable indications of the presence of a power in mental life which we call the instinct of aggression or of destruction according to its aims, and which we trace back to the original death instinct of living matter. It is not a question of an antithesis between an optimistic and a pessimistic theory of life. Only by the concurrent or mutually opposing action of the two primal instincts—Eros and the death-instinct—never by one or the other alone, can we explain the rich multiplicity of the phenomena of life" (Freud, "Analysis Terminable and Interminable," 242–43).

47. Roustang, *Dire Mastery,* 25.

48. Freud, *Introductory Lectures,* 451.

49. Dennison, *Lives of Children,* 4.

3. The Promise of a Social Pedagogy

1. 1. Gauthier, *Moral Dealing*, 95.
2. Starobinski, *Jean-Jacques Rousseau*, 302.
3. Paulo Freire, *Pedagogy of the Oppressed* (New York: Seabury Press, 1970), 59.
4. Jurgen Habermas, *Knowledge and Human Interests* (Boston: Beacon Press, 1971), 301–6.
5. Paulo Freire, "Extension or Communication," in *Education for Critical Consciousness*, by Paulo Freire (New York: Continuum, 1973), 113.
6. Freire, *Pedagogy of the Oppressed*, 68.
7. Ibid., 62.
8. Eric Fromm, *The Heart of Man* (New York: Bantam, 1966), 41, quoted in Freire, *Pedagogy of the Oppressed*, 64.
9. Freire, *Pedagogy of the Oppressed*, 64.
10. Ibid., 87.
11. Paulo Freire, "Education as the Practice of Freedom," in Freire, *Education for Critical Consciousness*, 3.
12. Freire, "Extension or Communication," 136.
13. Ibid., 132.
14. Freire, *Pedagogy of the Oppressed*, 88.
15. Freire, "Extension or Communication," 147.
16. Freire, "Education as the Practice of Freedom," 46.
17. Ibid., 81.
18. Freire, "Extension or Communication," 144–45.
19. Ibid., 105.
20. Freire, *Pedagogy of the Oppressed*, 51.
21. "Rethinking Critical Pedagogy: A Dialogue with Paulo Freire," in *The Politics of Education: Culture, Power, Liberation*, by Paulo Freire (South Hadley, Mass.: Bergin & Garvey, 1985), 198.
22. Freire, "Extension or Communication," 158.
23. Ira Shor, ed., *Freire for the Classroom: A Sourcebook for Liberatory Teaching* (Portsmouth, N.H.: Heinemann, 1987), 24.
24. Freire, "Extension or Communication," 100.
25. Ira Shor, *Critical Teaching and Everyday Life* (Chicago: University of Chicago Press, 1980), 162.
26. Ibid., 163.
27. Freire, "Education as the Practice of Freedom," 13.
28. Freire, *Pedagogy of the Oppressed*, 56.
29. Ibid., 75–76.
30. Ibid., 75.
31. Freire, *Pedagogy of the Oppressed*, 76.
32. Kyle Fiore and Nan Elsasser, "Through Writing We Transform Our World: Third World Women and Literacy," *Humanities in Society* 4 (Fall 1981): 395–409.
33. Freire, *Pedagogy of the Oppressed*, 80.
34. Ibid., 77–78.
35. Freire, "Education as the Practice of Freedom," 17.

36. Paulo Freire, *Cultural Action for Freedom* (Cambridge, Mass.: Center for the Study of Development and Social Change, 1970), 36.
37. Freire, "Education as the Practice of Freedom," 17–18.
38. Freire, *Cultural Action for Freedom*, 37.
39. Freire, "Education as the Practice of Freedom," 19.
40. Ibid., 20.
41. Ibid.
42. Freire, *Pedagogy of the Oppressed*, 101.
43. Shor, *Critical Teaching and Everyday Life*, 93.
44. Ibid., 161.
45. Shor, *Critical Teaching and Everyday Life*, xxv.
46. Freire, "Extension or Communication," 118.
47. Ibid., 121–22.
48. Ibid., 153.
49. Shor, *Critical Teaching and Everyday Life*, 98.
50. Paulo Freire, "The Educational Role of the Churches in Latin America," Washington, D.C.: LADOC 3, 14, 1972, 4.
51. Shor, *Critical Teaching and Everyday Life*, xiv.
52. Ibid., xix; and Paulo Freire, *Pedagogy in Process: The Letters to Guinea-Bissau* (New York: Seabury Press, 1978), 60.
53. Jean-Jacques Rousseau, "Man is born free and everywhere he is in chains," in *On the Social Contract: With Geneva Manuscript and Political Economy*, ed. Roger Masters (New York: St. Martin's Press, 1978), bk. 1, 46.
54. Freire, "Extension or Communication," 96 n. 5.
55. "Letter to North-American Teachers," in Shor, ed., *Freire for the Classroom*, 212.
56. Shor, *Critical Teaching and Everyday Life*, 98.
57. Donald L. Finkel, *Democracy in Education: Education in Democracy* (Olympia, Wash.: The Evergreen State College, 1986).
58. Freire, *Pedagogy of the Oppressed*, 68.
59. Rousseau, *Emile*, 120.
60. Che Guevara, *Episodes of the Revolutionary War* (New York: International Publishers, 1968), 102, cited in Freire, *Pedagogy of the Oppressed*, 169.
61. Freire, *Pedagogy of the Oppressed*, 169.
62. Soren Kierkegaard, "Love Abides," in *The World Treasury of Modern Religious Thought*, ed. Jaroslav Pelikan (Boston: Little, Brown, 1990).
63. Freire, *Pedagogy of the Oppressed*, 169–70.
64. Ibid., 134 n. 13.
65. Ibid., 171.
66. Ibid., 170.
67. "Rethinking Critical Pedagogy: A Dialogue with Paulo Freire," 178.
68. Ibid.
69. Ibid.

4. The Paradox of a Social Pedagogy

1. Rousseau, *Discourse on Inequality*.
2. Ivan Illich, *Deschooling Society* (New York: Harper and Row, 1970).

3. Ivan Illich, "The Futility of Schooling," in *Celebration of Awareness*, by Ivan Illich (Garden City, N.Y.: Anchor Books, 1970), 103.

4. Ibid., 105.

5. Illich, *Deschooling Society*, 43.

6. Ivan Illich, "School: The Sacred Cow," in *Celebration of Awareness*, 119.

7. Illich, "Futility of Schooling," 111.

8. Illich, *Deschooling Society*, 38.

9. Ibid., 1.

10. Ibid., 67–68.

11. Philippe Ariès, *Centuries of Childhood* (New York: Random House, 1965).

12. Illich, *Deschooling Society*, 42.

13. Ibid., 56–57.

14. Ibid., 58.

15. Ibid.

16. Ivan Illich, "A Constitution for Cultural Revolution," in *Celebration of Awareness*, 174.

17. Ibid., 45.

18. Ibid., 47.

19. Illich, "School: The Sacred Cow," 126–27.

20. Michel Foucault, *Discipline and Punish: The Birth of the Prison* (London: Allen Lane, 1977), 138.

21. Ibid., 194.

22. David Cayley, "Part Moon, Part Travelling Salesman: Conversations with Ivan Illich," Montreal: CBC Transcripts, 1989, 13.

23. Michel Foucault, "Revolutionary Action: 'Until Now,'" in *Language, Counter-Memory, Practice: Selected Essays and Interviews*, ed. Donald F. Bouchard (Ithaca, N.Y.: Cornell University Press, 1977), 230–31.

24. Peter L. Berger and Thomas Luckmann, *The Social Construction of Reality* (New York: Anchor Books, 1967).

25. Francis Galton, *Natural Inheritance* (London: Macmillan, 1888), 86.

26. Donald A. Mackenzie, *Statistics in Britain, 1865–1930: The Social Construction of Scientific Knowledge* (Edinburgh: Edinburgh University Press, 1981).

27. Letter from Florence Nightingale to Francis Galton, 7 February 1891, titled "Scheme for Social Physics Teaching," in Karl Pearson, *Life, Letters and Labours of Francis Galton* (Cambridge: Cambridge University Press, 1914–30), vol. 2: 418.

28. Mackenzie, *Statistics in Britain*, 76.

29. Michel Foucault, *An Introduction*, vol. 1 of *The History of Sexuality* (New York: Pantheon, 1978), 26.

30. Foucault, *Discipline and Punish*, 191.

31. Ibid., 191.

32. See Foucault, *History of Sexuality;* and William Ray Arney and Bernard J. Bergen, *Medicine and the Management of Living: Taming the Last Great Beast* (Chicago: University of Chicago Press, 1984).

33. Most schools have one or another forms of "in-house detention." These programs are for students who, in former times, would have been thrown out of school. Now schools keep in schools those that they throw out.

34. Ibid., 200–201.

35. Ibid., 228.
36. Ibid., 202–3; emphasis added.
37. Ibid., 203.
38. Ibid., 222.
39. B. F. Skinner, *Walden Two* (New York: Macmillan, 1948), 296.
40. Illich, *Deschooling Society*, 68.
41. Ibid., 73.
42. Ibid., 95.
43. Ibid., 14.
44. Ibid., 97, 101.
45. Ibid., 157.
46. According to Confucius: "The way out is via the door. Why is it that no one will use this method?" (quoted in R. D. Laing, *Self and Others* [New York: Penguin, 1969], 13).
47. Foucault, *Discipline and Punish*, 204.
48. Michel Foucault, *The Archeology of Knowledge* (New York: Pantheon, 1972), 205.
49. Michel Foucault, "Two Lectures," in *Power/Knowledge: Selected Interviews and Other Writings, 1972–1977*, ed. Colin Gordon (New York: Pantheon, 1980), 86.
50. Michel Foucault, "Intellectuals and Power: A Conversation between Michel Foucault and Gilles Deleuze," in Bouchard, ed., *Language, Counter-Memory, Practice*, 207–8.
51. Ivan Illich, "After Deschooling, What?" in *After Deschooling, What?* ed. Alan Gartner, Colin Greer, and Frank Riessman (New York: Harper and Row, 1972), 12–13.
52. Ibid., ix.
53. Cayley, "Part Moon, Part Travelling Salesman," 13.
54. Ivan Illich, "Toward a Society Without Schools," *Center Report* 4, no. 1 (1971): 4–7, 7.
55. Cayley, "Part Moon, Part Travelling Salesman," 32.
56. "The Concern for Truth," an interview between Michel Foucault and François Ewald, in Michel Foucault, *Foucault Live (Interviews, 1966–1984)* (New York: Semiotext, 1989), 305. Interview originally in *Le Magazine litteraire*, May 1984, 293–308.
57. Keith Gandal, "Michel Foucault: Intellectual Work and Politics," *Telos* 67 (Spring 1986): 121–34, 133.
58. But he thought of himself as a "teacher without students." In a discussion with a group of psychiatrists at Dartmouth College, May 1980, one psychiatrist pressed him to consider his own "position of power" in relation to his students and the administration of his college. Foucault laughed and said, "But I have no students; I have no administration."
59. "The Minimalist Self," an interview between Michel Foucault and Stephen Riggins, in Lawrence D. Kritzman, ed., *Michel Foucault: Politics, Philosophy, Culture: Interviews and Other Writings of Michel Foucault* (New York: Routledge, Chapman, and Hall, 1988), 3–4. Interview originally in *Ethos* (Autumn 1983): 3–16.
60. "Body/Power," an interview with the editorial collective of *Quel Corps?*, in Gordon, ed., *Power/Knowledge*, 62. Interview originally in *Quel Corps?* (October 1975): 55–62.

61. Allan Megill, *Prophets of Extremity: Nietzsche, Heidegger, Foucault, Derrida* (Berkeley and Los Angeles: University of California Press, 1985), 184.

62. Maurice Blanchot, "Michel Foucault as I imagine him," in *Foucault/Blanchot*, by Maurice Blanchot (New York: Zone Books, 1987), 80.

63. Foucault, *Discipline and Punish*, 308.

64. Ivan Illich and Barry Sanders, *ABC: The Alphabetization of the Popular Mind* (San Francisco: North Point Press, 1988), 279.

65. "Friendship as a Way of Life," interview in Foucault, *Foucault Live*, 203–4. Interview originally in *Le Gai Pied* (April 1981): 203–9.

66. "Sexual Choice, Sexual Act," interview between Michel Foucault and James O'Higgins, in Foucault, *Foucault Live*, 212. Originally in *Salmagundi* (Fall 1982–Winter 1983): 211–31.

67. "Friendship as a Way of Life," 204–5.

68. Illich, *Deschooling Society*, 56, 58.

69. Ibid., 146.

70. Ivan Illich, *Tools for Conviviality* (New York: Harper and Row, 1973), 11.

5. Turning Away from the Student-Teacher Relationship

1. Richard M. Jones, *Fantasy and Feeling in Education* (New York: Harper Colophon, 1968), 83.

2. Michael R. Katz, *Class, Bureaucracy, and Schools* (New York: Praeger, 1975), 191.

3. We have adopted the rhetorical device of referring to the authors of the two lectures as A and B for a particular reason. One of the results of teaching together collegially is a rather strong identification with the point of view of one's colleague. Each of us wrote the drafts on which these lectures are based long ago; we have since revised each other's drafts. The current lectures are ones we both identify with, and have each had a hand in writing. To call them Arney's and Finkel's lectures seems inappropriate. Moreover, as we further develop our conception of collegial teaching below, "A and B" will become emblematic of any possible collegial teaching team. To tie this pairing too closely to ourselves seems ill advised, and also misleading. The points of view we here identify as belonging to A and B indeed were born in each of us respectively. But collegial teaching has given them a life of their own to some degree, a certain distance from us, even a strange impersonality, which paradoxically, makes these points of view no less personal for us as they continue to inform our present teaching.

4. Gregory Vlastos, "The Paradox of Socrates," in *The Philosophy of Socrates*, ed. Gregory Vlastos (Notre Dame, Ind.: University of Notre Dame Press, 1971), 1–21. See also Gregory Vlastos, *Socrates, Ironist and Moral Philosopher* (Ithaca, N.Y.: Cornell University Press, 1991).

5. W. K. C. Guthrie, *Socrates* (Cambridge: Cambridge University Press, 1971), 4.

6. Bloom, *Closing of the American Mind*, 299.

7. Ronald J. Manheimer, *Kierkegaard as Educator* (Berkeley and Los Angeles: University of California Press, 1977), 16.

8. Umberto Eco, *The Name of the Rose* (San Diego: Harcourt, Brace, Jovanovich, 1983).

9. Manheimer, *Kierkegaard as Educator*, 35.

10. This characterization verges on caricature. We know of Foucault's work as a political actor and we know something of his demeanor. We know also that part of the reason he was interested in understanding the enormity of social power was that he believed he could only engage in judolike maneuvers with respect to social institutions. (And judo rests finally on a rigorous and total appreciation of the strengths of one's opponent.) But we must risk caricature to highlight the difference we speak about: the difference between Illich and Foucault *as writers.*

11. Ivan Illich, *Gender* (New York: Pantheon, 1982), 179.

12. Brann, *Paradoxes of Education*, 1.

13. We should not be tempted by the modern confusion that believes dialogue, at its linguistic root, has something to do with "two," as in "two people." It is formed from the roots meaning only "through" and "word." A dialogue is something that proceeds "through words."

14. Norman Gulley, *The Philosophy of Socrates* (New York: Macmillan, 1968), 69.

15. I. F. Stone, *The Trial of Socrates* (Boston: Little, Brown, 1984), 39.

16. Gregory Vlastos, "Socrates' Disavowal of Knowledge," *Philosophical Quarterly* 35, no. 138 (January 1985): 28.

17. Candace Lang, *Irony/Humor: Critical Paradigms* (Baltimore: Johns Hopkins University Press, 1988), 2.

18. Ibid., 28.

19. Cited in ibid., 21.

20. Ibid., 2.

21. See Daniel W. Conway, "Solving the Problem of Socrates: Nietzsche's *Zarathustra* as Political Irony," *Political Theory* 16, no. 2 (May 1988): 257–80.

22. Ibid., 260.

23. Ibid., 267.

24. Eco, *Name of the Rose*, 492.

25. George McFadden, *Discovering the Comic* (Princeton, N.J.: Princeton University Press, 1982), 38.

26. Peter France, introduction to *Reveries of the Solitary Walker*, by Jean-Jacques Rousseau (New York: Penguin, 1979), 15.

27. We would never endorse a pedagogy of play acting. Tactics such as playing devil's advocate when students fall under the sway of one or the other aim seem weak and flawed in comparison to having the tension between opposed aims embodied in one person who experiences the tension in all its wrenching force.

6. Collegial Teaching

1. We have heard it said that Kenneth Boulding once began an impromptu seminar on "peace" by saying, "I would like to argue that what exists is possible." That sentiment informs our entire chapter. Collegial teaching exists. We experience it when we teach together. We never lose sight of the fact that the existence of collegial teaching makes it continue to seem possible.

2. Hannah Arendt, *The Human Condition* (Chicago: University of Chicago Press, 1958), 8.

3. Richard M. Jones, "Enjoying Evaluation," unpublished MS, The Evergreen State College, Olympia, Wash., n.d., 46.

Conclusion

1. This is not to say that many won't think this anyway; they have spent their whole lives being treated as if this were so. It is to say that this is not what they see and feel going on around them. The experience they are having does not fit their own model of learning, whether they know it or not. But even most of those who don't know it begin to sense it as the course proceeds.

2. Of course, students and teachers *are* unequal in knowledge, in experience, and hence in authority. But the same is true, with respect to any specific issue, for A and B. These differences in knowledge and experience, hence authority, do not prevent A and B from conversing as equals, and taking into account these differentials as part of their dialogue. By the same token, students and teachers can converse as equals if they so choose.

3. Tocqueville remarked that this confusion was endemic to democracy, and documented the tendency among Americans to avoid difference at all costs for fear that it would have to produce inequality, a fate they feared even more than tyranny (i.e., they cherished their equality even more than their liberty).

4. Perry's scheme of intellectual development during the college years, as elaborated in William G. Perry, *Forms of Intellectual and Ethical Development in the College Years: A Scheme* (New York: Holt, Rinehart and Winston, 1970), demonstrates the crucial role that the discovery that "the experts disagree" is likely to have in intellectual development during this period of life.

5. Donald L. Finkel and William Ray Arney, "Collegial Teaching at Evergreen," unpublished MS, The Evergreen State College, Olympia, Wash., 1991.

6. Arendt, *Human Condition*, 177–78.

7. Illich, "School: The Sacred Cow," 134.

8. Maxine Greene, *The Dialectic of Freedom* (New York: Teachers College Press, 1988), 11.

INDEX

ABOUT THE AUTHORS

Donald L. Finkel is a Member of the Faculty at The Evergreen State College, where he has been teaching since 1976. He has published articles on teaching, learning, and the philosophy of education.

William Ray Arney is a Member of the Faculty at The Evergreen State College in Olympia, Washington. He is author of *Power and the Profession of Obstetrics*, *Experts in the Age of Systems*, and a statistics textbook. With Bernard Bergen, he is coauthor of *Medicine and the Management of Living*.